The Islands Time Forgot
Exploring the South Pacific Under Sail

Graham Morse

AuthorHouse™ UK Ltd.
500 Avebury Boulevard
Central Milton Keynes, MK9 2BE
www.authorhouse.co.uk
Phone: 08001974150

© 2010 Graham Morse. All rights reserved.

No part of this book may be reproduced, stored in a retrieval system, or transmitted by any means without the written permission of the author.

First published by AuthorHouse   8/20/2010

ISBN: 978-1-4520-0565-2 (e)
ISBN: 978-1-4520-0563-8 (sc)
ISBN: 978-1-4520-0564-5 (hc)

Library of Congress Control Number: 2010904284

This book is printed on acid-free paper.

Page 181: Chart of Suvarov Atoll from *An Island to Oneself*, used by permission of Ox Bow Press, PO Box 4045, Woodbridge, CT 06525.

Page 187: Chart of Tonga Group of Islands from *Landfalls of Paradise*, used by permission of University of Hawai'i Press.

Page 244: The Beaufort Wind Scale comes from the NOAA/NWS and is not subject to copyright protection.

For Janet:
my inspiration for the voyage, my encouragement for the book

Contents

A Serious Illness 1
Dreams Come True 8
All Change at Newport 15
Thar She Blows 21
Pirates in the Caribbean 27
Kuna Yala 43
An Engineering Miracle 58
In the Doldrums 66
Wildlife in the Galapagos 76
Alone in the Ocean 85
Mysterious Marquesas 94
Pearl Fishers of the Tuamotus 112
A Tragic Death 146
The Isolated Islands 172
Swimming with Whales 186
Aground on a Reef 213
Epilogue 236
Acknowledgements 239
Moonraker Plans 240
Appendix 1 Refit at Hinckley's Yard 242
Appendix 2 Replacing a Through Hull Fitting in the Water 243
Appendix 3 Beaufort Wind Scale 244
Sources 245

1

A Serious Illness

Valbonne, France, December 2004

I woke up at three in the morning with a pain in my chest. I lay still and hoped it would go away but it didn't. The pain came in waves every twenty minutes. After a while it became stronger. It was coming from my left side and I thought I might be having a heart attack. Then it became still sharper and more frequent. Now I was convinced that it was a heart attack and I felt very frightened. I had to get to hospital quickly but I wasn't sure how. My wife and I were staying in a rented house in the south of France and I didn't know the emergency number or how I would be able to explain my problem on the phone in French. The nearest hospital was in Grasse, about twenty minutes away, and I thought, stupidly, that the quickest thing would be to drive myself there.

Janet woke up and I explained what was happening. She was calm but felt terrible because she couldn't do anything to help. She wasn't able to drive because she was recovering from knee surgery and was still using crutches. I dressed quickly and made my way to the car. I didn't know where the hospital was, but I entered the name into the car's navigation system and to my relief it came up with a route. The streets were dark and empty, the road glistening black from overnight rain and reflecting the pale yellow street lights and the illuminated red and blue signs of shops and bars. As I drove, the pain got stronger and I tried to control my growing feeling of panic. When I got closer I saw the "H" traffic signs indicating that the hospital was near and I was comforted that I was not totally reliant on the navigation system.

I had no plan of what to do when I arrived. All I could think about was the pain and all I knew was that I had to be seen by a doctor quickly.

I abandoned the car where the ambulances pull up, thinking how odd it was to be walking through the emergency door and not being pushed in on a hospital trolley. I didn't know how to explain myself, but I needn't have worried. Although my French wasn't up to coping with a medical emergency, people in the hospital didn't need me to tell them what was wrong, and within minutes I was being treated. They wired me up to a heart monitor and I could tell that the doctors thought this was serious. I became concerned about what might happen to me. Was I really having a heart attack? Was I going to die?

It was difficult to understand what they were saying as I was wheeled on a trolley from place to place to have scans and tests. At one point I was left on my own, sitting on the side of the trolley, and felt faint. I instinctively cried out for help, and then slipped into darkness. The next thing I remember was seeing several staff peering down at me. I could hear Dr. Alain Tissot, the cardiologist, saying to one of the nurses, "What colour did he go? This is very important. Was it blue?" Although I didn't know what was happening, I felt strangely calm. There was nothing I could do and I was in expert hands. As I recovered, he turned to me with a smile on his face and a twinkle in his eye. "Yes, we know you are English, but don't worry, we are going to give you the best treatment anyway!"

Later the next day he explained, partly in English, partly in French, that he thought I hadn't had a heart attack but was suffering from a condition called pericarditis, which makes the envelope enclosing the heart harden, causing great pain. "The English have another name for this," he said. "They call it the iron fist. It is very painful, but you are not going to die."

Nevertheless the condition didn't improve as it should have done and I was in hospital for ten days. Janet came in a taxi to visit me every day. "Look what I've brought you," she said as she sat down next to my bed. It was the latest issues of *Yachting World* and *Yachting Monthly*, something she knew would cheer me up.

She was on crutches but she looked lovely, at least ten years younger than her sixty-two years, with short blond hair, a healthy complexion, and a good figure. She took care of herself. We had been young lovers, married when Janet was only eighteen and I was twenty-one, and our family, two boys and two girls, arrived before she was twenty-seven. The family was always the most important thing to Janet. She had dedicated herself to bringing up our children while I concentrated on a business career.

I grew up in a small market town in Berkshire, England, where my parents managed a pub. I left home for London at eighteen and began my career selling advertising space for the *Sunday Times*. I didn't have much idea of what I was doing, and I received no training, but it was rather glamorous and I did quite well at it. But after a while I began to think that there was more to life than calling on advertising agencies and taking clients to lunch. I wanted to learn what business was really all about and when I was twenty-one, although I had not been to university, I was accepted into the Unilever graduate management trainee scheme.

It was while I was working for Unilever in Manchester that we first became interested in sailing. I was spending too much time playing rugby, and one day Janet said, "I know you love playing rugby, but wouldn't it be nice if we could find a sport that we can do together?" I saw her point. I knitted my brows, puzzled, and wondered what sport that might be. I could only think of tennis, but I knew she didn't enjoy it. She said, "What about sailing? When I was young we spent summer holidays in Devon and I was taken sailing in dinghies by some of the boys. It was terrific fun." Impulsive and enthusiastic, I picked up a copy of the *Manchester Evening News* there and then, and we found a classified advertisement for a Mirror dinghy. Three days later we bought it and together we learned how to sail on the banks of Rudyard Lake, a reservoir on the outskirts of Manchester.

Janet hated living in Manchester, but she loyally supported me as she did in all the career moves I made: leaving Unilever, starting my own business—which I did three times—and coping with the risks, uncertainties, and house moves that went with my career changes. We had traditional and clearly defined roles, unspoken but understood, which made us a team: old-fashioned by today's marriage standards, but it was a relationship that worked for us.

When Janet left me alone in my hospital room I spent hours reading the articles in *Yachting World* and *Yachting Monthly,* and when I had read them all I turned to the advertisements in the back. My attention was drawn to one for a beautiful yacht. It was a 70-foot ketch called *Lazy Jacques* that had sailed around the world. It was for sale in Lymington, England.

As I lay there staring up at the ceiling, I thought of our dream of sailing across the Pacific. We had already achieved a long-held ambition to sail across the Atlantic after I had retired from business in 2000. Then we spent three years cruising among the islands of the Eastern Caribbean.

Janet had often suggested crossing the Pacific but I kept putting off the big decision. Perhaps I was nervous. Perhaps it was a step too far? "We can think about that next year," was usually my reply.

Now the urge to explore the world's largest ocean and visit remote islands returned, fueled by schoolboy memories of books I had read about the South Pacific—*Kon-Tiki, Mutiny on the Bounty,* and the explorations of Captain Cook. I felt that if I got better I shouldn't let the opportunity go by again. Perhaps a bigger, better boat was the stimulus I needed? When Janet visited me the next day, on an impulse I asked her to go to England to see *Lazy Jacques*. It must have seemed a strange request at a time like this, but to my surprise, she agreed. When she came back a week later she told me, "It is a beautiful boat and very well constructed, but not right for us. The accommodation was disappointing." I smiled and settled back on my pillow. It didn't matter. We didn't say any more about it then, but we had an unspoken pact that if I did get well again, we would make our dream come true.

But I didn't get better quickly. I had to return to Grasse hospital three times after new attacks. I developed pleurisy and my lungs were affected. I was deeply shocked to be so ill and for so long. Having been healthy all my life, and having never been in hospital before, at the age of sixty-five I was suddenly very aware of my mortality. When I finally left Grasse hospital I wanted to know what restrictions there would be on my way of life, and in order to avoid misunderstandings I asked my daughter, Nicky, to translate for me. She looked at my list of questions and smiled. The last two were, "Is it safe to have sex?" and "Can I drink alcohol?" When she posed these questions to Dr. Tissot, he paused, pursed his lips, and said, "Sex is okay, but no doctor can recommend alcohol." How French!

After three months of recuperation I was finally allowed to return home to Switzerland, where I was seen by Professor Françoise Spertini—a leader in the field of immune diseases—at the Vaud University Teaching Hospital in Lausanne. He concluded that my case was not a breakdown of the immune system, as he had feared, and that the cause was probably an unknown virus that had attacked my heart and lungs. Each time we met we talked about sailing and he encouraged me to be positive about our sailing dream. The panic attacks I had been experiencing receded and my confidence began to return.

Janet and I began to discuss the issues involved in sailing across the Pacific Ocean. It is true that some of the challenges of the early pioneering yachtsmen in the mid-twentieth century have disappeared—yachts are bigger, safer, and more comfortable. They are equipped with electronic navigation aids, water makers, furling sails, autopilots, and satellite phones. But the Pacific is enormous and a crossing is still a major undertaking, demanding experience, commitment, and self-sufficiency. If we went we would probably be away from home for at least three years.

Were we sure this was what we wanted to do? Of the hundreds of thousands of yachtsmen in the world less than two hundred cross the Pacific each year. Why do they do it? Probably for many reasons: for the sense of achievement it brings, to discover distant islands, to see other cultures, to enjoy its remoteness and escape from the routine pressures of life, or perhaps as George Mallory said of Everest, "Because it's there." For us, though, the overwhelming motivation was a yearning to explore remote places and meet people from very different cultures.

To understand more about the commitment we would be making we read books, including the excellent *The Pacific Crossing Guide* from the Royal Cruising Club Pilotage Foundation in association with the Ocean Cruising Club, which was our bible in those early days. It told us about the weather, winds, and currents that we could expect, the best routes to take, and the best time to go. The editors, Michael Pocock and Ros Hogbin, gave us an idea of what the islands were like and advised on how a yacht should be equipped for such a long voyage. Above all, it stressed the need to be self-sufficient in the maintenance and repair of the yacht. I remember the comment that you are far more likely to have to fix an outboard motor for an islander than for them to be able to help you. The more we read, the more we were convinced that it was what we wanted to do. But other big decisions would have to be made. Could we do it on our own, or should we have crew to help us? Should we sell our present boat and buy a bigger one? Would we need to move from our home in Switzerland if we were to be away so long? But the biggest discussion we kept having was whether we could do it on our own or would we need help to crew the boat.

We were certainly experienced sailors who enjoyed the freedom of being at sea, the achievement of being able to sail and navigate, the satisfaction of learning and using the skills of seamanship, and visiting quiet and remote anchorages inaccessible from the land. We had graduated from our Mirror dinghy to sailing a keelboat along the south coast of England and then made what seemed to us at the time the giant step of crossing the English Channel—our first time out of sight of land! When the children were older we sailed further afield, exploring the west coast of France and discovering the charms of southwest Brittany. Later we sailed as far as the northwest coast of Spain for our annual family holiday.

It had been fun teaching our children to sail and seeing them experience the sheer joy of the moment when the wind fills the sails and the boat shivers with expectation, but when the children left home we started yacht racing, encouraged by my sailing mentor, Ian Miller. We enjoyed the cut and thrust of inshore racing but Janet was less keen on offshore racing, which usually involved a weekend at sea, often in horrible weather, with the interior of the boat filled with wet sails. Offshore racing has famously been described as tearing up £50 notes under a cold shower, and it's an apt description. We competed in the Cowes Week regatta and sailed to Ireland for the Cork Week races. The highlight of my ocean racing, though, was taking part in the famous annual Fastnet Race from Plymouth to the Fastnet Rock, off the southwest coast of Ireland, and back to Plymouth. Many years later Janet and I sailed across the Atlantic in our own yacht. It had seemed like the pinnacle of our sailing achievements.

But now we were much older. The illness had shaken my confidence and made us realize that we were both vulnerable to illness or injury, which could be disastrous if there were only two of us on a boat alone at sea. We knew that we would have to be able to deal with any emergencies or mechanical problems ourselves.

I didn't want these responsibilities on my shoulders anymore. The one thing I had always hated about sailing was fixing things when they broke, which they frequently do. I disliked routine engine maintenance and dreaded the moment the engine stopped at a crucial moment. Many sailors love working on their boats, and spend winter weekends doing an endless list of jobs. As much as I tried, I simply wasn't one of those people, and it was probably this more than anything else that had always held me back from committing to sailing across the Pacific.

Another good reason to have crew was that we would be spending many days and nights at sea, and would have to take turns at watch keeping as we sailed through the night. It is very tiring, and although we did it when we younger, we didn't want to do it now.

Our first thought was that we might be able to ask friends or family to crew with us, but we soon realized this was not practical because it would mean asking them to take weeks and months out of their lives and that just wasn't going to happen. So we concluded that we would have a professional crew, trained, experienced, and able to take on the responsibilities and workload.

We realized that this would mean giving up some of our privacy and might diminish our sense of achievement, but there would be plenty of benefits. We would be free to explore the places we visited without being tied down by repairs and maintenance, cleaning and polishing, or waiting for spare parts to be delivered. There would be four of us to share night watches, cutting down the hours of sleep lost at night. We would be able to enjoy the sailing experience more knowing that we had someone else to take the responsibility for the safety of the boat in an emergency.

Having decided to have crew it wasn't hard to see that we needed a bigger boat. Our present yacht, *Ace of Clubs*, a Discovery 55, was perfectly suitable for two people to sail around the world, but wasn't big enough for us and two crew. So, with some reluctance, we decided to sell her and search for a new boat that would comfortably accommodate four people for long periods with a reasonable amount of privacy.

But the first step was to sell our own boat, which was in the Caribbean where we had been cruising. We had been unable to go there for the winter season because of my illness, so I contacted Professional Yacht Deliveries World Wide (PYD), and employed them to sail her back across the Atlantic to Palma, Mallorca. The skipper PYD employed was called Luke Windle, and we met him on the dock when he delivered our yacht to Palma on 1 June 2005. We had a long chat about the voyage and we liked him. He was only twenty-six, but was already very experienced, having been a delivery skipper since he was twenty-one. Janet and I stood on the dock and watched Luke walk off to the taxi that would take him to the airport and another delivery job. Little did we know that he would one day be the skipper of our next yacht.

2

Dreams Come True

Palma is the yachting capital of the Mediterranean, an ideal place for selling or buying a yacht, but none of the boats we saw seemed to fit the bill. The marina in Palma was a good place to meet people and we went out of our way to talk to owners and professional crew and ask them how they managed the relationship. In the warm summer evenings when work was finished and the marina was quiet, we walked up and down the dock chatting to crew. Often, over a beer at the end of the day, they told us that owners' expectations were unreasonable. It was no surprise to find that owners and crew had a different view of the relationship. Owners thought their crews were well paid, with all expenses taken care of, worked on a beautiful yacht, and sailed to fabulous places. Crew thought that the work schedule was too demanding, that they were paid less than they should be, and that when they went to wonderful places, they had no time off to see them. Most owners, it seemed, were modern versions of Captain Bligh.

The long Indian summer in Palma came to an end, and by December we had not had any luck selling *Ace of Clubs* or finding a new boat. I explained our problem to an old sailing friend, John Graham, who was a professional skipper who had sailed around the world. He suggested that we should come to see him in Fort Lauderdale, where there were several yachts that might interest us.

He met us at Miami Airport and as we drove to Fort Lauderdale to meet a yacht broker he told us that he was getting married. We were delighted, but realized that this would rule out any chance of him being our skipper, an idea we had been nurturing for some time. The broker drove us north on the busy I-95 to the exclusive West Palm Beach area and showed us two yachts, *Volare* and *Martha E*. We liked *Volare*, a modern classic that the world-famous yacht designer, Ron Holland, had built for his own use. What better recommendation could there be! *Martha E* was much larger with a light wood interior but didn't catch our eye as much as the head-turning *Volare.* We were very excited and asked the broker if we could see both boats again the next day.

Nineteenth January 2006 was a red-letter day for us—a complete turnaround! The negatives we had about *Martha E* melted away as we walked around her again. It was love at second sight! From the top of the dock we looked down at her lying alongside the pontoon. She was gleaming white with teak decks and a pilothouse that had black windows. *Martha E* looked purposeful, powerful, and ready to go anywhere. She was big too, 78 feet, much bigger than we had expected to be able to afford. But bigger has many advantages for a round-the-world sailing yacht: more space, more privacy for us and the crew, more stowage space, a more stable platform in a big seaway, and faster passage times. As we sat in the saloon, shafts of pale winter sunlight came streaming through the windows, reflecting off the warm honey-coloured wood interior joinery. We sat on the comfortable blue leather upholstery and looked around. She was so large, and beautifully finished. Could we afford this boat? And if we could, would we be able to manage it?

We flew home with our minds buzzing. Michael Nethersole, the broker, had been very helpful. He thought we might be able to get *Martha E* considerably below the asking price, which made her look very good value for money. John Graham was with us for the two boat inspections. His advice was invaluable, partly because he was totally independent, partly because he knew us and our sailing background, but most of all because of his ocean sailing experience. He pointed out the good and bad features on each boat and helped us understand what mattered when you were living on a boat for years at a time. He was careful not to make a specific recommendation about which boat to buy. At the end of the day that's a very personal decision. But after seven months of looking, we felt that *Martha E* was the one. It was time to make a move. After a series of rather tense negotiations we finally agreed on a price. We heaved a sigh of relief as we signed a binding contract, subject only to a sail trial and a survey.

On 28 January we returned to Palm Beach for the sail trial. It was a windy day with 25-knot[1] winds and big seas but Jeff, the owner's professional skipper, was calm and in control. It was challenging weather but a good day to test a boat's sailing ability and she handled it well. I was almost overwhelmed by the size and power of the yacht. She was so much bigger than what I was used to. John reminded me that we would have crew and we wouldn't be sailing the boat on our own. His advice reassured me. The decision was made. We put the survey in hand and began the formal process of purchasing *Martha E*.

Now it became urgent to complete the sale of *Ace of Clubs*, and we had a stroke of luck when an English couple we had been trying to reach for months phoned us out of the blue. They came to see the boat and a few days later made an offer. It was lower than I wanted but it had the effect of galvanising a Swiss buyer whom we had met earlier and he made a better offer. The deal was completed quickly to our great relief. I began to feel that my lucky star was looking after me again.

While we were in Palma for the sale of *Ace of Clubs* we interviewed a young married couple who had been recommended to us for the position of captain and first mate/engineer. We had been disappointed by the crew we had interviewed so far, but with this couple everything clicked from the start. The feeling was clearly mutual and we soon agreed terms and a start date of the 23 April 2006.

The structural and mechanical surveys on *Martha E* had been completed to my satisfaction and she formally became ours on 28 March 2006. One of the first things we did was change the boat's name. The previous owner named the boat after his mother, Martha Entenmann, who had founded the Entenmann cake empire. We chose *Moonraker* and submitted it to the British ship register of the Cayman Islands. A ship's name has to be unique, so it seemed a good omen when we received a letter saying that it had been approved.

---

1 *Wind speed is measured in knots. True wind is the force that is felt when the boat is stationary and is the speed that would be given in any weather forecast. The apparent wind speed is the wind as it is affected by the speed of the boat, e.g., if the true wind is 10 knots, and the boat is motoring straight into it at 5 knots, the apparent wind speed will be 15 knots. If the true wind speed is 10 knots and the boat is motoring with the wind dead behind, the apparent wind speed will be 5 knots. On Moonraker our wind instruments were set to show apparent wind speed, because that is what the helmsman wants to know, and that is generally what is quoted in the text. The exception was the wind instrument at the chart table, that was always showing true wind, which was recorded in the log book.*

The name *Moonraker* comes from my childhood. If you are born and bred in Wiltshire, as I was, you are known as a Moonraker. Wiltshire legend has it that one moonlit night, a group of farm boys smuggling contraband were surprised by a visit from the customs and excise men. They quickly dropped their bottles of brandy into the millpond, which was still as a...well, as a millpond, in which the bright full moon was reflected. When the customs men asked what they were doing standing in the pond with their hay rakes, they pointed at the reflection of the moon and replied, "We're rakin' that ther cheese outter the pond." The customs men went away convinced that they were dealing with country bumpkins, but the lesson is that Wiltshire boys are not as simple as they seem!

Ocean sailing is governed by the seasons. The best time to cross the Pacific is the summer, leaving Panama in March and arriving in New Zealand in September. It was now the end of April and we were too late this year. We decided to take a few weeks getting the boat ready and leave Fort Lauderdale on 23 May to sail up the eastern seaboard of America. After a week in the Chesapeake Bay, we would call in at New York where our son Stephen lives, before reaching Newport, Rhode Island, a base for a summer cruising on the New England coast. In the autumn we planned to have refit work done in Newport, sail to the Caribbean for Christmas, and then head west across the top of South America to arrive in Panama by March 2007.

Our crew joined the boat in Fort Lauderdale on 23 April and we arrived a few days later. The *Moonraker* name had been painted in gold and black on the transom[2] and the boom[3] and we felt proud as we gazed at it. It was our boat now and we were at the beginning of our great adventure. We walked around the interior of the boat and took stock of the accommodation in our new floating home. The cockpit felt deep, safe, and comfortable, with shelter from sun, wind, rain, and waves. The cockpit led to a pilothouse, a raised inside area with all-round glass giving perfect visibility. Although the main steering position was in the cockpit, and there was a navigation station below, it was also possible to steer and navigate from there. It would be a warm dry place to do a night watch and a pleasant place to sit in an anchorage and watch the world go by.

Down below, the accommodation provided everything that a small home might have. *Moonraker* was the same length as a tennis court, but only 18 feet wide at the broadest point and tapering to the bow and the

---

2   The transom is the flat surface forming the stern of the boat.
3   The boom is the spar that is connected to the mast and the bottom of the mainsail.

stern. We had a large saloon (living area), which was light, spacious and airy, with a dining table on one side and a coffee table with a settee on the other. The galley (kitchen) was well equipped with two large freezers and two refrigerators, giving us a great deal of fresh food storage capacity. The oven was gimballed, allowing it to swing and maintain a horizontal position no matter how much the yacht was heeled over, which meant that saucepans would stay in position when we were cooking at sea. Work surfaces were in blue Corian, and cups, plates, and bowls were nestled in specially designed lockers with wooden dowels holding the crockery in position.

Our cabin (bedroom) in the aft section of the boat had a double bed the same size as the one we had at home, and even had room for a small desk area and a TV. In the forward section in front of the mast there were two guest cabins and a crew cabin, providing a total of eight berths, all with their own heads (toilets) and showers. This was an ideal setup. We could occupy the back of the boat and our crew would be in the forward section, giving us all privacy.

One of the heads had a washing machine. When I told my daughter Nicky on the phone, she said, "You've got a washing machine on your boat?" and I replied, "Yes, don't you have one in your home?" We could generate our own electricity and produce our own water. The large fuel tank gave us a range of three thousand miles, which meant that we could be at sea for many weeks at a time without having to find places to take on water, fuel or food. As well as modern navigation equipment there were satellite communications, so we would be able to send and receive e-mail to keep in touch with family and friends.

There is never enough stowage space on a boat and every nook and cranny has to be used to store food, drink, clothing, books, charts, equipment, spares, and a host of things that might be needed in faraway places. We explored the possibilities in addition to the lockers provided—behind settees, under our large double bed, under the cabin soles (floorboards), and even in the bilges.

A steady stream of boxes arrived from Switzerland with the personal possessions we wanted to have with us to turn our boat into our home: books, CDs, DVDs (those that we would be happy see over and over again: favourite movies, Shakespeare plays, operas) and photographs of our children and grandchildren. Janet had included paintings from her Victorian watercolour collection, mainly seascapes, which immediately made the boat feel more like home. She had also brought beautiful artificial flowers from Switzerland, pale blue irises, which convinced most people that they were real. Although she would not be able to have fresh flowers in the months to come, they would be the next best thing, and it gave the boat that intangible female touch.

The crew had a long job list of work to be done before we could leave Fort Lauderdale. Most of it related to points raised in the yacht survey, but we also needed to attend to maintenance and servicing, as well as equipping the boat to the standard we wanted for our ocean crossing. At the life raft service center we saw our ten-man life raft taken out of its canister and inflated for checking and service. It looked brand new and I sincerely hoped that it was the last time we would see it open!

We made time to go sailing and learn how to handle our new boat, and after two weeks we left our crew to get on with preparing the boat and returned to Montreux to make the myriad arrangements necessary for us to leave Switzerland and move to the Cayman Islands.

How quickly sailing plans can change! I got a call from our skipper. "Graham, I'm afraid it's bad news. A rigger has been up the mast to tune the rig and noticed two cracks in the mast. They might be cosmetic, but he thinks it is more likely that there's structural damage. The head rigger is coming back to look himself." The owner of the firm later confirmed that he thought it was a serious problem. He sent photographs and a report to Matrix, the mast builders in New Zealand, for their comments.[4]

This was a bolt from the blue, particularly as prior to completing the purchase the yacht had been surveyed by a well-respected surveying firm. Our skipper thought it would probably mean having the mast taken out and repaired, which would delay our plan to sail to Newport on 23 May by at least a month.

Phew! There were now a lot of additional worries to think about: the cost, of course, and the negligence and potential liability of the surveyor. Then there was Florida sales tax. If the boat was not out of the state ninety days after the purchase date we would be liable for Florida sales tax, and this delay would take us past the deadline. In addition, our insurance company required that the yacht must be north of Morehead City, North Carolina, before 1 June—the start of hurricane season. Our sailing plans for the summer looked in tatters.

But two weeks later the news improved. Having seen the photographs and talked to the riggers in Florida, Matrix came back quickly and told

---

4 *Two cracks were found in the mast below the tangs that join the D (diagonal) shrouds to the mast.*

us that the cracks were cosmetic and should give us no cause for concern. What a relief! Our insurance company gave us permission to set sail, provided that we had the mast taken out, checked, and serviced in six months. Reassured by this good news we left Switzerland and flew back to Fort Lauderdale feeling excited about getting underway. When we arrived back the boat was fueled up, the vittling (provisioning) done, and we were ready to leave at last. It was eighteen months since I had been in my hospital bed in Grasse, dreaming of sailing across the Pacific. There had been many hurdles to cross to get to the starting line, but now we were there, and eager to begin our greatest sailing adventure.

3

All Change at Newport

At last the time had come for us to cast off the lines holding us to the dock in Fort Lauderdale and head out into the open ocean. On 6 June 2006 we rose at dawn. The early morning air was crisp and fresh, and as the golden orb of the sun rose above the horizon it seemed to promise not just another day, but the beginning of a new chapter in our lives. A frisson of excitement ran down my spine. It was already six days into the hurricane season but the forecast was fair. Just eighty miles to the east lay Freeport, on Grand Bahama, an easy one-day sail, and we motor sailed[5] across in a light breeze and sunshine. It was a stop necessary to satisfy the bureaucratic requirements of U.S. immigration and customs. As the boat was purchased in the U.S., it was necessary to clear *out* of the U.S. so that when we cleared back *in* we could obtain the necessary U.S. cruising permit! It was hard to grasp the logic of that.

We tied up in the commercial dock at Freeport, a surprisingly large container port with twelve giant cranes. The Customs and Immigration officers were very friendly, always a pleasant surprise, and even came down to the boat to give us the papers and clearance we needed, saving us the trouble of finding their office.

Because of the delay caused by the mast problem, we had to abandon our plan to spend a week in the Chesapeake Bay and instead sail directly to New York, but we were excited by the idea of docking in the shadow of the World Financial Center to meet our son, Stephen. The passage was a thousand miles, which we estimated would take about six days.

---

5   *Motoring with the sails up, which produces more speed in light winds and improves the motion of the boat.*

The first day out gave us a wonderful day's sailing. There was a moderate breeze, around 13 knots, with a relatively flat sea, enabling us to sail fast—ideal sailing conditions. I looked at the instruments and grinned when I saw we were doing a steady 8–9 knots.[6] *Moonraker* was performing much better than I expected for a 70-ton boat in light winds. In the early evening we caught our first fish, a large dorado weighing eight kilos. It was a perfect end to a perfect day. We were not to know then that storm clouds, both metaphorical and physical, were already building.

The next day brought a change in the weather. Low grey clouds covered the sky. The wind increased and the dark blue seas were lumpy as wind and current opposed each other, making the boat's motion uncomfortable. Although we were only two hundred miles off the eastern seaboard of America there was no sign of any shipping traffic. *Moonraker* shouldered her way powerfully through the bigger waves, again making good speed, but toward the end of the day we had a major setback. The vang[7] suffered a hydraulics failure, which meant that we could no longer safely use the mainsail, which had to be lowered and stowed. We were forced to motor sail the rest of the way using just the jib[8] and the engine. The motion of the boat changed. Instead of carving our way over the waves and bending to the wind, we were forcing our way through them. It was uncomfortable, and the joy of sailing was supplanted by the monotony of motoring.

Later we picked up the news of Tropical Storm Alberta on our weather forecasts. It was the first named storm of the hurricane season and came much earlier than usual. It moved over Cuba and affected the Cayman Islands, and quickly made its way north. It was forecast to continue up the eastern seaboard as far north as Newport. We were two days ahead of the storm and we expected to outrun it, but it was a nagging worry. How lucky we were that we got away from Fort Lauderdale when we did! Two days later and we could have been delayed by a week, or worse, caught in the storm.

---

6   *Knots is how the speed of boats, wind, and current are measured at sea. 1 knot = 1 nautical mile and 5 knots = 5.8 miles per hour. Distance is measured in nautical miles and wherever miles are stated in the text they are nautical miles. A statute mile is 5280 feet and a nautical mile is 6076 feet, i.e., a nautical mile is 15% longer than a statute mile.*

7   *The vang is a hydraulically-powered strut that controls the angle of the boom. It would be called a kicking strap on a small boat.*

8   *We had two head sails. The largest is the jib and behind that is the smaller staysail, which was mainly used for sailing upwind in strong winds. They can be used separately or in tandem.*

We decided not to call in to New York and sailed directly to Newport as the repair facilities we needed for the vang were more likely to be found there. This was a disappointment. Of more concern was a feeling I had that my relationship with the crew was not going the way I'd expected. We were not a happy ship. I decided to watch carefully and keep silent for now.

Moonraker slipped into the estuary leading into Newport at 10:45 AM on Monday 12 June. We had taken just over five days to cover the 1030 miles. The early morning mist was already being burnt off by the sun, revealing the buildings along the shore. The mansions of the Astors, Vanderbilts, and other industrialists who built modern America stood proudly on a hill, gazing down serenely at the river below. A traditional fishing boat with red sails and a green wooden hull sailed by, no doubt bringing out day-trippers from Newport.

Once we were tied up and settled down Janet and I had a chat with our crew about how things were going. They were a charming young couple and eager to please, but the main issue as I saw it was that they wanted to do everything entailed in sailing and running the boat, whereas I wanted to be actively involved myself. The situation was made more difficult because we were all in new roles. I was used to running my own boat and had never had professional crew before and they had come from a six-man crew on a superyacht owned by a wealthy Russian who used the boat solely to entertain his guests. We discussed the problem frankly and I hoped that things would get back on an even keel again. The crew began organizing the repair to the vang and attending to other jobs and we set out to explore Newport.

Newport was truly delightful and more charming than I could have imagined. The river estuary reminded me of Dartmouth, England. The harbour walls stretch out their arms to protect the hundreds of yachts bobbing at their moorings. On each side of the narrow cobbled streets are quaint old timber houses with blue and white clapboard. Thames Street (which the locals pronounce Thame, rhyming with fame) is a busy main street with boutique-style shops in traditional buildings.

The town has a similar sailing history and pedigree as Cowes in the Isle of Wight, but is much larger. Here, on immaculate green lawns that run down to the water's edge, is the country clubhouse of the New York Yacht Club, the historic home of the America's Cup—truly a yachting Mecca. From our mooring out in the middle of the harbour we watched sailing yachts of every kind: classic wooden yachts, the huge J Class yachts including *Valsheda*, twelve metre ex-America's Cup yachts, and the fast modern J-boats that are built in Newport. It seemed that everyone here just loves sailing. They were probably brought up to sail as children and their natural skills are there for all to see as they weave their sailboats in and out of the moored boats in the harbour without any thought of using an auxiliary engine (if they have one!).

Newport was a major commercial port two centuries ago, but in the early part of the twentieth century it became an exclusive and fashionable resort for the superrich, and the Astors and the Vanderbilts built what they called their summer cottages—in reality, mansions—on Bellevue Avenue. Janet and I took the famous 3.5-mile cliff walk that runs between the bottom of the gardens and the sea, giving us a close-up view into how the rich lived then. Some of the largest homes are now owned by trusts and open to the public, and we visited three, including the famous Marble House. It is hard to imagine how much money must have been spent on building, fitting, and furnishing these modern palaces. Seeing such opulence in those days must have made you either a committed capitalist or a communist!

We had to stay in Newport for two weeks whilst the vang was being repaired and fortunately for us this coincided with the 650-mile Newport Bermuda Race. It is a famous international sailing event and one of the highlights of the Newport yachting and social calendar. This year was the 100th anniversary and the town was buzzing all week with crews busy making final preparations. The race began off Castle Point, overlooked by the prestigious Castle Hill Inn, and we decided to watch the start there. It was about five miles away and I tried to book a taxi but it proved impossible because of the crowds in town for the race. Determined not to be beaten, I came up with the idea of renting a scooter from one of the bike and scooter rental shops you see all over Newport. I chose a two-abreast fiberglass green beetle with three wheels. We did the "shake, rattle and roll" over the bumpy country road and arrived at this very smart hotel on our green beetle, wearing crash helmets, to join the line of the good and the great of Newport arriving in luxury cars. The officially dressed marshal parking the cars looked at us in disbelief, then discreetly asked, "Would you mind parking over in the dustbins area, please, sir?" We hadn't come in quite the style I would have wanted, but we had got there.

The Castle Hill Inn is an elegant three-storied traditional wooden building with balconies billowing from all the floors, like a tall ship under full sail on a sea-green lawn. Hundreds of spectators, relatives, and friends of the competitors, dressed in bright nautical outfits of red, white, and blue, picnicked on the lawns and drank champagne in a scene reminiscent of an F. Scott Fitzgerald novel.

The day was warm with sun shining from a blue sky flecked with white cumulus clouds. A brisk breeze provided excellent sailing conditions for the three hundred starters. The yachts were divided into seven classes according to their size and so there was plenty of action as they jockeyed for position in the ten minutes leading up to each start. The noise of helicopters and light aircraft overhead added to the excitement. We were so busy taking photographs, watching the close-up action with our binoculars, and listening to the starter on our mobile VHF radio[9] that there was hardly a moment to eat the box lunch the inn provided. It had been an unexpectedly lovely day that made a complete break from our worries about the crew relationship.

At the end of June we left the boat in Newport to go back to Montreux for a week to pack up our home. Our furniture was being sent to the Cayman Islands and we planned to move there at the end of August while the boat refit was being done. The problems with the crew hung over us and soon came to a head. Although we were very busy packing up I was in regular phone and e-mail contact with the skipper. Through these exchanges it became increasingly clear that the relationship was not going to work, and finally we decided that we would have to replace them. It was a big decision. It wasn't a good time to change crew, but we knew that it was better than finding ourselves in a nightmare later on. We realized that total trust and a happy working relationship would be crucial when we were out in the middle of the Pacific; having crew with whom we were compatible would probably be the biggest single challenge we would face, one that could make or break our dream.

Now we had ridiculous time pressures—our eldest son Peter and his family were joining us on the boat one week later for a three-week family holiday. We also had to appoint a boatyard to do refit work in the autumn. Philip Coatsworth, the managing director of Professional Yacht Deliveries, knows a thing or two about crew, so I phoned him to discuss the situation and see if any of his delivery skippers might be looking for a career change. I thought that perhaps a skipper who had not run an owner's boat before might be a good bet—we could work out how we would operate together. He understood the problem, and told me, "A husband and wife crew can be difficult, Graham. If you have a problem with one it will always be

---

9   *Very High Frequency radio has a range of thirty to fifty miles. It is used to talk to other ships or to harbour control.*

defended by the other. If you have a male skipper and first mate, you can deal with each person separately. Do you remember Luke Windle? I think you should consider him."

I did, and had liked him when we met. Philip told us that he was young but had been given responsibility early on and was now very experienced. The reports he got from the crews who sailed with Luke were always excellent. It was a very strong recommendation, and as we had no time to spare we arranged to interview Luke at a hotel at London Heathrow Airport before we flew back out to Newport.

Luke strode into the lounge of the Jurys Inn hotel and immediately inspired confidence in us. He was tall, looked strong and fit, and was weather-beaten from months at sea. He told us that he had decided to make a career in sailing after completing a year's Atlantic circuit with his family. He skippered the boat for his father, and Luke felt that this helped him understand the relationship we were looking for. Naturally, Luke asked me what went wrong with the last crew, and it gave us the opportunity to be very frank. We picked up very good vibes and decided to offer the job to him then and there. He accepted enthusiastically. Three days later, he was on board in Newport, familiarizing himself with the boat. We went to the beaches in Newport with Peter and his young family and then sailed locally in Narragansett Bay.

4

Thar She Blows

When Peter and Lara left the three of us set off to cruise the coast of New England. We were one crewmember short but it didn't worry us. The three of us were interchangeable in all aspects of sailing the boat—anchoring, setting the sails, steering and navigating—and Luke had very quickly got the hang of how all the systems on the boat operated.

Off the coast of Massachusetts there are many lovely islands that are popular with cruising yachtsmen. The best known are Martha's Vineyard and Nantucket, but our first visit was to Cuttyhunk in the Elizabethan Islands. Cuttyhunk (not a name to say when you're drunk) is remote, totally unspoiled, and quite charming, a place where time has stood still. It has a year-round population of only twenty-three, but a few more in the summer when people come to their summer cottages. There are no cars, just golf carts. The tiny school is open only when there are children to teach and the one church serves three denominations, Catholic, Episcopalian, and Methodist. God must be a fisherman, because the church has a wind vane with the arrow in the form of a large striped bass! The only visitors are yachtsmen, so everyone is very friendly. Fishing is the main activity. A large table and fresh water tap are provided on the dock for yachtsmen to clean and wash their catch of the day. The climb along the path from the village to the highest point on the island was rewarded by magnificent 360-degree views. *Moonraker* was just a distant dot anchored outside the small harbour. There were no restaurants, so like most sailors in Cuttyhunk that night, we enjoyed a barbeque on board with the backdrop of a rich red sunset that spread slowly across the evening sky.

From Cuttyhunk we sailed up Buzzards Bay and took the cut through the Elizabethan Islands into Vineyard Sound, passing through Woods

Hole, a narrow channel that provided a dramatic moment. The pilot book had warned that the tide rushes through, but it still took us by surprise as the current pushed through the channel at 6–9 knots. With jagged rocks all around, it called for strong nerves and instant decisions. Janet sat at the chart plotter down below calling out the course and Luke struggled to maintain steerage as we picked our way round the buoys marking the channel. It was like white water rafting in the Canadian Rockies, but the boat wasn't rubber! We heaved a collective sigh of relief as we shot out into the calm waters of the Sound.

Martha's Vineyard is a famous and bustling holiday island about the size of the Isle of Wight. Although passenger and car ferries bring holidaymakers there, it is essentially a smart, exclusive island where the well off have summer homes. It is also remembered as the place where John Kennedy, Jr., was killed when his light aircraft crashed one misty night.

The Black Dog Tavern in the port is an authentic sea dog's tavern with scrubbed wooden floors, wooden tables, and old sepia photographs of tall ships and whaling boats. We almost expected Captain Ahab to come through the door at any minute. The only thing missing was the beer—Vineyard Haven is dry! A whole steamed lobster is the traditional dish, which we cracked open with our bare hands. In the heat of the battle bits of my lobster landed on Luke. I don't know who was more embarrassed, the owner or the new captain!

The following day we drove a Jeep round the island and by sheer luck found a splendid inland restaurant at a crossroads next to a mom and pop general store. It was called Cornerway and was run by Deon Thomas, a West Indian chef who also owns a restaurant in Anguilla, so the food had a distinctly Caribbean flavour. We realized that this place was a cut above the average when Wayne, our friendly Barbadian waiter, showed us the reservation that Bill and Hillary Clinton had made for the following week.

Martha's Vineyard is such a pretty name, and I was curious to know how the island had come by it. We expected that we would find the answer when we saw the sign to the Chicama Vineyards. So they do grow grapes here, I thought, but who was Martha? Eager to find out, we drove down a dusty track and arrived just in time for a tour of the winery. It was run by three generations of women, grandma, mom, and daughter. Aha! I thought. Which one is Martha?

It was none of them. It turned out that Chicama was a small family firm founded in 1971. The daughter explained that the island was probably called the Vineyard because the early colonial settlers found vines producing berries that looked like grapes. It was discovered by the English explorer Bartholomew Gosnold in 1602. From the ship's papers it is known that his captain was John Martin, and the original name of Martin's Vineyard probably derived from his name. It was later changed to Martha's Vineyard, perhaps because Gosnold's daughter was named Martha. Whatever, it was clear that there was no Martha and she didn't have a vineyard. Pity!

The warm sunny days with pleasant sailing winds had disappeared to be replaced by strong winds and a thick mist as we sailed up to Nantucket. It shouldn't have been a surprise. Mark Twain said, "One of the brightest gems in the New England weather is the dazzling uncertainty of it." We had certainly been dazzled, having already experienced thick fog, electric thunderstorms, torrential rain, 100-degree F temperatures, and bright sunshine.

The only ships we saw on our way up to Nantucket were trawlers, which were everywhere in these parts, and we had to watch carefully for lobster pots as their ropes could easily wrap around our propeller if we ran over one. As we crept up the narrow channel to the harbour on this misty day, we saw rocks on either side. The wreck of a sailing yacht with just the top half of its mast showing was an eerie reminder of the perils of the sea. Later I heard that this disaster happened only three weeks earlier when a single-handed sailor was motoring up the channel in very strong winds and his engine failed.

Nantucket is probably the best known of the islands we visited. It is most famous for having been the whaling centre of the world in the eighteenth and nineteenth centuries. From Nantucket, whalers went out into the North and South Pacific in search of sperm whale. Some would be away from home for three years, killing whales and boiling down their fat to make the oil for the candles that provided light throughout America and Europe. Whaling was certainly a cruel way to kill whales, but it was also incredibly dangerous for the whalers. When the cry "Thar she blows" went up, men would take to small rowing boats, eight to a boat, with the harpooner in the bow poised to drive his harpoon into the whale as they got on top of it. Then the angry whale would take off at great speed, pulling the boat behind in what they called the "Nantucket sleigh ride." At any time the whale might dive, and the mate would have to make a decision whether to cut the rope and lose the whale or be pulled under and die. This battle could last between two to eight hours before the whale eventually gave up the struggle, and then the exhausted men would have to row back to the mother ship, by now many miles away, pulling the whale behind them. If that were their first whale, they would have to do this forty-nine more times before the captain would finally turn the ship for home.

Nantucket was the leader in this industry for 150 years, as only the Nantucket men had the skills and were brave enough to go after the huge sperm whales. But in 1840 the industry went into a rapid decline when petroleum was discovered and found to be a much cheaper way of providing oil for light.

But Nantucket reinvented itself and is now a prosperous island with summer homes for the wealthy. It retains the heritage of its past with cobbled streets, along which are the homes that once belonged to wealthy whaling merchants. The attractive tree-lined streets now have fashion boutiques, art galleries, and restaurants in tastefully restored buildings. From economic disaster a new prosperity has grown up from the bare bones of the whaling industry, a tribute to the fortitude and business instincts of the Nantucket people.

From Nantucket we sailed 130 miles south to Sag Harbor on Long Island Sound. Sag Harbor is in the Hamptons, a fashionable area where wealthy New Yorkers go for weekends. Our youngest son, Stephen, and his partner, Kristina, came out by train from New York to join us there. It was great to see them again and enjoy glorious summer weather after the disastrous rain and fog we had when they came to the boat in Newport in June. We sailed out to Block Island, some thirty miles away, and anchored in the Great Salt Pond, which is an almost enclosed lagoon with a very narrow entrance. The pilot books told us that there was enough water depth in the entry channel but it was nerve-wracking. Like an aircraft taking off, once committed there is no turning back, but we passed safely through and into the deeper waters of the lagoon. I turned to Luke and said, "Were you worried?" "Yes" he replied, "especially when I saw swimmers standing in water up to their waists on either side of the boat." Inside, yachts were anchored everywhere, but we found a space with room to swing on our anchor chain. With so many boats so close together, there is always a risk of touching as they swing around, or worse, drag their anchor, which is what happened at four in the morning. Alerted by a high revving engine I went on deck to find a large motor yacht drifting down onto us and only fifty feet away. I watched helplessly, but to my relief the captain got the yacht under control and re-anchored a considerable distance away.

Our all too short summer cruise was at an end and it was time to sail back to Newport, where we were booked into the Hinckley boatyard at

Portsmouth, Rhode Island. The Hinckley Company is famous for building traditional sailing yachts, but they also have a fine reputation for refitting yachts, and it was here that we had arranged to do the work needed to get *Moonraker* ready for the Pacific crossing. The New England shakedown cruise had given us a good idea of the maintenance, upgrades, and changes that we wanted to make. Hinckley's experienced tradesmen poured all over the boat to prepare a plan on how best to do the work and what it would cost. Luke stayed on board to manage this while we returned to the Cayman Islands to move into our new home.

As we flew back to the Cayman Islands, Janet and I reflected on our short summer cruise and what we had learned about the boat and our new skipper. We were having a lot more fun, mostly because we were totally involved in sailing the boat. From the moment we dropped the mooring in Newport harbour, the three of us did everything together. We worked as a team and it felt like our own boat again.

The other thing we liked about Luke is that he loves sailing. His philosophy is that jobs have to be fitted around the sailing and not the other way round, and that was music to our ears. We kept the engine and generator off as much as we could and we sailed unless the winds were too light.

Although Luke was only twenty-six, his delivery experience in different types of yachts, in many parts of the world, and in all weather conditions, gave us confidence that he would safely take us anywhere. He had restored our enthusiasm and belief that we could live and work with a crew to realize our dream.

It was always our intention to have two crew members, a captain and a first mate, but things had gone so well on the New England cruise that we wondered if we could manage with just Luke. We broached the subject with him and, interestingly, he said he'd been wondering about it, too. Although we all knew that a fourth crew member would change the dynamics of our relationship, we agreed that the practicalities of maintenance, cleaning, and general help for Luke in running a boat of this size meant that we would have to take on a second crew member.

The job specification was agreed and it was left to Luke to produce a shortlist of candidates that he was happy with. He went back to England to conduct the interviews, and we later met with the final two shortlisted candidates. We chose Max Bowden. He had good sailing experience, was young, and had a positive attitude to life and an engaging personality. We felt that he would make a good companion for Luke as well as a competent work mate.

The refit was completed on 30 November 2006, fourteen weeks after the work began, a bigger and longer project than we expected.[10] There were 113 individual jobs on the Hinckley work schedule and the yard did a very good job. The quality of the work was excellent and they took only two weeks longer than the agreed completion date, although at one time Luke had ten men working on the boat as they hurried to get finished. In addition to the yard work, Luke and Max were able to tackle a long list of routine maintenance and cleaning work.

Sea trials were completed satisfactorily and Luke prepared to sail *Moonraker* from Rhode Island for the British Virgin Islands (BVI) in the Caribbean at the beginning of December. Janet and I had decided that we didn't care for a long winter passage in the North Atlantic so Luke asked Dana, a South African professional sailor he had met in the Hinckley yard, to help, along with his father, James. It was snowing hard when they left Newport in a weather window between the winter gales, so we knew we had made the right decision to sit this one out. The voyage was, as expected, cold, wet, and windy, but they made a fast passage, taking eight days to cover the 1600 miles. When we rejoined the boat in Tortola, BVI, she was nestled in the Nanny Cay Marina in bright Caribbean sunshine.

---

10 *See Appendix 1 for details of the work carried out by the Hinckley yard.*

5

Pirates in the Caribbean

Soon after we rejoined the boat in Tortola, our eldest daughter, Nicky, and her husband Gilles, arrived with their family for the Christmas holiday. Our grandsons, Tim and Luke, six and nine, were at an age when a sailing holiday in the Caribbean was an endless adventure. They snorkeled in twenty feet of crystal clear water, found a cannon from an old wreck, and identified angelfish, squirrelfish, blue tang, grunts, and parrot fish. Tim dived for a beautiful queen conch shell, much rarer and prettier than the usual conch. Luke spotted a human skull, and dived down to point it out to me. (It was an unusual piece of coral.) They learned to drive the dinghy and enjoy water sports. Max, who had been a sailing instructor, quickly had them mastering the wakeboard—a surfboard you kneel on while being towed at high speed. In a few days Luke graduated to water skis. How wonderful it is that young children have no fear! Luke shouted to Max, "Faster, faster," while his father called out, "Slower, slower." At the Bitter End Yacht Club we sailed Hobie Cats, which Luke and Tim steered with some help from an adult on the mainsheet.

When we sailed we put out fishing rods for the boys. They could hardly believe their luck when they caught two big fish, a jack and a king mackerel, both about three feet long. They were enthralled by the whole process of gaffing the fish and getting them onboard.

Christmas Day was certainly different. We flew the "Jolly Roger" and everyone had pirate costumes as presents. Sword fights broke out on deck all day. "Captain" Luke had dressed the mast with lights in the shape of a Christmas tree and Janet cooked a traditional Christmas dinner on board.

Pirates in the Caribbean

The Islands Time Forgot

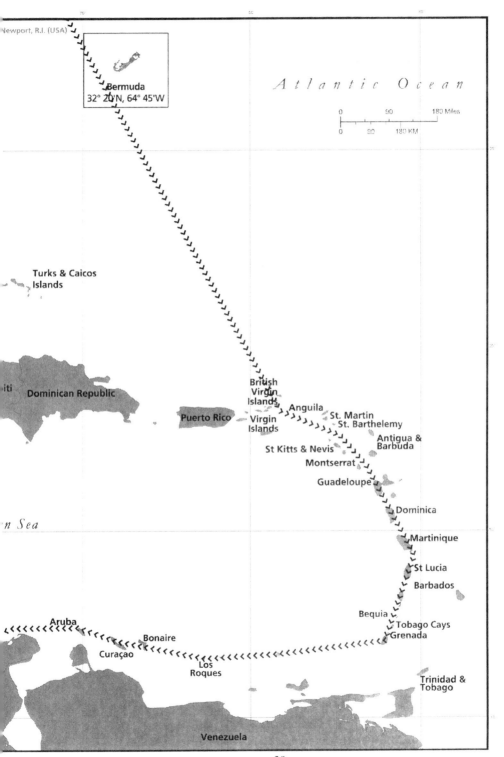

The BVIs are an ideal choice for family sailing with so many islands only a couple of hours sail away. We took the opportunity to visit several anchorages that were new to us, but Anegada remained our favourite. It is a small, flat island, reef protected, many miles from the rest of the BVI, and only accessible by yacht. The population is tiny, there isn't even a village, just a few sun-bleached cottages and some palm-thatched bars where yachtsmen can eat barbequed lobster and fish. The beaches are stunning—miles of white sand with clear turquoise water fringed by a coral reef. Here you can walk for an hour and see only diving pelicans and high-flying frigate birds before returning to a beach bar for a cold beer. At night, with no shore lights, the sky is lit by a canopy of brilliant stars, the sand sparkles with silver, and the sea gleams in the light of the moon. Anegada is a magical place.

It was here that our son-in-law, Gilles, found the ideal wind conditions for kite surfing, a sport in which the surfboard is pulled along by a large kite that you control as you surf over the water at high speed. It sounds difficult and it is! We watched a sponsored group from Holland who were experts and it was amazing to see them skimming the waves at speeds of around 30 knots.

Finally we said a sad goodbye to our family, and on 1 January 2007 set sail from Road Harbour, Tortola, bound for Antigua. The date was auspicious, the first day of a new year in which we would cross the Pacific Ocean. After champagne and red wine for our New Year's Eve celebration, we were not feeling great when we left. Luke and Max were fine, of course, despite going out to a party after dinner and returning in the early hours of the morning!

It was only 180 miles to Antigua, but what should have been a twenty-four-hour passage turned into thirty-six hours as we had 25-knot headwinds all the way. I was grateful not to succumb to seasickness, which I have been prone to in the past, and felt happier when Luke reminded me that headwinds should be a rarity from now on. Janet was brilliant, turning out great hot meals on time, despite the difficult conditions, which made her very popular with the crew. Max reeled in his first big fish, a three-foot-long dorado. It made eight steaks and two fillets, which we ate for lunch the next day.

Antigua is the St. Tropez of the Caribbean and *Moonraker* was dwarfed by the superyachts anchored in the picturesque Falmouth Harbour, including the amazing *Maltese Falcon*, a large modern square-rigger.

Clearing customs in nearby English Harbour that morning we had an amazing stroke of luck. We saw Michael Perham arrive, having just sailed the Atlantic single-handed at the age of fourteen in his 28-foot boat *Cheeky Monkey*. It was a world record. I was at boarding school when I was fourteen and my ambitions didn't stretch further than scoring a goal in the next school football match. I was a child in every sense of the word. But here in English Harbour on 3 January 2007, I met a boy who had bridged the gap and become a man, the youngest person ever to sail across the Atlantic alone. It is a feat that keeps alive the great British maritime tradition. We were privileged to be there in this little corner of Antigua while history was being made. We knew that this story, which was being covered by TV, radio, and press, would be all over the world in hours.

Janet and I met Michael and his father later in the day as they wandered around Falmouth enjoying the simple treat of an ice cream. The media circus had retreated like the tide, and they were left alone to reflect on an amazing day that had gone into history and the *Guinness Book of World Records*. Michael is a slightly built boy, quite shy, but with a maturity that the experience of being alone at sea had given him. I was struck by his modesty in everything he said. He was overwhelmed by the reception he received and seemed surprised. It was as if he had stepped ashore on the Isle of Wight having just sailed over from Hamble and found a reception committee waiting!

Later, when I asked him what had been his worst moment, he said that it was when his satellite phone died, which caused him to put into the Cape Verde Islands for a replacement. He missed his friends, but he could see no reason at all why a younger boy would not break his record. He didn't like cooking, but "Tesco cans were not too much of a problem." When I asked him the obvious question, "What next?" he replied quietly, "No plans at all, just back to school." (He made the news again in 2009 by becoming the youngest person to sail around the world single-handed.)

Some of the British press belittled his achievement. It is true that his father sailed in convoy with him in an identical boat and was never out of sight. It is true that he was in constant communication with his father on the VHF radio, and that they took turns at one hour watches during the night, and were able to give each other a radio warning if there was a collision risk or a squall. But how is that different from Ellen MacArthur, a courageous young British woman who broke the record for sailing nonstop around the world? It was an amazing achievement, but she had an expensive team of experts at the end of a satellite phone or a computer to give her weather routing and technical backup for any problems that arose.

Michael's father, a quiet and unassuming man who built the two identical Tide 28-foot boats for this record attempt, stayed in the background while his son rightly took the spotlight. Now the boats would have to be sold to pay for the venture. There was never any suggestion that there was any motive other than a loving Dad helping his son achieve a world record in the sport they both love. We were proud of them both.

* * *

Our friends Ken and Val Spedding joined us for a week cruising around the coast of Antigua, including the more remote reef-strewn north coast, and later Peter and Anita Wakeham sailed with us from Antigua to Dominica and Guadeloupe. Dominica (pronounced Dom-in-eeka) was a dramatic change from the coral island of Antigua. Antigua boasts 365 dazzling white sand beaches and looks just like the holiday advertisements, but is low, dry, and mostly barren. Dominica, a volcanic island, could not be more of a contrast, with mountains, volcanoes, rain forests, waterfalls, and, not to be outdone, claims 365 rivers!

Prince Rupert Bay is a tranquil anchorage sheltered by green mountains and the town of Portsmouth sits at the head of the bay. But it is the interior of the island that is most interesting. We explored the northern region with "Shadow," a Carib Indian who was our guide. The Caribs were a warlike tribe who killed off the peaceful Arawaks, the original settlers, whose ancestors came from the Orinoco Delta in 3000 B.C. When Columbus discovered Dominica in 1493 he found the Caribs living there. After colonisation by the Spanish, French, and British, brutal treatment of the Caribs resulted in the population being decimated. However, in 1903 the British granted them a 3700-acre territory in the northeast of Dominica. Now some three thousand survivors live there in eight villages, carrying on their traditional lifestyle and producing arts and crafts to sell. Other Caribs, like Shadow, live outside the territory and live a more integrated life. Elsewhere in the Windward Islands the Caribs were entirely slaughtered by the Europeans, so the Caribs here are the only survivors of these ancient people.

Dominica is a truly tropical island. We saw an amazing variety of fruits as we wound our way up the mountain in this green and pleasant land. Growing by the road we saw oranges, lemons, grapefruit, avocados, cocoa pods, coffee beans, mangoes, breadfruit, guava, yams, and, of course, bananas and plantain. The fruit trees are owned by small farmers with two or three acres who take the fruit to the local market. In the vegetable gardens you see cabbages, lettuce, and tomatoes. Everyone seems to have free-range goats and chickens, but the cows are tethered to stop them from straying.

The narrow roads climb up over mountain ridges and look down into deep river gorges and valleys with a prolific growth of plants, flowers, and trees. Many of the species growing wild would be expensive pot plants in England. The most fascinating tree is the tulip, which grows to thirty feet high and has a profusion of red flowers shaped like tulips. It was an interesting experience for Peter and Anita, who had not been in a tropical rain forest before.

Our intention that day was to reach the Chaudiere Pool, a little-visited waterfall well away from the tourist track. As Janet says, "Graham never wants to do things the easy way," so we took a long hike to the falls in the valley, then clambered over boulders on the edge of the river to get to the pool beneath the waterfall. When I plunged in I was swept away by the fierce current, but managed to stand up before going over the next waterfall! On my second attempt I was able to use a back eddy to float along the edge to the head of the pool and the waterfall. It was an exhilarating experience. Peter and Anita took a gentler plunge, and Janet was the official photographer. On our return we climbed 2,658 steep and muddy steps (I counted!) to get back to Shadow and our taxi and collapsed, exhausted.

Luke and Max visited the Titou Gorge, where there is a cave you can swim through until you reach the waterfall about two hundred metres inside. From there you can look up at the blue sky and see the torrent of water cascading down into the cave. Janet and I did this on our last visit in 2004, and it is probably the most dramatic adventure on Dominica.

But surely the most enchanting trip is a canoe ride up the Indian River, named after the Carib Indians. We started at dawn, with our guide, Albert, quietly rowing us into this eerie river in the early morning light. The silence was broken only by the call of unseen birds and the gentle swish of Albert's oars. At the river's edge the swamp bloodwood trees, with their incredible exposed twisted roots, created a canopy over our heads, but it was a relief not to see the boa constrictors that frequent the riverbanks. It didn't come as a surprise to learn that this area was used in a scene in the movie *Pirates of the Caribbean: Dead Man's Chest*.

Although Dominica is abundantly fertile, and any family can be self-sufficient for food, there is terrible poverty. Houses are mostly wooden shacks with tin roofs or concrete block houses, many partly finished or falling down. "No trespassin. I am comin back. Willi" was daubed in paint on one. Wrecked and derelict cars litter the roadside.

The poverty is most obvious in the towns. Walking through Portsmouth conjured up images from Africa. At the waterfront, two wrecked cargo ships dominated the skyline. They were victims of Hurricane Lenny in 1999, and apparently the owners, who are Dominican, cannot afford to move them, nor can the government!

But the people seem happy, and rarely more so than when they are watching a cricket match. By luck we happened upon the inaugural first class cricket match to take place in Portsmouth. The Windward Islands were hosts to Barbados. The pretty little ground, with the green mountains as a backdrop, provided a picturesque setting. It was a colourful and noisy event, with stalls selling food and drink and reggae music blaring. When a Barbados wicket fell, the crowd erupted and the man behind us blew a loud note on his conch shell. Perhaps typically for the laid-back Caribbean, the scoreboard was not finished and didn't work, but the cricket was enthusiastically followed, ball by ball, by a partisan but knowledgeable crowd. They may be poor, but they know how to have fun.

We raised our anchor to leave Dominica early on 22 January, bound for Le Marin, Martinique, a ninety-mile passage that should have only taken us twelve hours. But motoring out of Prince Rupert Bay the engine alarm went off. There was a strong smell of burning rubber and Luke soon established that it was from a degenerating fan belt. That was odd because it was new, so we decided not to use the engine again until we made the final approach up the windward channel to Le Marin. Using only the sails in the windy Caribbean should not have been a problem, but the wind dropped to a light breeze as we made our way down the coast in fits and starts. The coincidence of an engine problem on a day with no wind in the January trade wind season was bizarre.

As we drifted off the southwest corner of Dominica we saw the whale watching boats come out from Roseau, and with nothing better to do, we watched where they went. They must have tracking devices, because they soon found whales, which we could just make out through our binoculars. It was the blowing sound that first alerted us to a whale about three boat lengths ahead of us. What a thrill! We were making about two knots and the whale looked to be doing the same speed as it went across our bow. It was about twenty feet long, swimming lazily on the surface and blowing, and we could see it from nose to tail. Janet just managed to get a photograph before it dove. The moment quickly passed, and we were unable to identify the type of whale, but it was the closest we had ever been to such a large creature and we felt overjoyed and not in any way frightened.

Leaving the lee of the island we picked up the unobstructed trade winds blowing from the Atlantic, and were soon sailing fast again, but then, frustratingly, they dropped to nothing and wouldn't even fill the spinnaker. We reconciled ourselves to a night of gentle drifting in the knowledge that the wind would return at some time in the night or the next day. But a few hours later the wind gods smiled on us again and we picked up a gentle breeze that took us all the way to Le Marin. We tacked up the channel entrance, motoring only the last ten minutes, to anchor at 11:30 that night. The next morning, Luke and a French engineer diagnosed a faulty impeller problem that was easily resolved.

* * *

Cruising under sail is a nomadic life. We often made friends on other yachts but never knew when we would meet them again. On the small island of Bequia, our next stop after Martinique, we had the pleasant surprise of meeting up with our old friends Terry and Molly King-Smith, on *Dorado*. Janet and I first met Terry when we were on a radio course together in Burseldon, near Southampton, in 2002 in preparation for our Atlantic crossing. I don't think any of us remembered very much about the course! In the Caribbean we both based our yachts in Grenada so we got to know each other quite well. Now they were cruising north with children and grandchildren and our paths crossed in Bequia for the first time in over two years.

Terry came over to see our new boat, and later we climbed the hill to Coco's Place, a restaurant set up high in the hills overlooking Admiralty Bay. It was a wonderful evening, but tinged with sadness when we said goodbye, knowing that we probably would not see them again for some years.

While we were in Bequia we met Peter and Virginia Dimsey, an American couple who were about the same age as us. They began their voyage in the Mediterranean a couple of years earlier and cruised in the Black

Sea. Luke had met their crew when he was doing our refit in Newport in the summer and discovered that they were doing the same trip as us, and at the same time. The only difference was that their destination was Australia while ours was New Zealand. We looked forward to meeting again along the way, but strangely, we never saw them in the Pacific, although we were often in touch by e-mail. Such is the nature of the cruising life.

Tim Wright is a well-known marine photographer based in Bequia, and we asked him if he could take some pictures of *Moonraker* under sail. The conditions were perfect on the appointed morning, with a light breeze, so we were able to get the colourful red spinnaker up for the shoot. Tim is amazing. He drives his high-speed, rigid-bottom inflatable with one hand whilst taking photographs with the other, all the time zooming around to get the best angles. Later he sent us a DVD with 160 proof shots and we were delighted. It was impossible to choose the best, so we bought the whole DVD and put a selection on our blog[11] so that our friends could see what our new boat looked like.

* * *

Lying at the southern end of the eastern Caribbean chain is Grenada, the spice island, perhaps one of the most interesting of the Caribbean islands, with its mountains, rain forests, and beaches. The spices that have made it famous—ginger, nutmeg, and cinnamon—are grown all over the island in smallholdings and marketed collectively by co-ops to supply much of the world's demand. The harbour at St. George's is guarded by the formidable Fort George, built in 1705. Around the edge of the harbour is the delightful Carenage, the hub of the town, with its bars, cafés, shops, offices, and fishing boats. This is where everyone meets in Grenada, a noisy, colourful, happy environment—a place for shopping, doing business, selling to tourists, eating, drinking … or just hanging out. You cannot fail to be caught up in the friendly atmosphere of the Carenage.

We stayed in Grenada for two weeks, berthing at Secret Harbour, a small, rundown marina in Mount Hartman Bay. Our old friends Mark and Anita Sutton run a yacht management business there. It was where *Ace of Clubs* was berthed during Hurricane Ivan in September 2004, and they had helped to minimize the damage to her and manage the repairs that needed to be done afterward. Over a meal they told us what a terrible

---

11 *We kept up a blog so that a wide circle of family and friends could keep up-to-date with our news. It included photographs and an automatic position update.*

experience it had been. The island was ill-prepared for such a savage hurricane. Having been spared for the last fifty years, there was a feeling that "it can't happen to us." Even my insurance brokers recommended Grenada as a safe place to keep a yacht during the hurricane season.

With only a few days warning there was little that could be done, and an optimistic feeling that Ivan would veer away prevailed. It didn't, and 150-mile-an-hour winds smashed into the island. Houses crumbled, forests were stripped bare, the spice plantations were demolished, and boats ashore in the boatyard fell over like dominoes. Mark and his team struggled to provide extra mooring lines for the yachts in the marina until it was no longer safe to remain there. Their own house had the roof blown off and for days they lived on an undamaged boat eating only the canned food that was on board. They survived and we were glad to hear that they had got their lives back on track again.

One bright Sunday morning we went to a jazz brunch at Jenny's Place. Searching down an unlikely alleyway we squeezed past a group of men pouring concrete and finally found Jenny's Place, an unassuming single-story thatched wooden building on the beach. There was just a kitchen, a dining area, a bar, and few tables. We were greeted by a beautiful woman in an attractive lemon yellow dress. "Are you Jenny?" I asked as she showed us to our table. She nodded with a lovely smile. Somehow I wasn't surprised when the couple next to us told me that Jenny had been Miss World in 1970. Jennifer Holsten is still a truly beautiful woman with poise, magnetism, and elegance. But more than that she is a remarkable person. As we sat in the shade looking out over the beach she told me something of her extraordinary life—plucked from being a BWIA air hostess to become Miss Grenada and soon after Miss World, going on a world tour with Bob Hope, becoming Grenada's High Commissioner to Canada, getting a master's degree, working in third world countries for Canada's international aid agency—and much more. Jenny is an amazing woman. I thought "what a book she could write" and then found that she had! It's called *Beyond Miss World* and you can find out more about it at info@jennysplacegrenada.com.

The jazz was in full flow during the brunch with the deep rich base voice of David Emmanuel floating out over the water's edge. He was a big, warmhearted Grenadian with short fuzzy grey hair who made a minor claim to fame as a reggae singer in the UK in the eighties with two hits, "Police Officer" and "Lovely Day." Now, no longer expecting fame and fortune, he is back in his native Grenada singing what he likes and playing the guitar.

When he sang Bob Marley's "One Love," we all got up to dance. I looked around and for one surreal moment everyone seemed to be dancing, the guests in the bar ... *one love* ... the men pouring concrete ... *one love* ... the teenagers on a swimming platform ... *one love* ... young children on the beach ... *one love*. Everyone was swinging to the rhythm. I felt as if I were high on ganja! Did he change the last line from "Let's get together and feel all right" to "Let's get together and screw all night?" I looked over at David and he smiled back knowingly.

As the afternoon grew longer it became a jam session. Karen, David's girlfriend, sang beautifully, and Phil, a friend who is in the music business and was the manager for Showaddywaddy, sang "Blue Suede Shoes," then others got up to sing. Man, it was cool![12]

* * *

By a stroke of good luck Janet met Jean Renwick in the hairdressers. She is a member of an old Grenadian family that had been important plantation owners in earlier generations. Jean said that she allowed private tours of her garden at Sunnyside House. When Janet asked if we could join a tour, she told us that we could come the next day. The garden is quite lovely. It was featured on UK television's Channel 4 gardening program and is one of the most beautiful private gardens in the Caribbean. Sunnyside House is positioned high on a hill overlooking St. George's, set in three acres and with views in every direction. The garden was a riot of colour from a profusion of plants—bougainvilleas, of course, a rare hibiscus by Dr. Bertie of Tobago, many varieties of succulents, red bush plants, lilies, orchids, and so much more. There were specimen trees—calabash, mahogany, cashew—and more species of palm tree than I knew existed. Janet enjoyed it because the garden design had evolved naturally and she

---

12 *Jenny subsequently told me that the restaurant has been extensively renovated and is now managed by the woman who won the Best Caribbean Chef award in 2006 (www. jennysplacegrenada.com). Following legal proceedings, David Emmanuel no longer works there.*

could see that Jean had relied on her instincts rather than formal landscape garden training.

Jean had mentioned that she had kept a diary during the dark days of the revolution in Grenada in October 1983. It had made world headlines when the U.S. military intervened after the prime minister, Maurice Bishop, was murdered, and Bernard Coard, a Marxist, tried to take over the country. I had been very interested in the revolution and asked Jean if I could see her diary. She agreed and we made an appointment to come back the following day.

As we sat having tea in Jean's conservatory she showed me fascinating documents that would be of great interest to any historian. They included the Hansard transcriptions of House of Commons debates, memos from revolutionary leaders regarding plans to seize private estates, and her personal diary during the days of political intrigue, murder, violence, civil war, and invasion, which marked the lowest point in Grenada's history.

Her story began thirty-four years earlier when Sir Eric Gairy, the prime minister, gained independence from Britain in 1974, although he didn't have to try very hard. It was a time when Britain was shedding its ties with its colonies as fast as it could. "Grenadians wanted independence but not with Gairy," she told us. "He gained power as the people's champion. He was a rabble-rouser. I used to see him walking around town in white robes and a shepherd's crook, supposedly the savior of his people. But he was more interested in his own power than the welfare of the people. He got his way by violence and intimidation, and he had his 'mongoose gang,' a gang of thugs, who went round the country squashing any opposition."

Finally, the people could take no more and Gairy was ousted by Maurice Bishop in a coup in 1979. "Maurice was loved by the people. They all knew him. I knew him well. He was a lawyer. I remember meeting him at the tennis club one day. He was just standing by watching. He looked so sad and serious, so I said, 'What's the matter, Maurice? Come and play tennis.' 'I can't,' he replied. 'You don't understand. There are such big things happening.' I didn't know what he meant but a few days after that he forced Gairy from office, giving him the choice of leaving the country peacefully or being removed violently. Of course he chose exile."

"But," she said sadly, "Maurice was a socialist and he turned to Russia and Cuba to provide economic salvation for Grenada." Years of desperate internal political strife followed and their communist allies did little to support the economy in Grenada, although the Cubans established a military base. Then, on 19 October 1983, Bishop and seven cabinet colleagues were murdered in Fort George. The bloody killings were ordered by the deputy prime minister, Bernard Coard, who was a hardline Marxist, and it led to a short but bloody civil war. Coard had control of the army but the people fought for Bishop. Coard declared an island-wide shoot-on-sight curfew, but fighting continued until the dramatic intervention of U.S. forces—Operation Urgent Fury—and order was restored after five days. Jean showed us her diary for the days of the U.S. invasion. It brought back vivid memories for her. She told us that one day she saw Grenadian soldiers hiding in her garden, terrified, while a U.S. helicopter hovered so low that she could see the soldiers in the open door aiming their machine guns. As she talked I could imagine the thrashing of the chopper blades.

Who knows what led to the internal split between Bishop and Coard? Perhaps it was a serious difference over political strategies, perhaps the Russians or Cubans had a hand in the deed, or perhaps Coard simply wanted to take power. Whatever the reason, Bishop's body was never found and he is now a martyr. Coard remains locked up in a Grenadian jail with thirteen of his cohorts, and is hated by some of the people.[13] "I knew the Coards, too, of course," Jean told us. "I remember seeing Phyllis Coard sitting in the gutter at the side of the road with handcuffs on. It was very sad."

Driving back in the taxi I asked our driver, "Rock, do you remember the revolution?"

"Remember it? I was in it!" he replied.

Rock also knew Maurice Bishop and he was part of the People's Revolutionary Army, the militia that supported him when he ousted Gairy. A little older and wiser, he stayed on the sidelines when Bishop was murdered in 1983. I suspect that he knew a lot more than he let on. There are still dark forces underground in Grenada and political scores to be settled. For Rock, like many Grenadians, Maurice Bishop is a legend and a martyr.

---

13 *Bernard Coard was released from jail on 5 September 2009 following a review of his sentence by the Privy Council in London.*

He feels that the government should erect a statue in his honour or name the airport after him. I wonder why they don't?[14]

During our two-week stay Grenada celebrated Independence Day. In the buildup the week before, it seemed that every car and building was flying Grenada's yellow, red, and green flag. Cars had stickers in the back window, "I love me country." The enthusiastic celebration of independence was surprising considering the revolutionary past Grenada has had since cutting its ties with Britain. Perhaps it is a way of giving thanks for a stable government and a peaceful country since the dark days of 1979. The streets of St. George's were busy, brash, and bright. Everyone seemed to have the day off to start the party early. Women had made special dresses in red, yellow, and green, and the Carenage echoed with the ringing sound of steel bands. But surprisingly the next morning, Independence Day, was a more sober affair. The National Stadium was the venue for the formal events with a dais for the dignitaries and a march-past display. A large crowd had turned out but they couldn't all get into the packed stadium, so hundreds milled around outside. They were untypically subdued as they watched the marching groups arrive. The police, the army, and the prison service were all represented along with guest contingents from the Royal Navy, the U.S. Navy, and a large group from the Venezuelan Army. Slowly they took up their allotted places on the parade ground. The speeches were long and tedious but were respectfully listened to, even though the sound system was not adequate. There was no cheering or clapping. But when the time came for the national anthem everybody was ready to sing heartily. The band began to play but at that moment the sound system packed up. Even worse the wind was blowing the sound in the wrong direction, so no one could hear the music and they didn't know when to begin singing.

The mood picked up after the dignitaries left in their smart official limousines. The Venezuelan skydiver parachute team was announced to a great cheer. This was more like it! Choppers flew over with teams of skydivers and the first ten landings were on target in the middle of the stadium. Unfortunately two of the final batch of parachutists didn't quite make it. One landed on a garage roof just outside the perimeter fence, and the other went ignominiously into the sea just in front of the U.S. warship. The crowd loved it and a great cheer went up. This was entertainment! And then there were fireworks.

---

14 *On 29 May 2009, Port Salines International Airport was renamed in honour of Maurice Bishop.*

When the many representative contingents left the stadium we had a close-up view as they marched past us in the street. The Grenada police band got the biggest cheer as their leader, a big black man, swiveled his hips and shook his behind in a distinctly non-military style as he held his stick out to signal the right wheel. The women shrieked with laughter.

Grenada had been world news the week before because of a diplomatic incident involving this same band. The National Cricket Stadium, built for the Cricket World Cup that summer, was being officially opened. It had been completely financed by China, and five hundred Chinese workers had come to build it, so important officials had come from China for the opening ceremony. The police band struck up the visitor's national anthem. Unfortunately, it wasn't the Chinese national anthem they played, but of all things, the Taiwanese national anthem! Such a pity, as they had been practicing it for six months and played it beautifully.

Back in the marina Luke and Max used the time to catch up on a long list of maintenance work and collect the parts arriving from New Zealand and America. Getting parts for boats in the tropics is a problem. Only very basic items are stocked and parts usually have to be ordered from the country of manufacture. The most important job was replacing a pipe that passed exhaust water from the engine out through the bottom of the hull. The old one had a crack, which, if it had opened up, would have allowed seawater to pour into the boat. Max had made a board to fit over the hole if this happened, but we were all very relieved when the part arrived and Luke was able complete the job safely with the boat in the water.[15]

---

15 *See Appendix 2 for an explanation of how the through hull repair was done with the boat in the water.*

6

Kuna Yala

On 15 February *Moonraker* headed out to sea, again negotiating the reef-strewn channel that marks the entrance to Secret Harbour. We were leaving behind familiar territory in the eastern Caribbean islands and heading for the north coast of South America. Our destination was Los Roques, a small group of islands off the coast of Venezuela, lying three hundred miles to the southwest of Grenada. This was the first stage in the passage from Grenada to the Panama Canal, the gateway to the Pacific. Now we really felt that we were on our way.

The winds were from behind, bringing us good sailing. The next morning Janet was alone on the 6:00–8:00 watch and saw what appeared to be a fishing boat approaching out of the early morning mist. As it came closer a second boat appeared. We were eighty miles off the coast of Venezuela, in an area that has a reputation for piracy, so she was concerned and called Luke on deck to monitor the situation. As the boats got closer they appeared to be the kind of ramshackle vessels you see on TV carrying refugees. Some of the men were fishing with ordinary hand lines, but these certainly weren't working fishing boats. As they came still closer, men started to shout at us but she couldn't understand why. Luke told Janet to hold the course and go between the two boats. They looked at us and we looked at them. Nothing happened but it was a worrying moment.

The following morning Luke was on watch from 8:00–10:00 and I came up at 9:30 and chatted to him as I was due on watch next. I popped below to make a cup of tea and when I came back on deck Luke wasn't there. I looked all round the deck and down to the swim platform. There was no sign of him. My heart missed a beat. I ran below and threw open the door to his cabin and his heads. He wasn't there either. I rushed to the engine room. He would often be in there doing checks, but there was no Luke. With my heart racing I shouted to Janet, who was asleep in her cabin. "Get up immediately. I can't find Luke anywhere."

Without saying anything we both understood that Luke may have been lost overboard. It is one of the most dreadful accidents that can happen at sea because it is very difficult to find, let alone recover, a person once they are in the water. Janet went straight to the chart plotter and hit the Man Overboard (MOB), button, which marks the yacht's position on the electronic chart— the nearest known point to where the casualty went overboard. Then I called Max, who was asleep, to get on deck.

Before going into a full MOB procedure and beginning a search, some sixth sense made me run up the side decks to the bow of the boat. I don't know why, because I could see the foredeck clearly and there was nothing there except the dinghy stowed in its usual position. As I got to the bow I looked down and there was Luke, kneeling in front of the dinghy, fixing the strapping, quite invisible from the back of the boat and blissfully unaware of my shouts. "Luke," I screamed and he looked at me as if I had gone mad. I can't describe the overwhelming sense of relief that I felt.

Shaken by this, Janet asked Luke to go through a complete safety briefing for all the emergency situations—fire, man overboard, holing and flooding, dismasting, and abandoning ship—which he did very calmly and very well. It made us realize what a difference satellite communications have made to making a distress call in an emergency. The highest priority is the EPIRB, an automatic emergency position reporting system that would be used if the ship were sinking or if survivors were in a life raft. The EPIRB signal would automatically register our position and trigger a search by air and sea anywhere in the world. We also had a satellite phone that could be used to call coast guards and to seek help in other emergencies.

That afternoon we had a different sort of excitement. The two fishing lines whizzed out one after the other as the boys caught two dorados at the same time. The next day Max caught another one, but just as Luke landed it onto the swim platform, it gave a mighty leap and escaped.

They put the two rods out every day and had good results, usually around early evening. Our policy was only to catch fish to eat, so when we had filled the freezer we stopped fishing. Mostly we caught dorado (also called mahi mahi), magnificently colored fish that are about three to four feet long. They are gold when alive but the amazing thing is that they become a vivid blue as they are dying and then a silver grey when they are dead. I found it sad to kill such beautiful creatures and see their life slowly extinguished. We also caught large mackerel, about two feet long, and sometimes barracudas, which we didn't like to eat because of the risk of ciguatera (fish poisoning), so they were always thrown back.

But it was always exciting when the line flew out with a loud "whizz," and the cry of "fish" called everyone on deck. We would slow the boat down to two or three knots by reducing sail. It took at least thirty minutes to tire the fish and reel it in, and another half an hour to gut and fillet it. We were lucky that Luke had learned this skill from previous long distance sailing trips as it meant that Janet had beautiful fillets to put in the freezer.

The overnight passage gave us the chance to get used to the one-person night watch system we planned to use: each person did two hours on watch at night and then had six hours sleep, which gave us much more rest than the traditional four hours on and four hours off system. One person on watch can manage most things except reefing the mainsail, when help has to be called.

We reached Los Roques at 2:00 in the morning and crept around the side of the main island, Gran Roque, in pitch darkness. There was not a single light on the land and it seemed deserted, but as we came around the end of the island we saw lights twinkling in the harbour. Luke is very confident in making night arrivals if he is sure that the charts are accurate and show no dangers. It was good not to have to wait around for daylight.

Los Roques Archipelago consists of eight main islands and many smaller ones, surrounded by a large reef. It is probably the most beautiful natural area in Venezuela with amazing biodiversity, and in 1972 it was designated as a national park. The islands are eighty miles from the mainland and the only access is by private boat or light aircraft. The town of Gran Roque, where most of the population of twelve hundred live, has simple concrete buildings painted in red and yellow, giving it a truly South American atmosphere, and so different from the Caribbean we had left behind. A sandy road runs down the middle of the town. There are no cars, and as we strolled down the middle of the street the Venezuelan locals in brightly-coloured costumes smiled at us in a friendly greeting. The dirt airstrip on the edge of town has a control tower that must be one of a kind: it is perched on a lorry parked near the runway. I can imagine a pilot being asked, "Where would you like the control tower, sir?"

The weekend that we arrived was "Carnivale" in Caracas, so wealthy Venezuelans had come from the mainland to take advantage of the four-day weekend. As we explored the islands we came to appreciate the beauty and tranquility that makes them so attractive to the lucky few who can come.

Our second night was spent anchored in splendid isolation in the middle of a huge lagoon on the edge of a sandbar. We took the dinghy and splashed around in the shallow water in the middle of nowhere and ran around on the exposed sandbank. Bramble Bank, in the Solent, England, has something similar, where an annual cricket match is played for one hour at low-water spring tides, but it could not match this for its beauty or seclusion. The multicoloured crystalline warm waters stretched as far as we could see in every direction, and we were alone in the pale green shallow water of the sandbank. Luke took some spectacular photographs from the top of the mast.

The following day we anchored by an uninhabited island with a small bay and a pretty white sand beach. It was a popular fishing ground for pelicans and brown boobies and I watched mesmerized as they hovered over their targets, then swooped down into the water, reappearing a moment later with a struggling silver fish in their beaks. This is an easy way to while away the hours. Six other boats were anchored in the bay but it was no hardship to share this idyllic scene with them.

Later, walking along the beach, I met two young women from one of the yachts. They were from Caracas and told me how difficult life had become since Chavez had become president. Businesses were being nationalized at an alarming rate and the middle classes were financially very insecure. Crime in the city was rampant, but they live with it. They have to. Their homes are locked and gated and they drive to their offices with the car doors locked. No one walks the streets unless they have to. It seems that Chavez is modeling the country on Cuba, and is welcomed by Castro when he goes there. I asked one of the young women how they saw the future.

"It's okay for me," she said. "I'm young, and I'm at university in America. I'm training to be a lawyer, and I can work in any country. I don't imagine that my future will be in Venezuela. But I'm sorry for my parents. They are established there, they have their business and all their assets there. It is hard for them to move and they are very worried about the future."

Returning to Gran Roque we were delighted to see the blue hull of *Surcouf* anchored there. It belonged to Edmond and Yossi, a Belgian couple and their two children, Max, who is fifteen, and Roxanne, who is seven.

We had first met them in Grenada. When they had set sail from Holland to sail around the world they had relatively little sailing experience, and their 55-foot Contest yacht was the first sailing boat they had owned. Each part of their voyage so far—the English Channel, the Bay of Biscay, and then the Atlantic Ocean—had been major achievements that dramatically increased their experience and boosted their confidence. I was full of admiration for Edmond, who had the responsibility for his family while developing his sailing skills and learning about maintenance and repairs of his yacht.

It was such a pleasant surprise to meet friends again and they came across to our boat. Over a drink we shared our experiences and sailing plans. Janet asked Yossi if the children's education was a problem. Max was obviously bright, and at fifteen motivated to study on his own in order to be able to pass the exams to get into university. Yossi was teaching Roxanne the three R's and school routines were fitted into their life at sea. It was obvious that the children were enjoying the experience. The next day we watched them head off into the open ocean. We hoped we would see them again, as they were planning to go through the Panama Canal about the same time as us. We left a day later, sorry that our schedule meant that we could not stay longer in this unexpected and little-known South American paradise.

* * *

Take a strong Dutch stock, add a little South American flavor, stir in some Caribbean spices, and you have a recipe for Curaçao. This island seems to be the Netherlands best kept secret, along with sister islands Aruba and Bonaire—the ABC islands. It is surprising that the British have not made it a holiday destination as it has all the ingredients: all-year-round 85 F temperatures, little rain, it's outside the hurricane belt, and has wonderful beaches, diving, snorkeling, and sailing. It is also different from many Caribbean islands in that it has a strong economy, largely based on its oil industry, which is supported by a developed infrastructure and Dutch efficiency. They speak Dutch, Spanish, Piamento (the old slave language), and, thankfully, English.

Curaçao was the only one of the three ABC islands that we had time to visit. The main town, Willemstad, is a World Heritage Site that has colourful old buildings that have been preserved to create an Amsterdam in the Caribbean. The island is teeming with wildlife. Not far from the town we saw wild pink flamingoes on a salt lake. On nature hikes we often spotted an oriole, the national bird, which looks like a magpie but with a bright orange bar on the back and belly. We got close to a hawk resting on the ground in Shete Boca National Park. Here there are spectacular walks along rugged cliffs, with the sea crashing onto rocks tumbling into the sea. At the most dramatic viewing spot, "The Pistol," the sea surges through a hole in the rock, and then recedes, sucking the foaming wave back with a load bang like a pistol shot. It's so fascinating you could stand and watch it for hours.

The sheltered lagoon was full of yachts from many countries and we were delighted to see *Surcouf* again. Alongside her was *Bauvier,* the yacht that set sail with them from Holland. In fact three yachts set out together, the third one belonging to Yossi's cousin and business partner. The idea was that as none of them had significant offshore sailing experience they would travel in convoy and be able to help each other when needed, as well as provide company for each other and their young children. It seemed a sensible idea but already there were cracks in the relationship, with disagreements about where to go, how fast to go, how long to stay, and whether to sail in convoy. Finally the cousins had gone their separate way. Edmond and Yossi brought Bart and Dorothy from *Bauvier* over to *Moonraker* for drinks one evening and Janet made the Caribbean rum punches that are her specialty. It was one of those convivial evenings that the Irish would describe as good "craich." As the rum had its effect we reflected on where we had sailed from and where we might end up. Both *Surcouf* and *Bauvier* planned to sail around the world and were still confident about the challenge. Our own plans were less defined. The adventure for us was crossing the Pacific, but when we arrived in New Zealand, we would have to make a decision on our future. We thought we might sail back through South Asia, the Indian Ocean, and the Red Sea, finishing in the Mediterranean. But there was still a long, long way to go before we got to the other side of the world. As I looked around the table I wondered how it would all turn out for the six of us. I knew that it wouldn't be as we imagined it on this night.

The lagoon in Curaçao seemed to have an established yachting community of live-aboard sailors, mostly American and Canadian. The Americans, when they get together, often form a lively group, organizing events and keeping in touch on the VHF radio on social and domestic matters. We had seen a similar community of American yachts in Grenada, anchored in the lee of Hog Island. The locals there came to know them as the "Hoglydites," as they were generally an aging hippy crowd complete with graying pony tails.

Some of the American yachts in Curaçao had been there months and even years. It was as though they had set out on an adventure—many of them had sailed long distances to get to Curaçao—but for some reason got stuck. (When we got to New Zealand we met one of the American yachts we had seen in Curaçao, and were told that there had been wife swapping among some of the boats, and sometime later the whole community had broken up.) Unlike other yachts, we moved on after a week, sailing for the San Blas Islands, six hundred miles to the west. Already we had the feeling that we were racing through paradise, with only the briefest stops, when several weeks, rather than days, would be needed to really get to know the places and people. But we had decided to go through the Panama Canal in March, earlier than most boats we had met, so that we could maximize our time in the Pacific before heading south to New Zealand in October. However, I suspected that we would always feel that we wanted more time. Luke had been encouraging me to begin planning which Pacific Islands we wanted to visit and how long we would like to stay. With such a huge ocean, and so many islands, we would probably have to get used to the idea that we could only scratch the surface of the world as we sailed by.

Edmond, Yossi, Bart, and Dorothy were standing on the dock to wave us goodbye when we left on Sunday 25 February. The forecast was for strong winds, 20–25 knots, and some of the other skippers in port had questioned our decision to leave. They were waiting for the wind to ease, but with a large yacht and the wind behind us Luke felt that there was no reason to be concerned. We expected the passage to the San Blas Islands to take three days.

As we cleared the shelter of the land we felt the full strength of the wind and already had two reefs[16] in the mainsail. By early evening the wind had strengthened and we put in another half reef for the night. At 6:00 PM a military plane came up to us from behind, very, very low, made a sharp turn around us, and flew back from whence it came. We speculated on why we might have been the subject of this visit but it remained a mystery. Night drew on and we moved into our night watch system again, two hours on then six hours off. There is always a degree of anxiety setting off on an open sea passage, but this time I was more apprehensive than usual because of the strong winds that were building.

The wind blew hard at 25–35 knots in the night, much stronger than forecast, and the seas were increasing. At five in the morning Janet was on watch alone when the autopilot clicked off, almost causing an accidental gybe,[17] but she grabbed the wheel and steered by hand. The preventer, a rope that is rigged to "prevent" the mainsail from crashing over to the other side of the boat, did its job, and Luke was quickly on deck to help her. He switched to the backup autopilot in the pilothouse which meant that we were still able to use the autopilot, although it would be necessary to go from the cockpit into the pilothouse to change course, which wasn't ideal. The autopilot had been giving us trouble and Luke thought he had repaired it, but it had clearly not solved the problem. He had already ordered a new circuit board from the manufacturer, Brookes & Gatehouse in England, which was being delivered to Panama.

Early on Monday morning Luke put another half reef in the mainsail and reefed the staysail as the wind continued to build. It was blowing 30 knots and gusting to 35 knots. This was a now a gale force wind.[18] The waves were very large, probably sixteen feet high from peak to trough. The pilot books say that in this southwestern corner of the Caribbean the sea funnels into the V formed by the landmasses of South America and Central America, and it is not unusual to have very large seas relative to

---

16 *Reefing is how the sail area is reduced as the wind strength increases. Most mainsails have three reefing points to progressively reduce the sail area until there are three reefs in the sail in gale conditions. On* Moonraker *the mainsail has an in-boom reefing system in which the mainsail is reefed by furling it around a mandril inside the boom until it reaches a reefing point. The foresails, the jib and staysail, furl around the forestay, rather like a roller blind at a 45 degree angle.*

17 *An accidental gybe occurs when the boat is running down wind and the wind gets on the leeward side of the mainsail, forcing it over onto the other side. This can happen in a sudden wind shift or in a heavy swell.*

18 *See Appendix 3 for the Beaufort Wind Scale.*

the wind strength. Not that that was any consolation. The waves towered behind us, lifting our stern up, and the boat surfed down the waves at speed with a high-pitched whine from the hull and vibration ringing from the rigging. But *Moonraker* handled it well and we felt quite comfortable. Comfortable is a relative term, of course, as you need one hand to hold on all the time, so most jobs, especially cooking, are very difficult. Janet managed this brilliantly as she always does. She had precooked some meals for this eventuality so we were able to have hot food, which everyone looks forward to in a blow.

By midday the wind was blowing 35–40 knots, force 8, a full gale. The waves were twenty feet high. The sea looked spectacular, with breaking waves and a seascape of foaming white spume and a thick grey mist all around us. It was quite awesome. Breaking waves came crashing past the boat and still the stern rose up to meet the next towering crest and *Moonraker* slid down the wave. I took some photographs of the big seas from the relative comfort of the pilothouse and they gave an idea what the sea looked like. But pictures don't convey the savagery of the sea and it's difficult to describe in words.

One person who could describe the scene was Charles Pears, who was the first president of the Royal Society of Marine Artists. In 1914 he wrote an illustrated book, *From the Thames to the Netherlands*, which tells of a voyage he took in his small yacht, *Rose*. He poetically described a gale he encountered.

> *The cruel combers carried on by the grand grey motion of the heavy swells came crashing on towards the little yacht; fate like in their solemnity, merciless in their haste, like the tramping columns of some routed army bearing torn and disregarded flags of truce—bursting near the buoyant craft and gurgling under her, passing greedily to leeward, each wave's back a bride's lace train—away, away, harmless now, to grind the shingle of some distant shore.*

A large fishing boat passed quite close by us going in the opposite direction. They were battling into the wind and the waves, throwing up a huge spray as they crashed into each wave. We were lucky because we had the wind behind us. It makes an incredible difference. Sailing upwind in this gale would have been impossible. We watched the fishing boat for ages, fascinated and strangely comforted by the knowledge that other human beings were out here with us. We took in the reefed staysail and had just a pocket handkerchief of a mainsail now. Even with minimal sail set we were still going very fast and the noon run, the miles logged from midday to midday, was 196 miles.

Janet came down from her watch on deck to do the log entry and was amazed to find us relaxed and watching a DVD. The contrast between the quiet and security of the saloon and the noise of the wind and waves on deck was amazing. The watchkeeper has to be alert, all the time watching the wind speed and direction, keeping the boat on course, and aware of the huge waves surging up behind us. Down below we were insulated from this, resting, which is as it should be, because our spell of duty would follow soon enough.

Bizarrely the fishing rods were still out! Janet noticed it and was concerned about the boys' safety in the unlikely event that we did land a big fish, so she asked them to take the rods in. "How do you think I'm going to feel if I have to phone your parents to say we lost you overboard whilst fishing in a gale?" They smiled, but saw the sense in this and took them in. She felt much happier.

We were only ten miles off the coast of Colombia, but saw no boats, hardly surprising in this gale, until we spotted another offshore fishing boat battling its way through the big seas. They *were* trying to catch fish. What a way to earn a living!

By dawn on Tuesday morning the wind had started to ease but the seas remained big, so the sailing motion was uncomfortable as we corkscrewed around. Luke went on deck to take out a reef in the mainsail to give us some more power and discovered that the vang was losing hydraulic pressure. This was annoying because it was the same problem we had on passage to Newport and it had been overhauled since then. It was probably unsafe to have the mainsail up without the vang working, so we took it down and motored with only the jib up. I was worried that it might be a serious problem. Not being able to use the mainsail would be a disaster. I hoped we would be able to get it fixed in Panama, although when I discussed it with Luke he told me that there are few repair facilities there and I was worried that this might mean a long delay.

Later that morning we discovered that the boat had been covered in a horrible brown slime in the night. It was probably some kind of airborne emission as we were still running down the coast of Colombia. Was it smoke from the ganja factories? The same day we had another mystery to ponder. We moved from dark blue sea across a distinct line where the sea became green and it stayed like that for an hour, and then changed back to its usual blue. This would normally indicate a change in depth but the sea here was very deep with no shallow patches. Luke, with all his ocean sailing experience, had never seen anything like it. The four of us debated possible reasons but we were unable to come up with any explanation we could agree on.

The wind and seas were abating all the time but Luke did not want to risk using the mainsail in case we caused more damage to the vang, so we resigned ourselves to motoring the rest of the way to San Blas.

Our noon log gave us a 24-hour run of 189 miles, so we were still making good speed. There was plenty of shipping in the night as we passed close to the Colombian ports of Barranquilla and Cartagena. It made the night watch more interesting to be able to identify the ships in the vicinity and watch their progress on the Automatic Identification System (AIS). This is a new navigation system—mandatory for ships over three hundred tons—that is used to improve situational awareness in traffic separation systems and aid collision avoidance. It shows us another ship's name, course, and speed, but best of all gives us the closest point of approach (CPA) to our vessel and the time to go to the CPA. A radio signal provides an accurate and reliable position of other shipping.

But usually nothing much happens during a night watch and Janet and I were entertained by BBC Radio 4 plays. We were very lucky that Luke's father, James, had recorded over three hundred plays and loaded them onto the ship's computer when he sailed from Newport to BVI. Luke downloaded them onto Janet's iPod, so we were able to listen to voices in the night, and found this much more comforting than music when we were on watch alone.

When not on watch we slept a lot. Non-sailors often ask how we can sleep on a small boat at sea, especially when it is rocking and rolling in a gale as we had been. Oddly enough that is the one thing that is not a problem. When we finish a watch we are so tired we can't wait to get into our bunk and fall asleep. Because everyone has a different watch cycle, we are all asleep at different times. In the morning it was not unusual to be on deck on your own, while others were sleeping or reading below. In the afternoons we were all up and about, and everybody was certain to appear at lunch and dinnertime.

By Wednesday the wind and seas were back to normal and we had an uneventful day, motoring with help from the jib, which filled nicely. The only bit of interest that day was on my watch, when the AIS screen showed a ship coming toward us on a collision course. As I could see the ship's name on the AIS I called it up on the VHF radio when it was nine miles away. The friendly watch officer said, "Yes, I can see you," and he proposed that we pass starboard to starboard, which was unusual as the rule is normally to pass port to port. However, given our respective positions and courses, it looked the most safe and sensible thing to do and we both agreed to alter course accordingly. We had a brief chat. It was reassuring to talk to other ships when we were alone on the ocean.

Suddenly I saw dolphins. They came from nowhere and charged toward us to play under the bow. I called Janet and she brought up the video camera, but it was too late. They had decided to move on and were gone in just five minutes. It was such a pity as they usually stay longer and they always lift our spirits. The noon log showed that we did 191 miles in the last twenty-four hours.

We hoped to arrive in the San Blas Islands before midnight. The ETA on our navigation software fluctuated from 8:30 to 10:30, according to our speed. Having studied the charts, Luke decided it was safe to arrive at night, even though the anchorage would be unlit and was protected by reefs. He left the final decision until we were close in so that he could see how accurate the charts were—when we were in Los Roques the charts and our actual GPS[19] position varied by up to a quarter of a mile. He knew this because he had overlaid the radar onto the electronic chart to see if they matched. If they didn't we would sail slowly up and down away from the islands until first light.

By 9:00 that evening we were very close and Luke was satisfied that our GPS position on the charts was accurate. We were all up on deck, a little tense as we felt our way in the dark, seeing and hearing the white surf on the reefs around us. Looking through the Steiner binoculars, which have night vision, I could see three other yachts anchored, but only one had an anchor light on. It is hard to understand why so many yachtsmen don't show an anchor light at night to warn other boats where they are.

We dropped our anchor at 10:30. The boat lay still, strangely silent after days of violent motion, howling winds, and stormy seas. It was a

---

19 *The Global Positioning System (GPS) accurately gives the ship's latitude and longitude from a U.S. satellite network. Modern chart plotters show the ship's GPS position with a boat symbol on the electronic chart.*

relief to have arrived safely after what was one of the longest rough weather passages Janet and I had experienced. Sea passages can be frustrating, boring, fun, exciting, and frightening. This one had been exciting, but not frightening, and that was okay with me.

After a good night's sleep for the first time in four nights, we woke early as the grey fingers of first light crept into the anchorage to reveal a magical sight. We saw how narrow the gap was that Luke had brought us through: it was about three hundred feet wide with a reef on either side! There were small islands all around us.

The Comarca de San Blas, or Kuna Yala, as the country is called, is an archipelago of four hundred islands stretching for several hundred miles along the coast of Panama. We were totally unprepared for the primitive culture and simple lifestyle of the Kuna people. Arriving here from the relatively sophistication of Curaçao was like entering a different world, an enchanted kingdom.

I could see the village of El Porvenir, the capital, in the early morning light. Nearby was a small island with a tiny strip of land that served as the runway for light aircraft. The islands of Wichubhuala and Nalunega were completely covered by thatched huts that were toppling over each other into the sea. Every square foot of land was covered by the huts, which were made from palm fronds on frames of reeds or canes. When we went ashore we found that each village had a large community hut, the congreso, and a meeting hall, the chichi. The villagers gather there to drink chichi, which they brew for special occasions. The young women were beautiful and everyone was neatly clothed, the women in brightly-coloured dresses and the men in shorts and T-shirts. The women play a major role in the economy of the islands, making and selling mola art, usually embroidered quilts with vivid panels depicting fish, animals, and astrology. They make them in different sizes and prices range from one dollar for a one-foot square to fifteen dollars for a full-sized shawl, and sell them to yachtsmen and the occasional backpackers. The men go fishing or to the mainland, where they work in the forest or have farms along the rivers. All the crops, except coconuts, are grown on the mainland and have to be brought back by canoe.

The Kuna are of Indian descent and their features are distinctly South American, quite different from the West Indians in the Caribbean. An ancient race, they were driven out of South America by the Spanish, the conquistadors, and fled to the coastal forest and the San Blas Islands. The Kuna are a proud people and in 1925 they rebelled against attempts to govern them by Panama. A bloody war was only stopped by the intervention of the U.S., and in 1938 the government of Panama granted them autonomous rule. Now they all own the land in these islands and lead the traditional communal life of their forefathers. A Kuna man who spoke English showed us a carving that depicted their religious beliefs in the life cycle of man—on earth, being taken in a canoe to the next life, in heaven, and then returning to earth again.

Every village has a chief who is called the first sahila. You can tell which one is the first sahila: he is the one lying in a hammock at the congreso. His deputies attend to his instructions at the daily meeting at which village affairs are managed.

Life in the San Blas is a simple, self-sufficient existence. There is no electricity. Toilets are thatch cubicles that hang out over the sea. Water often has to be collected by canoe in barrels from the rivers on the mainland. This has to be used for drinking, cooking, washing the body, and washing clothes, although in the middle of some of the islands it is possible to find brackish water. The staple food is, of course, fish, caught with nets, bows and arrows, and hook and line. On the mainland the men hunt animals with bows and arrows, blowguns, and spears. They grow bananas, plantain, corn, and rice. Basic food is purchased in a hut that serves as the local store. Transport is by cayuco, a canoe dugout made from a single tree, and every family has one. Some have a small mast with a fore and aft sail, crudely made but effective and well sailed. A few have a more professional fishing canoe with an outboard motor. A small light aircraft arrives daily to bring supplies and the occasional "off the beaten track" tourist. It takes back the octopus and lobster the men catch to sell in the market in Panama, but only three of the 365 islands have an airstrip.

The vast blue sea is dotted with these tiny islands, a necklace of tropical jewels. As far as the eye can see there are islands with palm trees, sandy beaches, and reefs. Most are uninhabited and some have one or two huts housing a family. Life in the San Blas carries on as it must have done three hundred years ago. It is amazing how little civilization has touched these islands, with only the arrival of the daily aircraft connecting them to the twenty-first century.

This was quite different from anything that we experienced in the Caribbean and a major culture change that we struggled to absorb and understand. By the standards of the developed world it was a life with very limited horizons, surviving day by day, but the people seemed friendly, well fed, and clean. They have seen life in a relatively developed society like Panama and rejected it. Communism may be an outdated concept but the Kuna make a communal lifestyle work.

In the three days we were in San Blas we had only just begun to appreciate the people and their way of life, but it made an impression that will last a lifetime. We wished we had been able to stay for three months. Experiences like this make cruising in a small sailing boat uniquely rewarding. We were able to go to places that most people would never know about, let alone reach.

Sailing from San Blas to Panama, Max caught a big wahoo—forty pounds! It was the first time we had caught this game fish, which reputedly can strike a lure at fifty miles per hour. Max had good sport bringing it in, but we were amazed when we saw how big it was—nearly five feet long. It took nearly two hours from the fish striking to Luke completing the cleaning and filleting. Max cut some into giant steaks that we barbequed in the evening. They were delicious but more than we could eat.

As we got closer to Panama we saw large ships converging, drawn like a magnet to the Port of Cristobal, the entry port on the Atlantic side. The ship's VHF radio came alive as Cristobal Signal, the port control, issued instructions to the ships arriving and leaving. As we saw more ships our excitement mounted. Just ahead of us was the Panama Canal, the gateway to the Pacific Ocean. Luke called Cristobal Signal on the VHF radio to receive his instructions. As we passed through the gap in the breakwater walls we saw that there were fifty to sixty ships anchored, either waiting to pass through the canal or to load and offload cargo at the docks, where a forest of cranes beckoned.

We had arrived at the holy grail of all the great explorers—Magellan, Drake, Columbus, and Cook. This was what they had all been searching for—a way to pass from the Atlantic into the Pacific Ocean without having to go thousands of miles south to round Cape Horn. The Panama Canal stretched before us. There was a thrilling feeling that another new chapter was opening up in our life.

7

An Engineering Miracle

The huge black gates opened, silently and tantalizingly slowly, to reveal our first sight of the Pacific. The ocean stretched out before us, sparkling in the bright sunlight. We were quiet, each with our private thoughts as we gazed out over the largest ocean in the world—twice the size of the Atlantic, almost a third of the earth's surface, an area greater than all the earth's landmasses combined. We had come to cross this ocean and now it was laid out before us. There was no turning back.

I thought back to the hospital bed in Grasse, and how the germ of an idea there had grown into the reality of standing on this wonderful yacht looking in awe at the Pacific Ocean, wondering how the adventure would unfold. I turned to Janet and gave her a big, long hug. We had come a long way together and now we were going to make our dream come true.

It was five centuries ago, in 1502, that Christopher Columbus arrived on the coast of Panama in search of a natural passage to the east, but he did not realize how close he was to the Pacific and to the very spot where four centuries later the artificial passage across the isthmus would be open.

The creation of the Panama Canal is an incredible chronicle of man's determination to overcome seemingly impossible natural barriers, rampant disease, engineering obstacles, financial collapse, international political hurdles, and persistent failure, yet finally to succeed in building one of the greatest engineering wonders of the world.

The story began in 1513 when Vasco Nuñez de Balboa, an intrepid Spanish explorer, crossed the Darien Isthmus to the Pacific Ocean, and the Spanish Crown charged the new governor with the task of finding a passage to the "South Sea."

It was easily said, but not so easily done. Although the ambitions stayed alive, little was achieved until the end of the eighteenth century. The narrowness of the isthmus was a seductively attractive feature, but its geology and climate created enormous obstacles.

Ferdinand de Lesseps, who had already built the Suez Canal, identified the Panama route in 1879, and under his patronage millions of French people had bought shares to finance the effort to build the canal. Tragically, in 1889, amid accusations of corruption and collusion in political circles and in the press, the company went bankrupt. Although the French effort failed, much had been achieved, albeit at a cost of 6300 lives from tropical diseases.

De Lesseps had found the geography of the area a very different proposition to the sand of the Suez but remained committed to the idea of digging a canal. The Americans had other ideas. In 1903 the French company was acquired by the U.S., and in 1906 the decision was made to use the lake and lock solution—three Gatun locks lifting ships up into the vast artificially created Gatun Lake, then three more locks taking them down to the sea level of the Pacific. Perhaps the most significant step in the new era was the task of eradicating malaria and yellow fever.

Work then progressed at a rapid pace over the next ten years and on 15 August 1914, the steamship *SS Ancon* made history by being the first vessel to cross the isthmus. It was an engineering triumph that was the culmination of four hundred years of struggle. The goal had been achieved at great cost, both financially and in human lives. As generation followed generation—sweating, toiling, perishing—the dream had been relentlessly pursued despite every adversity and setback that could be imagined.

> *The credit belongs to the person who is actually in the arena, who strives valiantly; who errs and comes up short again and again, because there is no effort without error and shortcoming, who, at the best, knows in the end the triumph of high achievement and who, at the worst, if he fails, at least fails while daring greatly, so that his place shall never be with those cold and timid souls who know neither victory or defeat.*
>
> —*Theodore Roosevelt*

* * *

An Engineering Miracle

We entered the Port of Cristobal on the Atlantic side of the canal and motored past the armada of cargo ships. The new marina at Shelter Bay seemed a better place to berth than the town of Colon, which has a reputation as a dangerous and dirty place. There we waited for the completion of the extensive paperwork required before we were cleared to transit the canal. A short distance from the marina compound, the jungle was inhabited by puma, apes, monkeys, and snakes, as well as beautiful birds—the blue and yellow macaw, the harpy eagle, and the exotic keel-billed toucan. This was tropical jungle on a wild scale and not a place to go walking on your own.

Many yachts choose to pay for the services of an agent to manage the formalities required to make the canal transit. Our agent, Peter Stevens, was an expat "Brit" who had been in Panama since the sixties, and he "greases the wheels" to see that the lengthy administrative procedures are followed and approved, and that we didn't have to wait long to get our passage date. It normally takes about a week.

Finally the day came when we had finished all the necessary inspections and completed the endless forms—which filled a large file. Following Peter's instructions we motored out to "the Flats," an anchoring area off Colon city where the pilots pick up yachts (a pilot is mandatory for all yachts whatever the size). We had been told that we would be going through the canal with a catamaran and two small yachts in two stages over two days. Our first stage would be in darkness, up through the first three locks and into Gatun Lake, where we would anchor for the night. The pilots for the other two yachts duly arrived at the Flats and departed. An hour later we were becoming worried that we had been forgotten, but our pilot duly arrived and we set off in pursuit of the others at about 5:00 that evening.

There are three ways a yacht can pass through the locks: in the centre with lines to each side, alongside another vessel, or alongside the lock walls. Our pilot told us that we would be the lead boat, centre lock, with just the catamaran tied to us. In maritime law the pilot gives advice that he expects to be followed, but the final decision for the safety of the ship remains with the captain.

We motored toward the first of the Gatun locks following a large container ship that would be going into the lock with us. As we approached the lock our pilot dropped a bombshell. "I am not qualified to pilot a yacht of your size through the canal!"

There was a long silence until Luke finally asked, "What do you mean you're not qualified?" Looking rather sheepish the pilot replied, "I have been looking at my documents again and it says that you are rated as a seventy-one-foot boat, and I am only rated up to sixty-five feet." This was ridiculous, as we had just been measured by the Canal authorities as seventy-nine feet in length. We were at a complete loss to know what to do. He picked up his mobile phone to call his base. Finally he turned around with a grin. "It's okay. I have permission to continue."

The pilot seemed rather overawed by our boat and even asked if he could go below and take photographs to show his wife. This was not what we were expecting from a Panama pilot! As we rafted up with the catamaran in the first lock he seemed unsure of himself and ineffective in taking control. Strong leadership was certainly needed with two pilots, two captains, not to mention two female crew on the catamaran, who were shouting orders to everyone.

The lock was enormous—1072 feet long x 109 feet wide and 42 feet deep. A Panamax ship, the maximum permitted size, is 955 feet long x 105 feet wide, giving a clearance of just two feet each side of the canal. We shared the lock with a very large container ship!

Transiting the locks is essentially the same as anywhere else, just on a much bigger scale. The lock gates were opened when the water level inside was the same level as outside, then we motored in and four very skilled line handlers at the top of the lock threw down four messenger lines, one for each corner of the boat. (A messenger is a thin throwing line with a weight on the end.) Four of our crew then tied their messenger to a 125-foot long mooring line provided to us earlier by the agent. The dock line handlers hauled our ropes up and walked with the yacht as we slowly motored into the lock to the tying-up position. Then they secured their mooring line to the dock and we hauled in the slack until the boat was held securely in the centre of the lock by all four lines. When all the boats were ready the water rose quickly by some thirty feet and we continuously took in the slack on the lines until the chamber was full. The gate opened and we motored out and into the next lock.

Simple! Now that we knew how to do it next time would be easy, I thought. But in the next lock the mooring line I was handling snapped. The water in the lock was rising fast and wash from the propellers of the cargo ship in front was creating turbulence. With only three lines holding us to the top of the lock we began to swing around, but Luke maintained control using the engine. The pilot called out instructions to me and I

An Engineering Miracle

pulled the broken line in. Fortunately it was broken at the very top of the rope. I hauled it back in, a new messenger was sent down, I retied the mooring line to the messenger, and the man on the dock quickly pulled it back up. Phew!

Of course the big ships are not handled this way. Ships' lines are attached to electric towing locomotives known as mules, which weigh around fifty-five tons and tow, brake, and maintain the ship in the chamber, avoiding contact with the concrete walls. They are made by Mitsubishi and cost over $2 million each.

The third lock was incident free and we emerged into Gatun Lake in pitch darkness and followed the pilot's instructions to find a mooring buoy. He told us to be ready at 6:30 the following morning when a new pilot would arrive to take us the next thirty-seven miles to the Pacific. At 10:00 we were still tied up to our buoy with no pilot. The other yachts in our convoy had left at dawn so we thought that we had been forgotten. Luke called up the pilot control base but they assured him that the pilot was on his way. David, our new pilot, arrived half an hour later looking very relaxed. "Right, captain," he said, "we need to motor at ten knots for the next seven hours to get to the lock in time." Our maximum motoring speed is ten knots but we could hardly say to our Panamanian pilot that it wouldn't have been necessary to proceed at full speed if he had been on time. But David turned out to be very professional and usually piloted the big ships, so we passed the long day asking him about the pilot's job and the operation of the canal.

The Gatun Lake was created by using the mighty Chagres River to flood the Gatun valley. It is a bizarre landscape. The tops of hills peek up above the water creating small green islands. The narrow shipping channel winds its way between them, but it is well marked with red and green marker buoys all the way. The channel is narrow, two-way, and very busy. It is an unnerving experience to see a supertanker appearing round a small island and coming toward you at full speed. David told us a story of a large container ship that was unable to make the turn around one bend in the channel and ended up aground with its bow buried in the shore next to the railway line. The skipper was asked by radio if he needed assistance to get off. "No," he said, "but you might want to cancel the next train."

There is no speed limit in the lake section but fourteen knots is what the pilots usually recommend. An American warship captain told a pilot he could do thirty knots and stop in a boat's length. The pilot said "okay" and off they went. Approaching the lock the pilot said "Stop!" and the ship did stop dead in its tracks. The problem was that the thirty foot following surge wave smashed into the lock gates, causing serious damage. "Of course, those pilots don't work here anymore," David said with a smile.

The traffic through the channel was nonstop in each direction. The canal operates twenty-four hours a day, 365 days a year, taking forty-four ships through every day. It is big business for Panama and growing. A fair size container ship is charged $220,000 for the transit and must be booked at least a year in advance. By contrast we were charged $2000. The number of yachts passing through is negligible so they generate minimal revenue and are considered a nuisance. But we were treated well by David. Unlike our first pilot he was a consummate professional, and relaxed. He explained that being a Panama Canal pilot is extremely well paid, and one of the most sought-after jobs in Panama. To qualify you must first have several years experience as a captain, then there is a long wait to be admitted as a pilot.

There is much talk about the new canal being built to cater to the increase in world shipping and the trend for much larger ships. It will run parallel to the existing one and is already underway, with completion planned for 2015. The Panamax size of five thousand containers will then be raised to eight thousand containers to accommodate the new megaships. The existing canal is even now being widened to increase the throughput of ships.

Although the lock system appears to be straightforward, David explained that it was vital to keep the water in the lake at the right level. "If the water level in the lake is too low there won't be sufficient depth in the locks for ships to float, so before that happens more water is released from dams that stand by for this purpose. If we have had heavy rainfall the water level in the lake becomes too high and the locks would flood, so there is an overspill system to release water from the lake."

It sounds simple but it is managed by a computerized network of measuring stations that receive information from hydrological points the moment rain falls or when the river and lake levels start to drop. Reports provide data that is updated in real-time every fifteen minutes 365 days of the year, enabling control of the water level and ensuring the safe movement of shipping.

After motoring at full speed for twenty miles we reached the entrance of the renowned Culebra Cut, which at only 487 feet is the narrowest section of the canal. This section was cut through a mountain of rock that caused the greatest difficulty when the canal was built. Old sepia

An Engineering Miracle

photographs gave us some idea of what a gargantuan task it must have been. As we passed through the cut we could see that the canal was being widened. What looked like ants beavering away on giant mounds of earth were mammoth earthmoving machines. They might be modern diggers but they were still using the original technique of removing rock by trucks along the terraces that rise up from the sides of the canal.

To get down to sea level we descended thirty-one feet in one step at the Pedro Miguel lock into Miraflores Lake, and then motored a further three-quarters of a mile to reach the Miraflores double lock, which dropped our boat fifty-four feet to the sea level of the Pacific Ocean. In the final lock, David decided that instead of being held in the centre of the lock, as we had been so far, we should raft up with a Panama cruise ship, which was moored next to the lock wall. This meant that we didn't have to worry about getting four mooring lines ashore. We just had to tie up alongside the small cruise ship and then when the lock gates opened gently move away from it. It should have been simple but with just one lock to go our luck ran out. In this last lock, the warm fresh water from the lake and the cold water from the sea are mixed. The warm water rises and the cold water sinks, causing a circular current in the lock that can run at four knots. Coming alongside the cruise ship and putting our engine into reverse to stop, the current pushed our stern round the back of the ship. To make matters worse we had a gallery of cruise ship passengers watching our predicament. Luke recovered the situation but I felt sorry for him. He always maneuvers the boat very well, and it must have hurt his professional pride to have a mishap like that, which caused minor damage to the hull paintwork.

The pilot launch came to take David off and we waved goodbye. Then on an impulse, as we were about to motor round to the Flamenco Marina, I said, "Let's go sailing." Luke raised the sails and the yacht heeled to the wind like a racehorse eager to canter after having been shut in a stable. The sea was flat but there was a good breeze for sailing. I was steering, enjoying the boat's eager response to the wind, and Luke and Max handled the jib sheets snappily as we tacked in and out of the dozens of anchored ships waiting their turn to enter the canal. It felt good to be sailing again after so much motoring. Jock, an American who had joined us for the canal transit, had never been on a large sailing yacht before. He watched, fascinated. "Graham, I didn't know how a yacht was sailed and I have to tell you that I'm impressed with the teamwork." Coming from a U.S. military man I took that as a nice compliment.

Jock had been a senior officer guarding the canal in the seventies so he had come, along with my old friend Bob Paradise, to see what had changed since the handover of the canal to Panama, and we were glad to have his insight into the history of the U.S. management of the canal.

Over dinner that night Jock told us that not only did the Panamanians need the Americans to build the canal, they needed their expertise to manage and defend it. However, throughout the nineteenth century, the terms of the original treaty between the U.S. and Panama were the subject of frequent discussion and disagreement. Panama wanted the 1903 treaty to be renegotiated and things came to a head in 1964 with clashes that led to many deaths and injuries, culminating in Panama breaking off diplomatic relations with the U.S.

In 1973, the Panamanian government internationalized its claim for the return of the canal. This was discussed at the United Nations Security Council and finally, in 1977, Jimmy Carter signed the Torrijos-Carter Treaties leading to the return of the canal to Panama after a twenty-year transition period that ended on 31 December 1999. A key condition was a neutrality treaty allowing free access for the ships of all nations for as long as there is a Panama Canal. The treaty also acknowledged Panama and the U.S. as the main guarantors of passage.

Until Jock told us about his experiences working in Panama I hadn't realized how difficult relations had been between the U.S. military and the Panamanian government. Nevertheless, in the common interest, they had worked successfully together. It seemed to us, though, that the ordinary people still have a deep-seated resentment of the Americans. None offered to speak English, although they probably could.

8

In the Doldrums

The Flamenco Marina in Balboa is where yachts leaving the canal make their final departure preparations before setting out into the Pacific. From Balboa you can see nearby Panama City. Its modern skyscrapers, banks, and office blocks, dominate the skyline. Away from the downtown area the city is an endless sprawl of run-down tenement buildings and small shops with barred windows. Crime and poverty spread their ugly blanket over this teeming city. Janet and I decided we didn't want to visit the high spots or low life so we used the time to make a short trip to Peru to visit Machu Picchu, the lost city of the Incas.

We flew from Panama City to Lima, where we stayed overnight before boarding an internal flight to Cusco in the heart of the Andes. When we arrived at our hotel, which was at 11,800 feet, I felt ill and lethargic. The hotel called a doctor who diagnosed altitude sickness and rushed me straight into a small clinic where I was put on oxygen and an intravenous drip. I wasn't actually sick, but felt sleepy, had a tight chest, and was short of breath. I wondered if this was because of the pleurisy that had affected my lungs during my illness. The doctor examined me and pronounced that I would have to stay on oxygen for the night. Having paid for the best hotel in Cusco I felt rather sorry for myself in a hard bed in a small room with peeling white walls, eating simple food from a plastic tray, and watching TV in a language I couldn't understand. The clinic did the trick though, and next morning the smiling doctor announced that I was fit and ready to continue touring, but now I had more pills to take. Naturally Janet was relieved, although she too later suffered from altitude sickness when we were climbing around Machu Picchu.

The Islands Time Forgot

We thought Cusco would only be a staging post to reach Machu Picchu. How wrong we were. It is an amazing historic destination in its own right. Cusco was the capital of the Inca Empire and revealed fascinating insights into the historic legacy of the city and the nearby Sacred Valley. I wished we had been able to spend more than two days there and that I had been fit enough to enjoy it. The classic way to travel from Cusco to Machu Picchu is to walk the Inca trail, something that Janet's friend Gill Hodson had done on her own ten years before, so we knew that it was a tough three-day trek with overnight camping. It appealed to the heart but the head ruled and so we opted for the traditional but luxurious Orient Express train that winds its way from Cusco through the valleys of the Andes until it reaches the station at Aguas Calientes. From there a coach took us up the long and tortuous zigzag road to the only hotel at the top of the mountain.

Experiencing Machu Picchu in some ways reminded me of seeing the Grand Canyon for the first time. You have seen the photographs, you know what to expect, but nothing can prepare you for the awesome and beautiful experience. Our guide took us from the hotel to a high vantage point, so that our first glimpse of Machu Picchu was looking down on it, the classic view that the trekkers get on arriving from the Gate of the Sun. If you have seen a photograph of Machu Picchu it was almost certainly taken from here. It was breathtaking. We gazed on the scene for a long time without speaking. Although we had read about the historical and architectural significance of this lost city of the Incas, for us it was memorable because of its breathtaking location—built on top of a high mountain, surrounded by the river Urubamba far below, and set among the Vilcabamba Mountains high in the Andes. But more than this, there is an energy about the place, a spiritual feeling that draws you in and keeps you staring at it for hours. It is impossible to explain and impossible to ignore.

This city of grey granite and green grass lawns is shrouded in cloud and cloaked in mystery. Why was it built there? It was the only Inca city that survived the Spanish conquistadors, who destroyed every city and temple they found. Some speculate that it was built there to be hidden from the conquistadors, but it was built a hundred years before the Spanish arrived in 1530. It was out of keeping with the locations of all other Inca cities and royal palaces. And how was it built in this most inaccessible of locations? Why was it totally abandoned, in perfect condition, a hundred years later and thirty years before the Spanish arrived in South America? Every guide will tell you a different story. The real mystery is that nobody knows the

In the Doldrums

true answers to these intriguing questions and Machu Picchu remains inscrutable, refusing to give up its secrets.

Incredibly it remained hidden for hundreds of years until an American explorer, Hiram Bingham, discovered it by accident in 1911. It was completely overgrown by jungle, but otherwise completely intact except for the thatched roofs. It still remained almost unknown, accessible only to explorers using the Inca trail or scaling the mountain on horseback, until 1948. Then things changed forever when the government built the amazing "El Zig-Zag" road from Aguas Calientes that allows motor coaches from the station to make the long climb to Machu Picchu. Now a million visitors from all over the world come here each year. Its growing popularity creates a dilemma for the government, which wants to preserve the site but likes the tourist revenues. Several ideas for restricting the numbers have been suggested but it is hard to find a solution that is fair to everyone. Although the growing numbers of tourists diminish the spiritual experience, it seemed to us large enough to absorb the crowds, and we were glad to have had the privilege of visiting this enigmatic sacred site, truly one of the wonders of the world.

* * *

Back at the Flamenco Marina in Balboa, Luke and Max were making final checks on all the mechanical aspects of the boat and Janet set about the major task of restocking our provisions. Luke suggested we should have enough food for two months. Janet does this by working out the meals for four people and multiplying by the number of days. So, for example, if we had Weetabix for breakfast every day, and had two biscuits each, we would need 448 biscuits or eighteen packets, or some combination of this for different types of cereal. Looking at it like this you can begin to imagine the volume of food we needed to buy.

As none of us spoke Spanish, our agent had given us the name of a local taxi driver, Manuel, who spoke English and would help us do the shopping. He drove us to his local supermarket, which was large and well stocked with everything we could want. Janet filled six large supermarket trolleys with chicken, beef, and lamb, which would fill our large freezer, and staples like rice, pasta, olive oil, canned goods, cereals, and long-life milk that would be stored in lockers, and that, if necessary, could last us

The Islands Time Forgot

for months, especially if we were able to catch fish regularly. Although the fresh fruit and vegetables would only last two weeks, we hoped we would be able to buy more fresh food in the Galapagos, the first islands we would reach. Manuel fascinated the local shoppers when he commandeered one checkout for Janet's exclusive use. He organized the packing with military precision and helped carry the dozens of boxes back to the boat. We weren't going to starve.

I spent time with Luke poring over charts and pilot books discussing the route we would take and the islands we would visit. There are many ways to cross the Pacific. The route we chose was the classic east to west passage. It is described in *The Pacific Crossing Guide* which suggests good reasons for choosing it. It remains in the tropics for most of its length, it makes full use of the trade winds, and it calls in at some of the most beautiful islands and atolls on earth. Another attraction for us was that other yachts were likely to be taking this route, so we would be able to make friends and share the experience with fellow yachtsmen.

It would take us to the Galapagos, the Marquesas, the Tuamotus, the Society Islands, the Cook Islands, Samoa, Tonga, Fiji, and then New Zealand—a six-thousand-mile voyage that would take six months.

Janet had decided to fly back to the Cayman Islands to visit our daughter, Julia, whose first baby was due any day. She was disappointed to miss the first leg of the Pacific passage, but as a mother she felt that her priority was to be with her daughter. It seemed strange to be setting off without her, but she would be rejoining us in the Galapagos in a week, and as Bob Paradise was coming with us as far as the Galapagos, we still had four crew.

Our departure date was set for Sunday 18 March, but on the Saturday night the dock staff asked us to move the boat from the marina dock to fore and aft mooring buoys in the harbor. Luke wasn't very happy because of the lack of space in the outer harbor, but did as he was asked. Unfortunately, in the maneuver, directed by the dock master, the line from the forward mooring buoy was caught round our bow thruster.[20] Max had to swim down in the dirty harbour water to cut it free—not a nice job. Luke still didn't think the space we had been given was safe so we decided to move outside the harbour to anchor. Next morning Max cleared the remains of the rope from the bow thruster and the good news was that there was no damage, the last thing we wanted on the day of our departure.

---

20   *A propeller set into the bow that pushes the boat to port or starboard. It is most useful for maneuvering the boat in a confined space.*

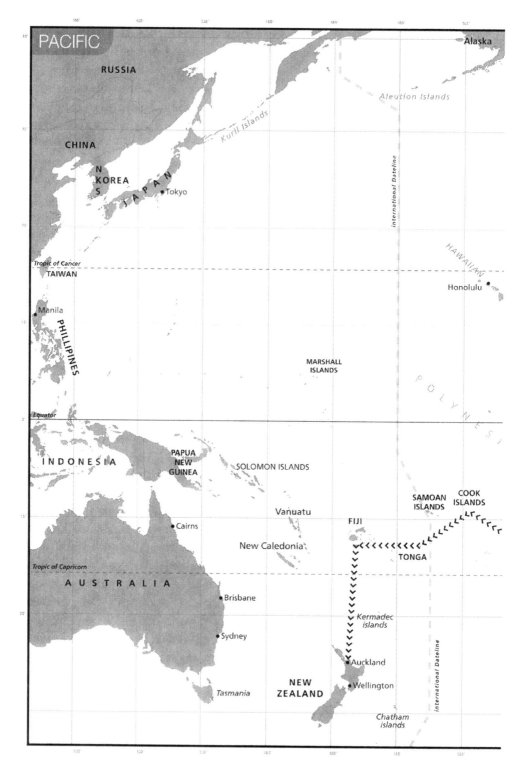

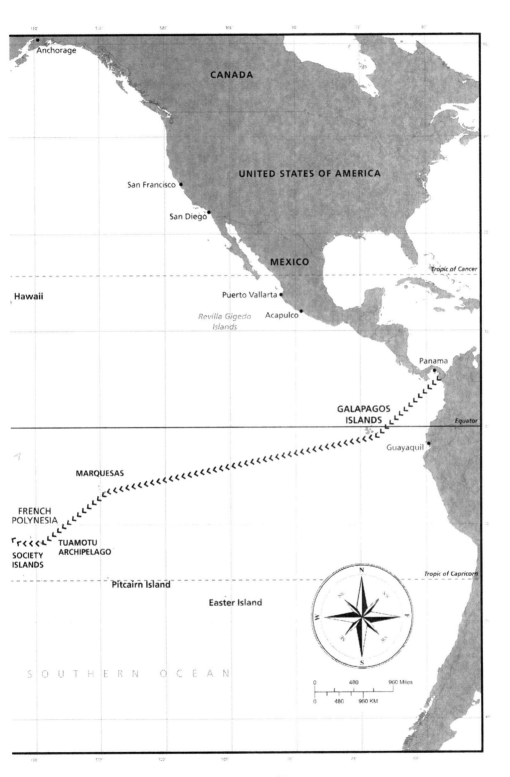

The bad news was that Max became very sick. The water in the harbour was blamed, but it was almost certainly a strain of gastroenteritis that Bob Paradise had unknowingly brought to the boat from New York. He was the first to go down and we all followed like a chain of dominoes while we were in Panama. It was extremely unpleasant but it only lasted a few days and at least it wasn't yellow fever!

At midday on 18 March we raised the anchor and motored out through the massed container ships waiting their turn to enter the canal. I wondered what the adventure would have in store for us, knowing that there would be highs and lows, unforeseen events, and that perhaps the experience would change us, but above all hoping that we would all arrive safely in New Zealand.

We had a good breeze for the first twenty-four hours but had to motor on the second day. It was hardly unexpected as we had entered the Doldrums region just north of the equator. The sea was flat and glassy calm with almost no shipping—just a big flat empty sea. It was mind-numbingly boring. Our life settled into a routine of watches, cooking and eating meals, sleeping, reading, and watching DVDs. At least we were able to motor. We pitied the old sailing ships with no engines; they could be stuck here for weeks.

Luke was optimistic that we would find wind somewhere, and as we were ahead of schedule we could afford to sail slowly if we found even a light breeze. The spinnaker was prepped and ready to hoist.

Max provided us with some entertainment when he caught a nice king mackerel. Later on he found a stowaway seabird on the radar scanner on the mast. It was very reluctant to leave but got the message after Max threw things at it. We didn't mind giving the bird a lift but didn't like the mess it was making!

We had plenty of reading time and took turns buried in *Lonely Planet*, learning about the different islands in the Galapagos. It sounded amazing. There was much discussion among us as to what the islands would be like. We had all seen film of the unique wildlife but would the reality live up to our expectations? What we did know about the Galapagos is that it is a bureaucratic nightmare. While we were in Panama, I read pilot books and went on to sailing Web sites to find out about the procedures for entry into the Galapagos and for sailing in those waters, because we already knew that there were burdensome restrictions.

> *The passing sailor used only to be granted permission to stay for 72 hours but in 2001 the regulations were modified to allow a 20 day stay and transits between San Christobal and Santa Cruz providing permission and clearance has been obtained...yachts are still not allowed to cruise independently without a special permit. These are expensive to obtain and heavily restricted."*
>
> —The Pacific Crossing Guide

But this was six years ago and we didn't know how the regulations might have changed since then, so Peter Stevens, our agent in Panama, had given us the name and contact details of an English-speaking agent in the Galapagos and recommended employing him to help us overcome the red tape of the Ecuadorian government. I e-mailed the agent from the boat and he replied promptly. Apparently there were two ways that we could make the visit: either by leaving the boat anchored, and then going round the islands on a small cruise ship, or by cruising the islands on our own yacht with a pilot on board—but this required various permits. As Stephen and Kris were joining us for a sailing holiday, we wanted to cruise on our own yacht, so I requested more detailed information and an itinerary.

Having motored all Monday night and most of Tuesday, we were resigned to our fate of motoring through the Doldrums, but early in the evening a good 15-knot breeze unexpectedly set in. We crossed our fingers that it would take us all the way to the Galapagos. The wind gods were kind and we continued to enjoy the sailing. In the night our furling spinnaker, which was left on the forestay ready for use, started to unfurl as the wind picked up. It could have been ripped to pieces, but Luke and Max jumped on deck instantly and were able to refurl it and get it down and stowed away without any damage.

The agent in the Galapagos e-mailed me a detailed itinerary. It sounded wonderful but there was no mention of the price. I was suspicious and fired back a short reply. "But what is all this going to cost?" The answer came back quickly and I stared at it for a long time. I just couldn't believe it. But there it was on the screen—eighteen thousand dollars! This was just for the hire of the mandatory pilot and all the license fees required. The joy of sailing is the freedom to go where we want, when we want, and without paying for it. This was piracy! I sent a curt reply. "This is way beyond my budget and totally out of the question. We would love to explore your beautiful islands but we will have to forget the whole thing." I left it at that for now.

In the Doldrums

Crossing the equator on a boat for the first time is a special moment that superstitious sailors mark with gifts for King Neptune and a bizarre but memorable ceremony that usually involves dressing up or a sacrifice. Luke and Bob had done it before but Max and I had not, but sadly the moment passed without us realizing it. I wasn't superstitious but I secretly hoped that King Neptune was not angered. The southern hemisphere looked much the same as the northern. Amazingly it was cold in the night and the watchkeepers all wore fleece jackets, even when the sun came up. We wondered if we were in the right place.

To my surprise, the agent sent a contrite e-mail saying that the trip could be done on a much smaller budget in a different way. By now I was confused, suspicious, and rather angry. I decided that we would wait until we arrived in San Cristobal and then consider our options. At least the agent promised to have someone meet us there and help us clear customs and immigration.

There was a buzz of excitement as we sighted Isla San Cristobal in the early afternoon. As the land became clearer we could see that it was high and rocky and seemed totally deserted. We picked up a sea breeze to sail down the coast. It was dark when we entered Wreck Bay, Port Baquerizo Moreno, but it wasn't a difficult entry. To our surprise the harbour was filled with the lights of boats of every type and size, making it difficult to find a place to anchor. Luke finally picked a spot and we crashed out for a good night's sleep, grateful for no call to go on watch in the night.

We had come 878 miles, and taken just over four days at an average speed of 8.3 knots. Not bad for the Doldrums. Thank heavens for powerful engines in modern yachts.

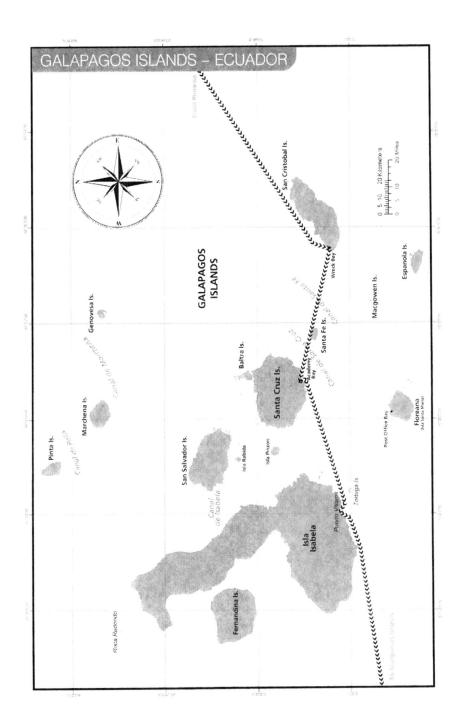

9

Wildlife in the Galapagos

I rose early the next morning to go on deck to take in the new surroundings. I could hardly believe my eyes! A sea lion was asleep on the platform at the back of the boat. Creeping around quietly, so as not to disturb it, I took some photographs. It wasn't until I went ashore that I discovered that sea lions were everywhere—on the beach, on the dock steps, on the rocks, and in the water. It was fascinating to watch them swimming. Not so much fun was the calling card our sea lion left behind. Removing the mess wasn't a pleasant job so Luke rigged up netting to cover the back of the boat to prevent them from returning to us for free board and lodging each night.

Bob and I went ashore to explore Port Baquerizo Moreno while Luke went with the agent's representative to sort out the customs and immigration formalities. The hub of the town is the well-built new dock, where boats of all sizes jostle for space to pick up or disembark tourists of many different nationalities. It is a small town, just one street really, with shops offering souvenirs, tours, Internet cafés, and a few bars and restaurants. The sun beat down out of a bright blue sky, bleaching the red, white, and yellow Spanish-style buildings into washed-out colours. There were few people about in the noonday sun; the locals had gone to lunch and siesta and the tourists had gone off on their boat trips. It was quiet, hot, and dusty. The cacti growing everywhere made the street look like a scene from a Spanish cowboy movie.

We went into shops, hoping to arrange a boat tour, but it was difficult because we couldn't find anyone who spoke English, but then I heard an English yachtsman talking to some locals. He directed me to Ricky, who runs a café on the seafront. "It's great," he said. "You can get lunch there for three dollars." Ricky turned out to be Mr. Fixit, who spoke reasonable English and said he could provide whatever we wanted, like Delboy from the TV show, *Only Fools and Horses*. He arranged for supplies of fresh fruit and vegetables to be taken out to our boat, fixed a land tour and a snorkel/diving trip, and directed us to the Internet café run by his cousin. Lunch was cooked by his wife. It *was* only three dollars and very good.

Bob and I went for a boat trip the next day. The snorkeling was excellent, but the water was freezing. How very different from the Caribbean. It was strange to be on the equator with a sea temperature that felt like England. I could only stay in the water for ten minutes for my first snorkel, and at the second dive site, where it was much deeper, I could only manage five minutes. The reason for the extremely cold water is the Humboldt Current, which comes up the west coast of South America and then turns west to pass through the Galapagos. It is the effect of this cold current meeting the warm water at the equator that contributes to the unique wildlife environment.

Although I was only in the water for a short time, the diversity of marine life was amazing: turtles, sea lions, stingrays, a huge school of spade fish, and sharks. I have only been in the water near sharks twice and, like most people, am very wary of them. Our guide told us we would see larger ones at the second spot, Kicker Rock, further out to sea. "If you are lucky you may see hammerheads," he said. I decided I didn't want to be lucky so I stayed in the boat. After everybody else got into the water, I thought, "I can't sit this out. I'm here for adventure," so I gingerly slipped into the water. One of the snorkelers pointed below him and shouted, "Shark here," and when I apprehensively swam over and looked down, sure enough there were five or six big sharks gliding by about ten feet below us. In fact they were quite uninterested in the swimmers above and strangely I didn't feel at all frightened. Perhaps it was the relaxed attitude of the dive master that gave me confidence. It was my first experience with sharks in the Pacific but I could not have guessed at the encounters that were to come later.

The only airport in the Galapagos Islands is on San Cristobal, so we made our crew changes there. Bob was leaving to go back to New York, Janet was returning from the Cayman Islands, and Stephen and Kris were arriving.

I met Janet at the tiny airport and gave her a big kiss. It was the first time for a long while that we had spent a week apart, and it was wonderful to have her back with the news of our new grandson. Julia was overwhelmed by the surprise visit and grateful that Janet had been there just two days after the baby was born. She just cried and hugged her mother. It had to be a surprise because it would have been awful to have made a commitment and then not be able to keep it because we were at sea. The photos of Matthew with his exhausted-looking mother were very loving and made us all feel closer together.

The next day an open truck arrived, courtesy of Ricky, to take us on a land tour. We saw the giant tortoises at a nature reserve. They are curious creatures: large, old, and wrinkly, but quite approachable. Our guide then drove us to the interior of the island, where there is an extinct volcano. Climbing a long boardwalk that zigzags its way to the summit, we were rewarded with a 360-degree view across the island. It was a bleak landscape of harsh terrain, mostly brown and barren rock, scrubby vegetation, and giant cacti.

Climbing a little further to the summit we were treated to a pleasant surprise. The old caldera had filled with rainwater to create a large lake. Magnificent frigate birds hovered over it, delicately dipping their wings in the fresh water before flying high, then dropping like a stone, shaking their wings dry before pulling up just above the surface. Some years ago I learnt from a nature guide in Tobago that frigate birds are unable to fly if their feathers become saturated with water. This is why, unlike most seabirds, they cannot dive for fish in the sea. It seems a cruel trick of nature. They feed by attacking other birds and taking the fish from their mouths or by catching fish that have jumped above the surface of the sea. In Tobago we had seen high-flying frigate birds get wet in a heavy rain shower and then drop, shaking their wings to get rid of the water on the surface of their feathers. However, we had never seen them washing themselves above the surface of fresh water like this before. It was a thrill to be so close to them and it must have been half an hour before we were able to pull ourselves away and walk back down the boardwalk.

But it is underwater that Galapagos has most to offer the visitor. Following the success of our first trip to Kicker Rock we went again with Stephen, Luke, and Max, who all wanted to scuba dive. This tall, strangely-shaped, and beautiful old rock, split in two to reveal dazzling white, yellow, and orange rock strata, is divided by a narrow channel, and it is here that one can often see the sharks, rays, and big fish. The water was very cold at 66 F. Even the dive master was frozen! Conditions were unusual and getting worse and a thick fog blew in. This was not what we expected on the equator! The boys dove to sixty feet but visibility under the water was poor, so they did not see as much as they had hoped for, although they did encounter hammerhead sharks. Even snorkeling I saw two spotted eagle rays.

For me the underwater highlight was swimming with seals and sea lions (it was hard for us to tell the difference). In the shallow waters off the Isla Lobos they gave us the impression that they welcomed our company, the young ones especially. They were wonderfully playful, swimming straight at us like a torpedo, then swerving away at the last second. Max got an amazing movie shot of this on his underwater camera and you can see the seal come right up and try to take a bite out of the camera. You can even hear the sea lion's jaws snap. However, no one got bitten, and I believe that they're essentially friendly and harmless as long as you stay away from the big bulls. The young ones behave just like puppy dogs. We watched in astonishment as they climbed up the anchor chain of the boat by wrapping their fins around the chain, trying to snatch a loose piece of rope in their mouth, and then sliding down the chain again.

Here at Isla Lobos we saw marine iguanas on the rocks and the lovely but aptly named blue-footed boobies. They look as if they've dipped their feet in a pot of blue paint. It was the mating season and the magnificent frigate birds were nesting, so we were treated to the extraordinary sight of the males puffing up the big red pouch on their chest to attract the females, who would then decide which mate to choose.

The dive boat on which we did this trip was small and uncomfortable but fast and fun. There was room for just twelve passengers and we shared it with the Kiwi crew of *Odysseus,* a 56-foot yacht sailing from New Zealand to Spain. We gave them tips on the Panama Canal and they whetted our appetite for New Zealand. Much of their sailing had been upwind, probably with a lot more to come, and I was so glad that we had mostly downwind sailing to look forward to. Everyone got on very well, although we would probably never see one another again. It was fun to spend the day together and be with kindred spirits in this remote environment.

Finally the long-running saga with our agent to obtain the restricted cruising permit we wanted was resolved and we were allowed to leave San Cristobal. From the extortionate figure of $18,000 I was offered a restricted permit for $800. It allowed us to go to the ports on the four main islands but we would be unable to move the boat from these ports and would have to take day-trip boats to explore further afield. It seemed our best option, so I accepted it.

The bureaucracy in the Galapagos is unbelievable. Every yacht is told a different story. Essentially the authorities don't want yachts in the

Galapagos so they are either heavily restricted as to where they can go or are charged a king's ransom. The excuse is conservation of the environment, but it is hard to imagine what damage yachtsmen might do, and I suspect that the idea is to make the interisland cruise ships the only way of cruising the islands.

Ricky (Mr. Fixit) told me how corrupt life is in Ecuador. He explained that initially the development and commercial benefits of tourism in the Galapagos were meant to be for the local people. In order to conserve the environment it was sensibly decided that boats taking tourists around the islands and to the dive spots should operate only under license, and these licenses were initially given to local boat operators. When international commercial tourist operators saw the opportunities, however, they got together with the Ecuadorian government and suggested that it would be in the best interests of the environment (and commercial interests, no doubt) if they were given the exclusive rights to operate interisland boat trips. They bought out the contracts of the local boatmen cheaply and now the locals are left with only the small day-trip boats with which to make a living. Much of the wildlife in Galapagos is endemic, but so, it seems, is corruption.

It was a pleasant forty-five-mile sail from San Cristobal over to the island of Santa Cruz, although there was some fog around. We passed very close to the uninhabited island of Santa Fe, which might have been better named Desolation Island. Santa Cruz is the centre of the ecotourism business. Port Ayora, Academy Bay, was packed with interisland ships of every kind and price—from five-star luxury cruisers to small boats with shared cabins. The town was teeming with tourists and there were shops offering souvenirs, tours, and diving. The Internet cafés, bars, and restaurants were all busy. Also popular was the Charles Darwin Research Station and museum. We went there hoping to learn more about the influence of the Galapagos on Darwin's work, *The Origin of Species*, but it was disappointing and told us little new. Further out of town we found the municipal market with stalls piled high with fruit and vegetables as well as live cattle and chickens. This is where we would come to stock up before we left on the three-thousand-mile passage to the Marquesas.

We took an open truck to the national park for a guided hike. It was a welcome contrast to San Cristobal because it was so much more fertile. Every kind of tropical fruit grew in abundance. We even ate baby tomatoes from a wild bush. Walking down the shady paths with overhanging trees we saw giant tortoises hidden in the bushes and cooling off in small ponds.

They are about four to six feet in length and our guide told us that some of them reach an age of three hundred years. As we approached they made a loud hissing sound. Although scary at first it is not an aggressive noise, simply air being expelled from inside their shell as they draw their head in. We entered a labyrinth of very old caves created by lava flow from the volcano, and at one point had to crawl under a gap just three feet high—not exactly Janet's idea of fun. The bones of dead cows (well, the guide said they were cows) were piled up inside. Apparently they had strayed in by accident. We were glad to emerge from the dark cave into the bright sun and fresh air.

The anchorage at Puerto Ayora was open to a nasty swell from the south, the worst I have ever known. The long swells came on our beam and rocked the boat from side to side. We came to anticipate the motion. It would begin slowly and then build in momentum until finally the boat was rolling over at an angle of 40 degrees. Then it slowly subsided until it was calm again. We waited, wondering when the next swell would come, dreading it when it did. It made sleeping almost impossible because the swell was worse at night when the wind dropped. These were the most uncomfortable nights at anchor that I can ever remember, and on top of the swell there was fog at night and a cold damp atmosphere.

The conditions finally became unbearable, but we were not permitted to move the yacht, so Janet and I took a break from the boat and stayed two nights in a very comfortable hotel in the Highlands area where we just relaxed by the swimming pool. A bed that stayed still in the night was a very attractive feature. It was a tonic that relieved some of the pressures building up among us from living so close together for so long. We resolved to do it more often.

After six days we were glad to leave the hustle and bustle of Santa Cruz and the agony of the swell in the harbor at Puerto Ayora to sail to Isabella. Only forty-five miles away, this is the westernmost and largest island but it was not in any of our pilot books. The charts proved to be half a mile out, with some parts of the island not charted at all, so we crept slowly into the shallow lagoon. Ten yachts were anchored in Puerto Villamil.

Next morning the surf was up outside the lagoon, with huge breakers crashing onto the town beach and the rocks surrounding the lagoon. It was clear that this tiny lagoon was the only tenable anchorage for this island and if it had been full we would simply have been unable to stay.

We were anchored in the deepest spot, near the lagoon entrance, because the rest of the lagoon was so shallow that even the water taxis had to take a careful winding route to the dock to avoid the shallows and the breaking waves that were finding their way right up to the seaward side of the dock. A small cargo ship had anchored behind us, and local boats and barges were ferrying cargo from ship to shore. I saw one with a load of new mattresses. It is the only way that goods can get ashore here. Even the shallow barges can't come alongside the small dock, and we saw men wade out to the barges through waist-high water and return carrying heavy sacks on their backs.

Isabella was much more to our liking than busy Santa Cruz. There were no tourists and a sandy track led into the small town, which was deserted. We found a shop and booked an afternoon boat tour. It was difficult to know what we were getting as nobody spoke any English, but it only cost $15 a head so we took potluck.

The trip turned out to be an unexpected pleasure, perhaps the best we had in the Galapagos. We were taken to the islet of Los Tintoreras (Tintorera is the Spanish word for tiger shark). Ironically this island was right next to our anchorage but it is part of the national park and was not open to us without a guide. A whale was wallowing in the shallows, but sadly we learned that it had come there to die. Then at last we found what we had been searching for in the Galapagos: the unique Galapagos penguins. We saw two or three from the boat, swimming and diving for fish, and then as we got closer to the shore we saw more preening themselves on the rocks. Our guide was able to get the boat up really close to watch them. They were small—only about twelve inches tall—but quite beautiful and very captivating. Our cameras were clicking for a long time.

After landing on the small rocky island we walked single file up a path that looked down on a narrow gully, about 115 feet wide, with sea water entering at each end. It was full of white- tipped reef sharks (but no tiger sharks!) We couldn't believe our eyes. There must have been fifty or more just milling around in ten feet of water. It was mesmerizing to see so many sharks so close, and in their natural environment. It was hard to understand what brought them all together in this enclosed space.

There were eagle rays in the same spot, and as we walked along the beach we saw marine iguanas and sea lions. The marine iguanas, about twelve to twenty inches long, looked prehistoric, as their ancestors were, and the sea lions seemed aggressive. Our guide told us not to approach them too closely. The expedition only lasted two hours but we were amazed by what we had seen, and enjoyed it all the more because it was totally unexpected.

Because of language difficulties, we also had no idea what to expect when we took a mystery tour inland. After a one-hour drive over rough roads the open truck began the climb up the side of a mountain. When the dusty track ran out we were asked to get out and given the choice of continuing the climb on foot or on horseback. Having never been on a horse before I didn't think this was a good place to start, so I had no hesitation in opting for "shank's pony." The guide told us in very broken English that the walk to the top of the Sierra Negra volcano would take two and a half hours up and then the same down. I was concerned about the idea of five hours climbing and thought, "I can't do that in this heat." The four of us discussed it and thought perhaps we had misunderstood her. Perhaps she meant a two-and-a-half-hour walk in total? We weren't sure but decided to walk anyway.

It was a long hard uphill trek through pleasant countryside with deserted farms, overgrown orchards, and pastures where cows wandered freely. It was a shock when we met them grazing on the narrow path with no room on either side. We realized they were harmless, but the thought of wandering through them and perhaps getting kicked was daunting. After a standoff of a few minutes they didn't budge, so we shouted and clapped our hands and thankfully they galloped off into the bush.

On reaching the top we were stunned by the incredible sight of a huge oval caldera, nearly six miles wide and four miles long, filled with a flat black bed of lava—a solidified lake. It looked as if this seething black mass had just poured out yesterday, which I suppose in geographic time it had, as it last erupted in 2005, just two years ago. We gazed in silence, imagining what this scene must have looked like when the volcano was erupting. Now it looked like the surface of the moon. Our walk continued around the rim of the caldera. By now we had been hiking for two and a half hours and I was already tired. Janet and the boys were fine, but I was finding breathing difficult so we turned back.

It seemed a long time before we saw the welcome sight of our truck waiting for us, a tiny speck hundreds of feet below. We were frequently passed by groups cantering by on horses. It was obvious that horseback was the best way to explore this territory and I felt stupid that I wasn't able to ride. Finally I jumped in the back of the truck, exhausted. Halfway down the mountain we began to smell burning and to our dismay the truck ground to a halt, the overheated engine hissing in complaint as it slowly cooled down. Then there was silence, broken only by the sound of birds singing in the trees. Our situation looked dire. We were stuck in the middle of nowhere, tired, thirsty, and hungry. No one had a mobile phone and there wouldn't have been reception out here anyway. Reluctantly the driver pulled up the bonnet and poked around, but we could tell from the long faces and weary tones of the driver and guide that this was not something that was going to be fixed in a hurry. We sat for a few minutes quietly discussing our predicament. Then, hallelujah! In the distance was a cloud of dust coming our way. We watched as it came closer and closer and finally saw that it was another truck. Our spirits lifted as it came to a halt alongside us. The two drivers chatted away in Spanish, and then our guide turned to us with the welcome news that we could continue our journey in the other truck, which would turn around and take us back. It was a huge relief to get back into town. I wanted to give the driver money—we were truly grateful for his help—but he firmly refused to take any and we could only thank him profusely for his kindness.

We left the Galapagos Islands for the Marquesas with mixed feelings. Galapagos is not for everyone. If you are a naturalist or just love nature, you cannot fail to be thrilled by the wild life. We had been up close and personal with unusual birds, animals, and fish that had left us with wonderful memories. But the restrictions and bureaucracy put a damper on the experience. The joy of sailing is the freedom to go wherever you want. Our experience was also spoiled by the frequent fog, damp evenings, and very cold water. The bad swell in Santa Cruz will remain a painful memory for a long time and will be the benchmark by which we judge swell in the future.

10

Alone in the Ocean

On Wednesday 11 April 2007 we set out on the three-thousand-mile passage to the Marquesas. We estimated that it would take about two weeks, the longest period we would be at sea on the Pacific crossing. As usual I felt apprehensive. The inescapable fact was that if there were an emergency we would be on our own in the loneliest place in the world, with help thousands of miles away. How we would handle it would depend on the nature of the emergency, how we reacted, and the leadership of the captain.

The weather was our main concern on this part of our voyage. For the first week the weather was perfect, with a pleasant breeze of 10–15 knots on the beam and a moderate sea, giving us 8–10-knot boat speeds under a blue sky and fluffy white clouds. At these speeds we were regularly able to beat the magic two-hundred-mile-a-day goal, which was very satisfying. Now that we were clear of the cold Humboldt Current the nights were warmer, although we continued to wear light jackets on watch at night.

We were at 5 degrees south and heading southwest, not a direct course for the Marquesas, but we expected to pick up stronger winds at between 7–10 degrees south before turning west with the wind behind us. The weather forecast and the pilot charts seem to agree that this was a sensible strategy.

Here in the ocean, clear of the distraction of light from the land, the night sky was perfect for stargazing. The heavens were thickly dusted with stars and we spent a lot of time staring up at them. Luke had loaded a software program onto the ship's computer that showed the night sky at our position for each hour of the night. Looking at the screen in the cockpit in conjunction with the compass made it easier to make out the constellations and the stars above them. I had no problem identifying Rigel Kentaurus

Alone in the Ocean

and Hadar and, above these, the Southern Cross. From this I could pick out Orion, Ursa Major, and the planets Venus and Saturn. As the night progressed the stars moved up and across the sky, so the vista constantly changed. Star identification isn't easy, but practice makes perfect.

The two fishing rods were out all the time. Between six and eight in the morning was the time when fish were most likely to bite. The boys lost three big ones when either the line broke or the fish got off the hook. The problem was slowing the boat down in time. At eight knots our boat speed seemed to pull the hook out of their mouths. We discussed the problem and decided on a plan to slow the boat down more quickly.

The next time the line whizzed out and the watchkeeper cried "fish," we all rushed on deck and took up our stations to slow the boat down. I took the wheel and put the boat dead down wind, Janet and Max furled the jib and the staysail while Luke played the fish. Half an hour later it began to tire and Luke was able to slowly reel in. Max was standing ready with the gaff hook like the bowman on a whaler, ready to plunge the gaff in so that the fish could be lifted onto the bathing platform. As it came closer we could see that we had caught a big tuna, not long but chunky, like a rugby prop forward. It weighed eighteen pounds and made enough steaks for nine meals. Luke and Max had so much fun and the excitement was contagious. It lifted everyone's spirits.

The winds were indeed stronger at 8 degrees south, and with 15–20 knots true wind we were able to turn to the west and sail downwind directly for the Marquesas, which were now 2121 miles away. With a third of the distance behind us we still had a long way to go. It became warmer and we needed only shorts and T-shirts on the night watch.

On our sixth day the weather changed. We had a wet and windy night, logging one of our fastest twenty-four-hour runs—228 miles. There was plenty of rain and wind the next day, too, which developed into a very boisterous downwind sleigh ride. The wind was twenty-five knots, gusting thirty, which caught us out as it was only forecast to be fifteen knots. We had to close the hatches, which made it very hot and stuffy below deck.

The next morning at 7:30 Janet and I were suddenly awakened by a loud crash and the boat heeling over violently. We would have been thrown out of bed if we didn't have the lee cloths rigged.[21] We struggled out of bed and made our way up on deck as fast as we could, with the boat still pinned over at a crazy angle. We had no idea what had happened. When

---

21 *The lee cloth prevents one from falling out of bed. A canvas sheet is fixed under the mattress and taken up the side of the bed and fixed by cords to hooks in the ceiling.*

we came on deck Luke was fighting with the wheel, trying to get the boat back on the original tack. The boom had come across in an accidental gybe, but fortunately the preventer did its job and stopped the boom from going all the way over and causing serious damage. Luke was able to get her back on the correct tack again and nothing was broken, but it had given us quite a fright.

When things were sorted out Luke told us that the reason for the accidental gybe was that the autopilot had failed again, and gone into standby on its own. By Murphy's Law it had happened when Luke was down below at the navigation station doing the log, so he had to get back up on deck before he could get to the wheel to hand steer. This autopilot failure had also happened earlier in the night, so we knew we had a problem again. When Luke tried it half an hour later it was working, but of course now it did not have our full confidence! Luke decided to e-mail B&G, the manufacturer, to troubleshoot the fault. It seemed to be a different problem to the one that occurred before we reached Panama and it had now happened four times.

A ship appeared from nowhere and passed about 3.5 miles away from us going fast in the opposite direction. It was a shock, as we hadn't seen it until it was quite close. It hadn't shown up on our navigation screen with the AIS system and it wasn't visible on the radar screen because of the amount of clutter from the rain squalls and breaking waves. It was worrying to realize how close we could get to another ship in bad weather without knowing it. After days of seeing nothing it served as a sharp reminder to keep our eyes open. We learned later that some of the large factory fishing ships switch off their AIS so that other fishing boats don't know where they are, which is illegal and dangerous. This was probably why it wasn't showing up on our AIS.

After three days of strong wind the heavy clouds lifted but the sky was still a wall of grey. It had stopped raining and the wind abated to twenty knots, which made the boat's motion more comfortable. Completing the log at the end of her watch, Janet announced that we would soon be at our halfway mark, which raised a cheer.

The next morning we shook out the one reef left in the main. The wind had been easing all night and at noon we put the spinnaker up, which gave us a very satisfactory increase in our boat speed from 5.5 to 8 knots. At last we had blue sky, sunshine, and pleasant winds again and we were cracking along, making 210 miles in the next twenty-four hours. What a change in mood this created on board! We were able to keep up this good speed for the next few days, consistently beating the magic two-hundred-mile-a-day mark with the exception of one day.

Although we were sometimes lonely and very conscious that we were thousands of miles from land, we were still in regular contact with our friends and family. Each day we checked our e-mail, which was downloaded by satellite to the ship's computer, to hear the news from our children and friends. Some of them, like Jen Sizzey, were following our progress daily using the "tracker" we had on our Web site. It showed them our boat's position on a chart, and was automatically updated every twenty-four hours.

An occasion arose that caused me to reflect on how much technology has revolutionized communications at sea. I received an e-mail that said that the U.S. dollar had reached $2 to the British pound for the first time in fifteen years. I wanted to buy dollars immediately, so I e-mailed my bank in the UK with questions and arranged for them to phone me on the ship's satellite phone at 6:00 AM, when I finished my watch (2:00 PM in the UK). I got the phone call and did the deal, but they needed my signature on a letter confirming the instruction. Max scanned the letter for me (I didn't know how to do it) and I e-mailed it back to the bank. The transaction was completed at 6:15 that morning in the middle of the Pacific. Amazing!

Our weather forecasts came from MaxSea, a software program that runs our electronic navigation charts and provides other resources including weather forecasting. To get the forecast we e-mail them a grib file—a condensed e-mail specifying the weather information we want for the area we select. Normally we got a response within twenty minutes, giving the wind speed, direction, and sea state for the next three days, and we did this every day. We then overlaid this onto our navigation screen, so that we could see the arrows showing the wind direction and speed on our electronic chart.

We also had historic weather information from pilot charts that showed the percentage likelihood of the wind speed and direction all over the Pacific each month. These are based on hundreds of records from the old sailing ship days until recent times, but include data from a wide range of other sources. They are surprisingly accurate. If I compared a current weather forecast to the pilot chart it was amazing to see how similar the predictions were.

Many of our friends asked what we do when we are on watch. Even though we go for many days without seeing anything, we have to be alert in looking out for other ships. To help us, we have radar and AIS.

If another ship is coming too close it may be necessary to take avoiding action by changing course. When there are other ships around this is an absorbing activity and time flies by. The wind speed and direction has to be monitored all the time. If the wind increases, the jib and the staysail may need to be reefed. If the wind has increased significantly, the mainsail will need to be reefed and Luke will need to be called. If the wind drops, we might want to put out more sail. If the wind direction changes, we may need to alter course. The log has to be completed every hour. The latitude and longitude, log (miles sailed), wind speed and direction, boat speed and heading, barometer reading, battery reading, sail changes, and whether we are using the engine or generator are entered. Still, time passes slowly at night when nothing much is happening, and two hours can seem an age. It is a relief at four in the morning, when, with five minutes to go, you see the glimmer of a light below and the stirring of the next person coming up for a chat before taking over the watch.

We enjoyed 15–18 knots of wind with blue sky and sunshine for some days. It was perfect trade wind sailing, which made us all happy. I was reminded of the lines from "The Homeric Hexameter" by Coleridge.

Strongly it bears us along on
swelling and limitless billows,
Nothing before, and nothing
behind, but the sky and the ocean.

The only complaint was that there had been no fish since we caught the big tuna. The boys changed the lures to see if that would help. Meanwhile there were plenty of fish in the freezer and the meals were wonderful. Although Janet usually plans the menu, at sea we had a cooking roster tied to the watch system. The person coming off watch at 6:00 in the evening cooked the main meal of the day, which we ate around 7:30. We were creative in finding many different ways of serving fish. Luke made a particularly good fish curry and Janet's fish pie was something to look forward to all afternoon. Breakfast was "help yourself," as we all got up at different times. Lunch, part of the cooking roster, was typically pizza, pasta, or a wrap with cold meat and salad. Because of the constant motion of the boat we ate on our laps in the cockpit from what we called dog bowls—large plastic pasta bowls. We took turns washing up.

I amused myself by keeping a record of how we spent our days between joining the boat in the BVI on 16 December and our estimated arrival in the Marquesas at the end of April. Surprisingly, only one in five days had actually been spent at sea (defined as requiring overnight sailing).

- 25% of our time was spent sailing in the day but anchored at night
- 22% was spent at sea and sailing through the night
- 46% of the days we were in harbour or anchored
- 7% of our days we were away from the boat

One morning I saw the sails of another yacht, very close by, only about three miles off our port side. Having been alone for so long it was an exciting moment. I was about to make contact with it when a voice came through on the VHF radio. It was from the yacht I was watching, *Saraband*, a South African 36-foot monohull, also bound for Fatu Hiva, the nearest island in the Marquesas. Eager for company, we chatted for a while. I was surprised to learn that they left Galapagos on 1 April, whereas we left on 11 April. They expected to take twenty-eight days while we estimated fifteen. It made me appreciate how significantly a larger yacht cuts down passage times.

With three days to go, the wind began to drop and a nasty swell developed, creating a confused sea. There wasn't enough wind to keep the sails filled and we rolled in the troughs. The sails flogged as the boat rolled and the wind spilled from the mainsail. As it rolled back again the boom crashed out against the full extent of the mainsheet. The sails were banging and crashing in this way for some time, which was not good for the sails or our morale. To counter this, we put the boat more on a beam reach to increase the apparent wind speed and keep the sail filled, but we still had an uncomfortable night. None of us got much sleep. The next morning the wind dropped further and we had to motor, but at least the swell had eased and we were able to head directly to our destination.

At noon we put our clocks back one hour for the third time. Like airline passengers, we also have to take account of time zones. We did it in one-hour increments when we felt like it, trying to keep the daylight period roughly the same, and ensuring that we would be on local time before we arrived at our destination.

That evening at dusk the line whizzed out and we could tell from the sound that we had a big one. Luke had hooked a marlin. This is a sport fish, a big fighting fish, perhaps six feet, and its first leap in the air after being hooked was a gesture of total defiance. We prepared the boat for a long fight, quickly getting the sails down and the engine on so that we could try to match the boat speed to the marlin's runs. It would appear to be worn out, then fight back and take out more line again. Luke was in a fighting mood, too, as he and the marlin matched wits. The two boys loved it. At last Luke got the fish up close, but it darted alongside the boat and created slack in the line and managed to break it. Free of the line, it heaved itself up onto the surface of the water and did a mysterious power glide, almost upright, using its large tail fin to propel itself across the water, perhaps not believing it was free, and then it dived and was gone. I had mixed feelings. The boys were mad at losing the fish, and missing the challenge of gaffing it and getting it on board, which would have been no mean feat for a fish this size. But I felt uneasy about hunting such a beautiful fish. I am not a vegan, I enjoy eating fish, and I am not anti-fishing, but I could not bring myself to kill such a magnificent creature. Privately, I felt glad that it had lived to fight another day.

Around midnight we passed another yacht, *Aventura.* Luke called the yacht on the VHF radio and spoke to the skipper, who was an American, also out of Galapagos and bound for Fatu Hiva. It seemed that we were all converging on the same destination and we looked forward to the gathering in the anchorage where we could rest and compare notes.

For two days we had no satellite coverage, which meant no e-mail. The Inmarsat satellite system we used, although a global system, has some blank spots in parts of the Pacific that prevent data transmission, which requires much higher speeds than voice transmission. Fortunately the satellite phone worked fine. It was difficult to see exactly where the blank spot was on the satellite coverage map, as they don't give the latitude and longitude, but we were hopeful that we would have coverage back when we left the Marquesas. We felt rather peeved and it was ridiculous how dependent we had become on e-mail.

The evening after the first marlin strike we had another one. We were motoring and so in a better position to react quickly to slow the boat down when the fish struck. Luke had learned a lot from the experience of losing the one the day before. Oddly, it was at exactly the same time, early evening, about 5:30. He played it for longer this time, giving me instructions on how I should maneuver the boat to keep the fish behind us with the right tension on the line. The line has a breaking strain of fifty pounds, and this was a powerful fish weighing over one hundred pounds, so it would be very easy for the fish to put on too much tension, or slack, which would break the line. The battle went on for nearly an hour, and the marlin got tired, but it was still playing tricks, pretending to be dead and then giving another mighty run. As the fish was gradually reeled in, Max, poised with the gaff, speared it and then hauled it onto the bathing platform. There, still defiant, it thrashed about so much it got free from the gaff and back into the water. But Luke reacted quickly and managed to keep the fish on the line.

Max got the gaff in again and heaved the marlin back onto the bathing platform. It was huge, and it took two gaff hooks, one near the head and one near the tail, before they could pull it from the swim platform up onto the aft deck. The excitement and sense of achievement was electric and I took a memorable photograph of the two boys shaking hands with wide grins on their faces. They hung the marlin from a rope at the end of the boom for our traditional photograph because it was too heavy for Luke to lift up. It was also too heavy for our scale, which has a maximum of one hundred pounds. Luke estimated that this one must have been over 130 pounds and six feet long. It was an immense achievement for the boys to land such a huge and powerful fish, the biggest they have ever caught by a long, long way. It will be a day they will remember for many years to come.

Luke and Janet bagged up 187 individual marlin steaks and put them in the freezer. It was more than we could use but we thought we could go round the boats in the anchorage at Fatu Hiva and offer some to those who had not fished or not been so lucky. Meanwhile the fishing rods were decommissioned until our fish stocks were depleted.

At dawn on 25 April we were hit by a squall that caught us unawares with the full mainsail up. It gusted up to 33 knots and caused an accidental gybe. The preventer again did its job in stopping the boom from slamming over to the other side of the boat, but the sail was held in the middle of the boat, pinning us over at an angle of 45 degrees. The three of us below were thrown around and Janet was propelled from one side of the saloon to the other, crashing into the dining table and badly bruising her legs. Otherwise we were all unhurt. Luke managed to get the wheel over to get us back on the right tack and we continued, a little shaken by our experience. Max cheekily cracked, "Luke, why does this always happen on your watch?"

As soon as this squall passed we put a reef in the mainsail and a succession of squalls with heavy rain went through. The trouble with these squalls is that although you can see them coming on the radar, they are mostly harmless, only adding three or four knots of wind, but then one comes along that doubles the wind speed. It seemed impossible to know which one packs a punch and it made me nervous. We had been lucky not to have had any damage or injury but it was always a possibility.

Still chastened by our experience of the dawn squall I asked Luke to put a reef in the mainsail in preparation for our last night, even though it was only blowing eighteen knots and was not really necessary. It turned out to have been a wise precaution, because on Janet's midnight watch there were gusts reaching thirty knots plus, and even with a reefed main the boat was hard pressed. She always kept the foghorn next to her at the wheel in case she needed to summon help in an emergency. Seeing that the gusts were increasing, and concerned that another reef was needed, she gave the foghorn a sharp blast, which brought Luke running up on deck. He did the rest of her watch with her but although they were bombarded by squalls for the next two hours the situation remained under control.

At six in the morning the dark clouds cleared to reveal a bright windy morning, with the island of Fatu Hiva only thirty-five miles away. Max called "Land ahoy" two hours later. It was a wonderful moment after fifteen days at sea! We all stared at the tall dramatic cliffs of the southwest headland. As we rounded the headland the yacht came under the shelter of the land, giving us our first close views of the landfall. Fatu Hiva was just how I imagined the Marquesas—steep mountains dropping down to the sea with clouds clinging to the mountain tops, lush vegetation and coconut palms covering the lower mountains, tropical fruits and flowers adding bright splashes of red and yellow to the vivid green vegetation.

In the anchorage at Hanavave Bay yachts bobbed at anchor. Strong winds blew off the mountains, through the valley, and into the bay, whipping up the calm water and rattling the rigging, then subsiding as quickly as they came, returning the bay to perfect tranquility. It was an idyllic setting for our arrival in French Polynesia.

11

Mysterious Marquesas

After we anchored I calculated that the passage had taken just over fifteen days, and that we had sailed 2999 miles, averaging 8.25 knots per hour and 199 miles per day. We had only motored for forty-six hours out of 360, 12% of the time. Although it was the middle of the day, we were all very tired and crashed out on our bunks.

Waking the next day, we appreciated how spectacular and dramatic Hanavave Bay was. From the deck we gazed at the tall volcanic pillars rising from the thick green vegetation. Because of their strange phallic shapes, early explorers named the bay "Baie des Verges," which literally translated means "Bay of Penises," but when the missionaries arrived they were outraged by this, so they added a letter "i" to make the name "Verges" into "Vierges," which means virgins. Perhaps the original description was more appropriate.

The Marquesas, Les Iles Marquises, were our first taste of French Polynesia. There are ten islands, six of them inhabited, with wonderfully lyrical Polynesian names, like Fatu Hiva, Hiva Oa, Tahuata and the largest one, Nuku Hiva. The volcanic mountains, millions of years old, rise dramatically from the sea with razor-sharp ridges and cathedral-like spires reaching up three thousand feet into the clouds. Geographically, culturally, and economically they are unlike the other island groups in French Polynesia, and are more remote and isolated from Tahiti, the capital.

When our dinghy reached the stone jetty Janet and I were greeted by dozens of small children who were as excited to meet us as we were to meet them. Fatu Hiva is the most southern island in the Marquesas group and many miles from Nuku Hiva, the main island. The only links to the outside world are a small bonito boat that makes trips twice a week to

The Islands Time Forgot

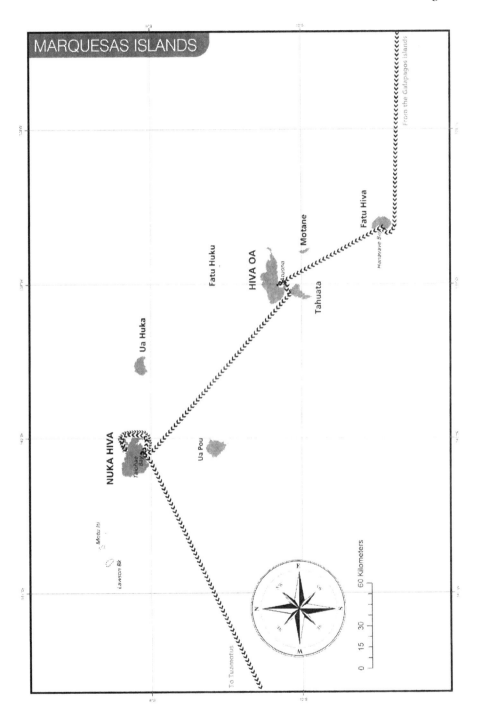

Hiva Oa, the nearest island, and a supply ship from Tahiti that calls once a month. Visitors are a curious novelty and the few yachtsmen are the only Europeans that the children meet. They gathered round us asking for "bonbon." We hadn't brought any sweets or small gifts with us so we went back to the boat and returned with colouring crayons, pads of paper, and balloons, and they screamed with delight. More children appeared from nowhere. We wished we'd been better prepared. The villagers invited us into their homes and showed us craftwork they had for sale. The wood carvings of idols were beautifully made. Janet was relieved to find that French is spoken by most people, especially the younger children and the women, and it was proper French, not pidgin, so she was able to have normal conversations and we learned a lot more about the people than we did in the Spanish-speaking countries. Polynesian, the native language, was impossible for us to understand.

A crowd of young children gathered around Janet and she asked one of the women with them to explain the school system. She told us that on a small island with a population of only 631, it is impossible to have the proper school resources. But education is a very high priority, so at the age of seven these children playing on the dock with us, along with the children from other outer islands, are sent away to boarding school on Hiva Oa. Even there the school facilities are limited, and at the age of fourteen they have to go to school in Tahiti, many hundreds of miles away. If they are clever enough they will remain to attend the university. The cost is met by the French government, but it must be a terrible wrench for the parents, although they seem to accept it. Like families all over the world, they aspire to improve their children's way of life. Of course some children return to their home island if they can find work, but many never return.

A few days later we talked to Marie, a schoolteacher on Tahuata, who didn't come back from Tahiti until she was forty-eight years old. When we asked why she came home, she told us, "I came back for the beauty of my homeland, for peace and tranquility, the freedom to do what I want, and to get away from the bureaucracy, crime, and friction there is in Tahiti." It summed up our first impressions of the Marquesas.

The path through the village of Hanavave took us past simple single-story stone houses, neatly tended gardens with flowers and vegetables, and free-range chickens and pigs. We took the only track out of the village, beside a fast running river into a narrow valley, frequently stopping to stare at the phallic mountain pillars that presented a different view at every turn. The track led to Omoa, the only other village on the island, but it was ten miles away, further than we thought we could manage across the mountains. So we turned around and strolled back, eager to know more about these rarely visited islands in the middle of the Pacific. When did people come here? Where did they come from? How do they live?

Thor Heyerdahl, the Norwegian anthropologist, came to Fatu Hiva on his honeymoon in 1937 and later wrote a book about his experience. He speculated that the Polynesians in the Marquesas had come from Latin America, and in 1947 he undertook the famous *Kon-Tiki* expedition on a balsa wood raft to prove it. I read his account of the voyage when I was a boy and remember how it influenced my image of the South Pacific. Who would have thought that I would be following in Heyerdahl's wake fifty years after reading his book?

Sailors will easily understand why he thought the migrations may have been from South America to the west. They would have followed the favourable trade winds and currents that had taken us from the American continent to the Marquesas, but his theories were later abandoned in favour of a body of opinion from contemporary scientists who provided evidence that the Polynesian migration came from the South China Sea.

It is now generally accepted that the Polynesians originated in Southern Asia, possibly Taiwan, and over thousands of years slowly migrated east across the Pacific, driven by man's urge for discovery, sailing east into the vast unknown Pacific Ocean with only the stars, the sun, and the moon to guide them. The first settlers arrived in Tonga and Samoa around 1300 BC. The next wave pushed on to the Cook Islands in 300 BC and it was another hundred years before they crossed the thousand miles of open sea to reach the Marquesas.

There they lived undisturbed for eighteen hundred years until the discovery of the Marquesas by the Spanish navigator Alvaro de Mendaña in 1595. Captain Cook rediscovered the islands in 1774 on his second great voyage in HMS *Resolution*.[22] Other explorers followed, and the islands were claimed for France by Admiral Abel Dupetit-Thouars in 1842. French missionaries arrived about this time and established their church.

Earlier missionaries had not been so successful. The story goes that in 1797 two Protestant evangelists from the London Missionary Society arrived at Tahuata on the good ship *Duff*. The young vicars, William Pascoe Crook and John Harris, were taken ashore, and on their first night the high

---

22 *Captain Cook made three great voyages of discovery to the Pacific. The first, 1768–1771, in the* Endeavour, *the second, 1772–1775, in the* Resolution, *and the third, 1776–1779, again in the* Resolution. *He was killed in Hawaii in 1779.*

chief graciously sent his wife to sleep with Harris. He, of course, rejected her advances, so the puzzled woman and her friends crept back into his hut to satisfy their curiosity regarding his sex. Poor Harris awoke surrounded by females and was terrified. He jumped out of bed but found to his horror that the women had hidden his clothes. They fell about laughing while the poor fellow spent the rest of the night huddled naked on his sea chest. Early the next morning he returned to his ship and left the Marquesas forever. Sadly I cannot report that this hospitality continues and we have to assume that these customs have long since died out.

Exposure to sailors from the west and visits from whaling ships and sandalwood traders introduced syphilis, arms, and alcohol, which had a devastating effect on the population. It dropped catastrophically from an estimated fifty thousand in 1804 to only 4865 in 1880. Today it is around ten thousand, reviving a race that almost entirely disappeared.

Strictly speaking we should not have been in Fatu Hiva, as the official clearing in port is Atuona, on Hiva Oa, but Fatu Hiva is usually a yacht's first sight of land, and after several weeks at sea it is very hard to sail past this beautiful island. But now we had to clear in at Atuona.

The town of Atuona has a small harbor that is quite shallow, and the few yachts already there made it impossible for us to enter, so we anchored outside the breakwater. This position was exposed to a swell that rocked the boat from side to side—not bad on the Santa Cruz scale of swell but still very uncomfortable—so after Luke had been ashore to visit the gendarmerie to complete the customs and immigration formalities, we left for a more protected anchorage at the island of Tahuata, only a few miles away. We anchored in Vaitahu Bay, the anchorage that Cook found in April 1774. We also arrived in April, just 234 years after Cook. It was a remarkable moment to be anchored in the very bay where Cook had arrived in the *Resolution*. I looked up my copy of the book "James Cook, The Journals," for Cook's account of first sighting the Marquesas and his landing in Vaitahu Bay.

After nineteen weeks at sea, calling in only briefly at Easter Island, Cook arrived in the Marquesas and ran through the narrow channel between Hiva Oa and Tahuata in unsettled squally showery weather. They were searching for Vaitahu Bay, the anchorage discovered by Mendaña in 1595. At last they found it but whilst attempting to anchor were attacked "… by such Violent Squalls from the high lands that we were within a few yards of being driven on the rocks to Leeward." When they had successfully anchored they were surrounded by canoes. "We had no soon anchored then about 30 or 40 Natives came round us in a doz or fourteen canoes, but it require some address to get them alongside, at last a Hatchet and some large Nails induced the people in one Canoe to put under the quarter galley, after this all the others put alongside and exchanged Breadfruit and some fish for some small Nails and then retired ashore."

The natives' caution was hardly surprising. These were the first Europeans they had seen. The next day they seemed intent on stealing whatever they could from the ship. One took an iron stanchion from a gangway and Cook told the officers to fire muskets over their heads as a warning. Sadly one of the natives was shot and killed by accident and Cook realized they did not understand the effect of firearms. He was a caring man and went to the home of the family of the dead man with gifts.

The following day a man of some consequence returned with a pig on his shoulder "which he sold for a Spike nail as soon as he got along side." and trading recommenced. Cook went ashore with the boats from the *Resolution* looking for a watering place and an important chief came down to the beach with many people; gifts were exchanged between Cook and the chief, good relations were established, and trading for pigs and fruit continued.

But three days later the natives seemed to lose interest in trading for some reason that Cook did not understand, and it was clear to him that the place was not likely to supply him with sufficient food, fresh water, or wood for repairs, so he decided to leave.

Cook, who pioneered the treatment of scurvy in the Royal Navy, was not unduly concerned about the inadequate provisioning because the men were in good health "… this was undoubtedly owing to the many antiscorbutic articles we had on board and the great care and attention of the surgeon who took special care to apply them in time."

On Tuesday 12 April, 1774, the *Resolution* weighed anchor and after cruising along the islands to understand the coastline better, set sail for Tahiti. It may have been only a brief visit but it was a significant one, increasing navigation knowledge and providing an understanding of the Polynesian people and the lands they lived in.

The bay and tiny village of Vaitahu, set against the steep slopes of the mountains we gazed on would have looked very similar to Cook. Probably very little has changed since he first saw it. He would not have seen the Catholic stone church that dominates the seashore, the influence of the missionaries, or the memorial marking the spot where the French admiral, Dupetit-Thouars, met Chief Iotete in 1842 and took possession of the

Marquesas. A few village houses and copra drying sheds were scattered around and there were traditional canoes pulled up on the shore, probably very similar to the ones that came out to meet Cook. It was very quiet—no roads, no cars, no shops and no jobs. The people harvest copra and noni (a small green fruit) to sell to the market, rear pigs and chickens, grow vegetables, pick fruit, and catch fish.

It was in this village that we met Marie, the schoolteacher mentioned earlier, and sat in her garden chatting about the history and culture of the islands. When we left she gave us baskets of fruit to take back to the boat and wanted nothing in return—quite a contrast to the reception that Captain Cook experienced. The next day we moved to Hanamoenoa Bay where Cook had found the surf too great to anchor. In contrast we found a calm sea and a white sand beach fringed by coconut palms. We swam to the beach and found a copra shed but no people or evidence of habitation.

Returning a few days later to Atuona, the swell was no better, so Luke took Janet and me ashore and then sailed back to the shelter of Hanamoenoa Bay, leaving us to explore Hiva Oa. Perched high above the town, with magnificent views over the bay, is a small resort called the Pearl Lodge, where we decided to stay for a few days rest and relaxation. It gave us another opportunity to take time away from the boat and I am sure Luke and Max enjoyed some time on their own.

The Pearl Lodge was an unexpected treat, totally in sympathy with its surroundings. A dozen palm-thatched cottages had comfortable but simple rooms furnished in Polynesian style. The dining room was in an open-sided thatched building with tall, carved wooden pillars that overlooked a terrace with spectacular views of the sea and the mountains. At the end of the terrace the calm pale blue water of an infinity pool contrasted with the dark blue sea beyond. We stayed for three days. It was the perfect antidote to sea fever and a restful base from which we explored the small town.

The Marquesas have been home to many creative spirits, but perhaps none more renowned than Paul Gauguin, the French painter, who made his home in Atuona. It was here that he created some of his best work, and where he died and was buried. Although his original house, *Maison du Jouir* (House of Pleasure), has been destroyed, we walked around a perfect replica of the place in which he lived his bohemian lifestyle. Above the door is the wooden panel he had carved with the enigmatic inscription, "Maison du Jouir. Be mysterious. Be in love and you'll be happy."

Next door to the house a Gauguin Museum has been built (it is much better than the one in Tahiti), and although it cannot contain any of his original paintings, which are in the most famous museums and art galleries in the world, there are seventy-five perfect copies of his work, which helped us to have a real feeling for the man and his life's work. Also on display are many original letters and other biographical details that gave us an insight into the person: a man who believed he was a great artist but was not given the recognition he deserved; a man who sought the commercial success he was due; a man who was disturbed, unstable, passionate, misunderstood, angry, and often in ill health.

The evocative paintings of Paul Gauguin have become synonymous with Tahiti and are largely responsible for Polynesia's enduring reputation as a paradise lost. Toward the end of his life, and after a failed suicide attempt, he took refuge on Hiva Oa, where he defended the inhabitants against the colonial administration and the all-powerful Catholic Church. Although weakened by old age and illness he did not stop writing, drawing, sculpting, and painting. He felt that Hiva Oa was nearer to the "noble savage" ideals he had sought in Tahiti. It was here that he painted the Polynesians who were his friends, and it was during this period that he produced one of his most beautiful nudes, *Barbaric Tales* (1902). At this time his paintings were being bought in Europe in the knowledge that his impending death would increase their value. He died in 1903 and was buried in the Calvary Cemetery above Atuona.

Back on board *Moonraker* a few days later we sailed round to the north of Hiva Oa, and in the isolated village of Hanaiapa we enjoyed an unexpected introduction to Marquesan hospitality and bartering. William, who met us when we walked ashore, was an unusual-looking character with a big black beard tinged with white, which was tied up under his chin. His craggy features and intelligent enquiring eyes were covered by a large wide-brimmed straw hat. He told us that he was the president of the "Hanaiapa Yacht Club," of which we were made honorary members. Since 1975 he has been welcoming yachts that visit the bay and asking them to record their details in his books.

We walked back to William's house and sat on his porch, browsing through his books, reading about the yachts that have passed here over the years, wondering what became of the crews with smiling faces that stared out at us from photographs from over thirty years ago. It seemed surreal that we were following in their footsteps so many years later. We added our own photograph of *Moonraker* with a message for those who follow after us. William brought us a drink of water in plastic tubs into which he squeezed lemon and lime juice. He told us that a few years ago he and his friends were drinking and playing cards when the house caught fire. With no firefighting facilities it quickly burnt down. Since then he's been gradually rebuilding as far as his time and money to buy materials allow. We saw that the white-painted concrete walls appeared to be intact but there was no roof, just a blue tarpaulin providing shade and shelter. The furniture consisted of crude wooden benches and a table. It didn't bother William and somehow in this serene and beautiful tropical environment it didn't seem to matter.

While we sipped our cooling drinks and chatted, William kept producing gifts—a hand of green bananas, red bananas, giant grapefruit, peppers, and a lettuce. The gifts overwhelmed us at first, but as we talked more we came to understand that this was part of a barter system or gift exchange, and he soon enquired about the things we might have for him.

We invited him back to the boat, which he was very interested to see, and settled on a bottle of whisky and a *Moonraker* T-shirt as a fair exchange. Over lunch on board we learned more about village life in the Marquesas. He didn't speak French well, as many of the younger people do, but he did speak some English, which was amazing, as his only way of learning English was from passing yachts, and he only sees about thirty each year.

The population of Hanaiapa is around one hundred, so everyone knows each other and are interrelated. William has nine children and seventeen grandchildren, although they don't all live in his village. There are no shops and the nearest town, Atuona, is fifteen miles away, a two-hour drive along a rough track. Only fifteen people own trucks, so they car pool when they need to go to town. Like everyone else there he makes a living from growing and exporting copra and noni.

Noni is a small green fruit the size of a lemon that grows wild everywhere and is used to make a new miracle health drink. The fruit is pulped in Tahiti and shipped to America, where the juice is extracted and flavours added. It is reputed to reinforce the immune system and ward off cancer. Copra is the dried nut meat from which coconut oil is extracted for use in cosmetics, soaps, and beauty oils. The world price of copra was twenty-five cents per kilo, but the locals receive one dollar, thanks to a subsidy from the French government. He told us that the next day we would see the interisland ship, *Aranui*, make its fortnightly call to collect the copra and noni exports bound for Tahiti.

Walking down the narrow road that runs through the village, we came upon a rehearsal for a Polynesian dancing competition that was to be held in Atuona on 14 July, Bastille Day. Polynesian dancing is a great tradition and was very popular everywhere we went. The rehearsal was held in the community hall, which was open on all four sides with just a roof to provide protection from the sun. The whole village had turned up to watch. A team of twenty boys and girls were having only their second rehearsal so they were a little self-conscious, but gave an enchanting display of dancing to a haunting Polynesian melody played by a live band. They grinned coyly as we clapped and cheered when they finished. It all seemed very natural and fun. I captured it on video and it still makes me smile every time I watch it.

The next day saw the supply ship *Aranui* (a Polynesian word meaning "great highway") call in at the village. It is the lifeline to the Marquesas, delivering food, diesel, trucks, building materials, livestock, and furniture, not just to every island, but to every village that has an anchorage, because roads are few and of a very poor standard, making road transport difficult. The *Aranui* also fulfills a vital function in collecting the exports that provide the livelihood for most of the islanders. The current boat is the third in a line that stretches back to World War II.

We watched the *Aranui* glide into the bay and then we anchored close by to watch the procedures for landing passengers and cargo. She is a modern but strange looking purpose-built ship of 343 feet. The front end is a cargo freighter, with holds and cranes, and the rear is a mini-cruise ship that carries a hundred passengers from Tahiti on an idyllic sixteen-day round trip to the Marquesas. The shipping company also provides steerage tickets for islanders wanting to travel from island to island.

Hanaiapa Bay has no proper dock, just a stone wharf about twelve feet long that is open to the swell that rolls in, so the ship has to anchor in the bay and her cranes drop two vessels into the sea. One is for passengers, and is like a military landing craft with seats, the other is for cargo and takes large crates that can be dropped in and out of the hold by the cranes. The process took most of the day.

A small shed by the wharf holds the sacks of copra and barrels of noni that are ready for export. These are lifted into the small boats by strong men, and the two boats ferry back and forth. The passengers come ashore to stroll around the village and visit the artisan gift shop that has been set up for their arrival. Everyone is out to greet the visitors or help with loading and unloading. The ship's visit is a big event in the life of the village.

Mysterious Marquesas

* * *

The northernmost and largest island, Nuku Hiva, has a large sheltered anchorage, Taiohae Bay, and a small town with a population of seventeen hundred. *The Pacific Crossing Guide* recommends that this is where yachts should spend most of their time in the Marquesas and there were over twenty anchored there when we arrived.

The first thing we did was to find the only hospital in the Marquesas. Luke had been suffering from an acute swelling in one leg for some time but it had become increasingly painful and was moving up his leg. Medical emergencies and illness at sea, or away from the reach of doctors or hospitals, were always a major worry and I had subscribed to a twenty-four-hour emergency medical service when we set out. It linked the yacht by satellite phone to a hospital in Aberdeen and then connected the patient to whichever specialist doctor was appropriate. His computer had access to a list of our extensive medical supplies, drugs, and equipment, so the doctor could assess the problem in relation to the yacht's resources and advise the treatment or procedure required. (It's best not to think what procedures Luke, our designated first aider, might have to carry out in a real emergency!)

Luke had already called the emergency service about his leg before we arrived in the Marquesas and got through with minimal phone connection delays, which was reassuring. The doctor thought the swelling was due to a tropical infection and prescribed an antibiotic, but suggested that Luke should find a hospital if the condition didn't improve. Well, it hadn't, and here was a hospital, so Janet took him ashore immediately so that she could translate for the French doctors.

The hospital in Taiohae was very small, just three or four single-story buildings, and perhaps no more than a dozen beds, but it appeared to be well equipped and Luke was seen quickly. The French doctor puzzled over his condition and seemed concerned. A more senior doctor was called. "We are unappy zat ze swelling is now moving above your knee. We don't want eet to get to …," he glanced down at Luke's private parts, leaving the sentence unfinished, and a female doctor present blushed. Was this the French sense of humour or was he serious? They explained to Janet that they thought it was a rare tropical infection, perhaps a bite from an insect in the Galapagos, and suggested that Luke should be airlifted to Tahiti. That didn't please Luke or Janet and, after further discussion, the doctor proposed that a new course of antibiotics should be tried first and thankfully the condition improved after a week.

While Luke and Janet were in the hospital I was in the post office in Taiohae waiting in a long line stretching back from the counter. I only wanted a stamp to post our clearing-in documents. A man at the front of the line could see my predicament and said, "Let me take that for you." When I thanked him, he said, "You can buy me a beer later," and we struck up a friendship. His name was Sean Myers, an American who was sailing with his wife, Jennifer, and their two young children on a big catamaran, *Soul's Calling*. They wanted to escape from the daily routines of life, and were looking for a unique bonding and life-changing experience with their children, Jake and Michaela. Sean didn't have a lot of sailing experience and Jennifer had almost none, but they were not deterred by the challenge. They bought a new Beneteau Lagoon 54 catamaran to make the trip to Australia. He took delivery of their yacht in Brittany and set off with friends to cross the Atlantic to the Caribbean, where Jennifer joined them. He was plagued throughout by endless mechanical problems, repairing or replacing almost every system on the boat himself. Fortunately he has a very positive personality and is resourceful and cheerful in adversity, but it wasn't what he was expecting when he bought a new yacht. As he said to me, "I didn't sign up to be a boat mechanic. In the last year I have not been able to read a single book that wasn't a systems manual." He overcame problems that would have turned many people's dream into a nightmare, and emerged as a stronger person with a great sense of achievement.

Relieved that Luke was recovering, we rented a 4WD Ford truck for two days to explore the island. A road rings the outside of this mountainous land. We knew that the scenery would be dramatic and the terrain diverse but had no idea that this would be a driving experience the likes of which we had never known before.

The road surface was concrete to begin with, and we made good progress on the narrow road as we climbed into the mountains, enjoying spectacular views over Taiohae Bay, where we could see *Moonraker* anchored. After an hour we came to a place where heavy machines were being used to build the road and lay the concrete. From there on we were on rough tracks. It was a surprise to pass through pine forests, reminiscent of Wales, which had been planted years ago by the government but never cut because it was uneconomic to truck them to the harbor for shipping. Hmmm, a lack of planning there? Our speed dropped to around ten miles per hour at times and we were thrown from side to side on the heavily rutted surface of clay, rocks, and stones. On the occasional straight stretch we were able to get into third gear and reach forty.

The astonishing vista of a long, deep chasm with a river running through it made me pull over so that we could get out for a better look. It is called the Grand Canyon and although it can't compare with Arizona the name does convey an impression of its scale. Quite soon after this the terrain changed to farmland with meadows where cattle grazed. After half an hour the scenery changed again and we reached a scrubby desert area in the northwest corner of the island—the only land flat enough to provide an airstrip. After three hours driving, but covering only twenty-two miles, we had reached the airport. I have had some unusual drives from the airport to the town around the world but nothing that compared with this for spectacular scenery.

Knowing that the track we had just driven along was the main road between the airport and Taiohae, we feared that as we continued our drive along the north coast of the island it could only get worse. And it did. It became single track and the surface became more difficult to drive on. First gear was the norm with the occasional step up into second as we wound our way up and then down a mountain ridge. The hairpin bends came one after the other, often with loose stones or wet, slippery mud. I soon worked out how to use the 4WD, and that helped the wheels to get a grip on the loose stones. I needed it when I had to stop to change into first gear to get round narrow 180-degree hairpin bends. On one bend, with a cliff edge on the side, I had to stop and reverse in order to get round. Janet just closed her eyes, accepting her fate. "Well, if we both go over the edge I don't mind. We've had a good life."

Now we were driving down the sides of mountains into green valleys, through lush tropical jungle, crossing riverbeds and climbing up the other side to see waterfalls and stunning views of the coast. After three more hours we reached our destination, the small north coast village of Hatiheu, which has a population of just two hundred. We stopped outside a thatched building by the seashore. This was the restaurant Chez Yvonne. It seemed like a mirage that had revealed an oasis. We had driven for hours through rough country and seen no one, and now in the middle of nowhere we sat in our truck staring out on a thatched terrace full of lunchtime diners eating a meal and drinking cold beer. I rubbed my eyes in disbelief.

We discovered that the other diners were Europeans, who like us had driven out from Taiohae, but from the other direction. The cold beer was good and the poisson cru, a Marquesan specialty, was even better. Yvonne told us how she made it. Raw fish, usually tuna, is cut up, marinated and chilled in salt water. Then she adds chopped carrots, onion, tomato, and cucumber, some lemon juice and coconut milk, and voila! It was delicious eaten in the cool shade on a hot sultry day and washed down with cold beer!

After lunch we collapsed on the bed in the "bungalow" we had rented from Yvonne, resting our shattered nerves and shaken bodies. Well, to call it a bungalow was like calling the track we had driven on a road. It was a small, one-room wooden hut with a low bed and a plastic curtain hiding a shower and toilet. The construction looked like a DIY nightmare. I said thoughtfully to Janet, "Sometimes we have to remind ourselves how lucky we are not to be pampered in five-star resorts."

Janet woke up screaming in the night. "There's a cockroach in the bed!" I soon caught it and flushed it down the toilet but it left us lying in the dark wondering if his brothers and sisters were around. We had no problem waking up for breakfast at the appointed hour of 7:30 as the cockerels, or "alarm cocks" as we called them, lived right next to us. Isn't it funny? In the civilized world one would find these conditions unacceptable, but here in the third world it is an experience.

The next day was Pentecost and Yvonne suggested that we attend the early morning service in the village Catholic Church if we wanted to hear Polynesian singing. We were glad to, because it gave us the feeling that we were joining in with this close-knit community. The women and small girls wore white dresses and had white camellias or red hibiscus in their hair. The men wore white smocks and the boys had white Coca-Cola T-shirts. The singing was magnificent, with every man, woman, and child taking a full part. Two guitars provided the music and everyone sang in harmony, filling the church with their nostalgic songs and swaying rhythms, which drifted out of the open doors and over the bay. Prayers were chanted over and over again in Polynesian. It was a very special and uplifting experience.

Yvonne Katapura is not only the owner of Chez Yvonne and the pension we stayed in, she is also the mayor of Hatiheu and has been for many years. A remarkable woman, she has single-handedly been responsible for the initiatives that have built the school, the town hall, and the new Catholic Church we visited. She is modest and charming but an influential woman who gets things done and engenders a great spirit of community amongst all the villagers.

After the church service we enjoyed so much, we took a stroll round the well-kept village and could not fail to see the white statue of the Virgin Mary, "The Madonna of Hatiheu," which is perched one hundred feet up on top of a jagged rocky peak, reminiscent of the statue of Christ the Redeemer overlooking the bay in Rio de Janeiro. It was painstakingly built in 1872 by a priest, Michel Blanc, who carried all the materials up the rock face himself and created this enduring monument, and perhaps his place in heaven.

Driving back into Taiohae later that morning we passed through the valley of Taipivai. It was here that the writer Herman Melville hid with a friend when they deserted from the *Acushnet*, a whaling ship whose captain was a tyrant. Melville became accepted by the Taipivai tribe and later wrote *Typee*, a book loosely based on his experience. It was published in 1846 and became a popular bestseller that was in its time more famous than *Moby Dick*. Although fiction, the book provides a revealing insight into the people, their customs, and the culture. He was only there for three weeks, but in the book it seems as if it were a much longer period.

As we drove up the hill out of the village we reached a headland from where we looked down on the small village of Taiohae and the spectacular Comptroller's Bay. A river meandered through the valley and into the village before flowing over a sandbar, into the bay, and out to sea. A narrow path wandered across the ridge and I followed it to contemplate the incredible views.

Arriving back in Taiohae we felt that we had emerged into the sunlight of civilization: tarmac roads, concrete houses, shops, cars, all felt oddly welcome. We had been shaken and stirred, but our overriding memory of this two-day drive was of an incredibly beautiful island with hugely diverse natural features and awe-inspiring views.

Luke had left the boat when we arrived back in Taiohae Bay and flown home to England as a surprise for his father's sixtieth birthday. It was his first holiday since joining us nearly a year before. We didn't plan to go far in his absence, but there were a number of anchorages around Nuku Hiva that we wanted to visit. Perhaps the best known is Anaho Bay, just twenty miles away.

To our delight we were accompanied by dolphins for much of the way. First there were bottlenose dolphins, with four or five swimming under the bow of the boat, with others waiting to take their place. There are apocryphal stories of dolphins leading ships away from impending dangers, but here they seemed to be leading the way to Anaho Bay.

They are aptly named, with their distinctive bottle-shaped nose. These were over six feet long, although some grow as long as twelve feet, and we could see them clearly as they swam just below the surface. Sometimes they flipped over on to their backs, showing their white underbelly. We could hear loud squeaking noises that suggested that they were having a good time. Then, as suddenly as they arrived, they disappeared. It was as if the leader had given a signal that they had all instantly obeyed.

Shortly after, they were replaced by spinner dolphins. They have a similar nose, but are much smaller, only three feet long and grey in colour. We had no doubt that they were spinners when we saw them do their amazing trademark leap out of the water, jumping and spinning at the same time. Just when we thought the display was over, pygmy killer whales came to join in the fun. It was the first time we had seen them. Despite their fearsome name they are members of the dolphin family, but have a blunt nose, distinctive white lips, and grow to six to nine feet. The dolphins were with us for over an hour, an unusually long time. We took photographs, but it is impossible to capture the magic of these moments on camera.

Robert Louis Stevenson and his wife, Fanny, visited Anaho Bay in 1888 on the schooner *Casco*, and he wrote about it in his book about the voyage, *In the South Seas*. Stevenson was entranced.

> *I have watched the morning break in many quarters of the world…and the dawn that I saw with most emotion, shone upon the Bay of Anaho. The mountains abruptly overhang the port with every variety of surface and inclination, lawn, and cliff, and forest. My favourite haunt was a cove under a lianaed cliff. The beach would be all submerged; and the surf would bubble warmly as high as my knees. As the reflux drew down, I would grasp at it and seize shells to be set in gold upon a lady's finger.*

It is probably quite unchanged since Stevenson was there. It is indeed lovely, with pure white beaches fringed by a coral reef. Palm trees overhang the beach and green mountains rise high into the sky. I wish now that, like Stevenson, I had forsaken my comfortable bunk at dawn to experience that moment.

The next day we were joined in Anaho Bay by *Surcouf*. We had last seen Edmond and Yossi back in Curaçao. This wasn't entirely an accident, because we had been keeping in touch by e-mail, and then radio, and planned to meet in Anaho Bay when we knew they had arrived in Nuku

Hiva. It was wonderful to see them again, to socialize, and catch up with their news.

The next bay along from Anaho is Hatiheu, where we had previously enjoyed such a good lunch at Chez Yvonne. To get there by foot we had to climb over a mountain ridge. The *Guide to Navigation in French Polynesia* said, "Courageous hikers can walk to Hatiheu along a mule trail … it should take about one hour." *Lonely Planet* noted, "The ascent and descent are quite steep but the track is in good condition and is well marked. Bring mosquito repellent and plenty of water." I should have listened.

It was a beautiful sunny Sunday morning, so undeterred by these warnings I suggested to Edmond and Yossi that we should all walk across to Hatiheu and have lunch at Chez Yvonne. I wish I had taken more notice of the words "courageous hikers." Climbing through the thick bush and forest that covered the mountain was hot, sticky work and the path was steep and muddy. My shirt was drenched in sweat. An hour had gone by, and we were still nowhere near the top of the ridge. "It can't be long now, can it?" I complained, as we took another rest on a rock. I struggled down the path on the other side fantasizing about cold beer and poisson cru for lunch and finally we walked past the neat gardens and houses of the village. It seemed awfully quiet when we reached Chez Yvonne and I had a sinking feeling that there was nobody there, and sure enough the restaurant was closed on Sundays.

What despair! Thankfully one of the staff came along and took pity, giving us cold drinks. I knew that there was no way that I would be able to walk back across the mountain and asked if there was a fisherman who could take us back by boat. The village jungle telegraph must have been humming because to my very great relief, a fisherman appeared in his 4WD and agreed to take some of us back by boat while the younger members of our party set out to hike back. Oh, to be young again!

* * *

The unspoiled archeological ruins of ancient civilizations are seen throughout the Marquesas. Some are as much as two thousand years old and fascinate scientists, anthropologists, and visitors alike. A guide took us to see the most important relics, and explained the meaning of the stone ruins—the tohua (meeting place), marae (temple), paepae (stone platforms for houses), and tiki (stone or wooden statues). The most common are the tiki, Buddha-like figures that can be up to ten feet high. They are seen everywhere, and have remained untouched for thousands of years, mysterious reminders of a lost civilization.

A visit to a marae, built deep inland to be safe from raiders, was a sinister experience. The jungle had crept over the ruins and the large grey stones that still form the base of the temple were black with damp and moss. The trees had closed in as if imprisoning the community. The slopes rose steeply, folding into dark, jagged mountains. Bright sunshine was eclipsed by black clouds bringing rain and squalls. The absolute power of the taua (priests) and hakaiki (chiefs) hung over the sacred stones and we were reminded that they were cannibals.

> *Thus it was that regularly in the Marquesas the people ate all or part of the famous 'long pig,' the victims of war, an offering to the gods, or of simple vengeance. It is also well known that the eyes, choice morsels, were reserved for the notables (chiefs, priests) ... The victim, who could also have been chosen from his own clan, as well as from another tribe (that is when he wasn't killed in combat), was clubbed by surprise and shared amongst the eminent members of the clan. The women and the manuhane (lowly men) did not eat human flesh.*[23]

For all its raw beauty, its majesty, and the friendliness of the people, we found the Marquesas to have a disquieting atmosphere. Perhaps we stayed too long (nearly four weeks), perhaps we were unknowingly shocked by our first exposure to cannibalism, perhaps the high mountains and dense jungle combined to inhibit our movements, perhaps the remoteness and feeling that we were far from modern civilization and close to ancient civilizations all conspired to create a strangely forbidding environment.

---

23 *Guide to Navigation in French Polynesia*

12

Pearl Fishers of the Tuamotus

From the Marquesas we made the five-hundred-mile passage to the Tuamotus, three days away. It's strange: if we were sailing in Europe, five hundred miles would be considered a long passage. Now we think of it as a short hop. We were in the groove of ocean sailing. The weather was hot and sunny and we were able to fly the spinnaker in the light winds on the first morning.

Luke had returned from his visit to England only the day before we left, jumping back on board looking as fresh as a daisy and ready to go after his long and tiring flight. I don't know how he does it. I never cease to be amazed at the energy of youth. We had been discussing the news from England, and indeed the world, with which we were very much out of touch. Somehow it didn't seem to matter much to us, cocooned in our own little world in the middle of the Pacific.

The wind gradually died and we motored, which was very undemanding for the watchkeeper and boring for the rest of us. We used the time to read up on the Tuamotus, a group of islands we had hardly heard of. *Lonely Planet*, always our first source of information, gave us an idea of what to expect.

> *Strung like pearls across the Pacific, the Tuamotus (too-ah-moh-toos) are a world apart. These rings of coral were witness to what was once, according to Darwin's theory of atoll formation, an archipelago of high islands, as mountainous and grand as perhaps the Marquesas or Society islands today. The 77 atolls, scattered like confetti on an ocean of ink, stretch 1500km northwest to southeast, and 500 km east to west. The closest islands are about 300km from Tahiti. The*

atolls, coral crowns not reaching more than a few metres above the water, surround a central lagoon. No atoll is like another. For 30 islands, the outer ring is cut by one or more deep passes, while others are completely enclosed. Some are huge (Rangiroa is 75 km long), while others are minute.

It rained in the evening, making the night watches unpleasant. Although we think of the tropics as an area of endless sunshine, the truth is that it is a region of high rainfall. Fortunately even with the rain we didn't need protective clothing, because it was so warm and the bimini covering the cockpit kept us dry. Shorts and T-shirts were all that was needed, and when there was a heavy squall we kept watch from inside the pilothouse. It rained for most of the night, and there were dark clouds and rain for most of the next morning. The winds were light and variable, so we continued to motor and read up on the Tuamotus.

These islands were known as "the dangerous archipelago" in the days when landfalls had to be made with the help of the sun, moon, and stars. It was dangerous because the atolls are only as high as the tallest palm tree, so nothing could be seen on a clear day until a ship was very close. At night land couldn't be seen at all until the ship heard the thunder of the surf and saw the white of the waves before being crushed on the reef. But this was not something that worried us because we had charts, GPS, and radar.

On his first great voyage in *the Endeavour*, in 1769, Cook went into the Pacific via Cape Horn, and in April passed through the Tuamotu Islands on his way to Tahiti. It was the first land he had seen in sixty-six days. Curious as always to extend his knowledge he came close but found no place to anchor.

> *Tuesday the fourth of April 1769. A Steady fresh Trade and clear weather. At ½ past 10 AM saw land bearing South distance 3 or 4 Leagues; hauled up for it and soon found it to be an Island of about 2 Leagues in circuit and of an Oval form with a Lagoon in the Middle for which I named it Lagoon Island ... we approach'd the north side of this Island within a Mile and found no bottom with 130 fathom of line nor did there appear to be any Anchorage about it. We saw several of the Inhabitants, the most of them Men, and these March'd along the shore abreast of the Ship with long clubs in their hands as tho they ment to oppose our landing, they were all naked except their privy parts and were of a dark Coper colour with long hair ... This*

island lies in the Latitude of 18° 47' and Long 139° 28' West from the Meridian of Greenwich. Variation 2° 54'East.

—James Cook: The Journals

The island Cook describes was not one we visited but was very similar to those we did call at. Cook felt that it was not safe to enter the lagoon but nowadays yachts have modern navigation aids and where there are narrow passes they have usually been charted. But great care still has to be taken. The tide pours in and out of these passes, often at five knots or more, so it is essential to time entry for slack water or just when the tide starts to flow out.

The time of slack water can be predicted from the time of the moon's rising and setting, as the locals have known for hundreds of years. Slack water is five hours after moonrise, followed by the inflow, and then slack water comes again four to four-and-a-half hours before moonset, when the outflow begins. The tidal flow can be greatly affected by swell and wind, and local knowledge is helpful in understanding how they will affect the tide on any given day.

In Lonely Planet it says that an atoll usually has one village and the main activity is pearl diving. It sounded like the image of paradise I had as a small boy. Now I was going to see it for myself. After much discussion we decided to make our first landfall at the island of Ahe.

It was nine in the evening and I was on deck, alone on my watch. The clear sky was swathed in a canopy of a thousand stars and the surface of the sea was bathed in bright moonlight. A song from the musical *Evita* kept running through my head: "On this night of a thousand stars, let me take you to heavens door"—sung by Agustin Magaldi (Jimmy Nail), a tango singer who has an affair with Evita (Madonna).

The wind on my face was warm and balmy, with little humidity, the breeze an antidote to the hot sun of the day. The wind was blowing steadily at fifteen knots on the beam, giving the boat good speed and a comfortable motion, guaranteeing a good sleep for those off watch. Things can change quickly at sea, but I sensed that the conditions would be exactly the same when I came on watch again at four in the morning. All was well.

At 4:00 AM, after a deep undisturbed sleep, I was sitting at the wheel again, still in my shorts and T-shirt. The boat was silent except for the hiss of the sea and the hum of the wind. Down below, everyone was sleeping. The dimmed lights of the instruments were glowing in front of me. The moonlight sparkled on the sea and the phosphorescence glittered like diamonds spilled over the waves.

Dawn crept up from behind in the east, a soft grey lightening of the night sky at first, followed by the slow flood of daylight and the first sight of the sun spreading its warmth across the sea toward me. The boat was still silent, everyone asleep. I was alone in the universe. It was a new day. A night like this was simply ... heaven. I was still humming the song. It was one of those magical moments that make sailing something very special.

But on our third day out the weather changed, as it always does, bringing rain, clouds, and strong winds. There were two reefs in the main, partly because of the wind strength and partly because we wanted to slow down to time our arrival in Ahe for slack water at six on Monday morning, so after the squalls passed through we kept one reef in to keep the boat speed down.

At nine that morning both rods had a strike at the same time. It was action stations and all hands on deck for the routine we had developed. Luke and Max could only land one fish at a time so they decided to go for Max's first. It was a lovely tuna weighing fifteen pounds, but while they were landing it, the fish on Luke's line, almost certainly another tuna, got away.

On the last night we slowed down again, sailing with the reefed main only to make sure we arrived at slack water. Soon after dawn we caught our first sight of Ahe, which appeared as a long band of palm trees, and with the help of our radar and GPS we had no problem identifying or entering the Tiareroa Pass, a narrow gap we negotiated without any difficulty.

The navigation charts are often out of date and inaccurate so we usually use Warwick Clay's *South Pacific Anchorages* as our pilot guide into an anchorage. He often paints a very black picture, making the dangers sound overwhelming when in reality it never seemed as bad as he warns.

Although we had Warwick Clay's directions, eyeball navigation was essential. Max was positioned in the bow with the sun behind us, looking out for coral heads. He could judge the surrounding water depths by the colour of the water—dark blue is deep, lighter blue is getting shallow, turquoise is very shallow, brown is aground! With Max calling out the dangers we motored slowly across the lagoon to the village of Tenukupara, as tranquil an anchorage as we could ever wish to find. Then I caught sight of three other yachts anchored there. We cheered when we recognized two of them, *Free Spirit* and *Sora*. *Free Spirit* is a 45-foot catamaran owned by Russell Eddington, and *Sora* is a 45-foot ketch crewed by Terry and

Cass, a father and daughter team who we had met in the Taiohae Bay in Nuku Hiva.

It was such a nice surprise to find *Free Spirit* tucked up in this remote anchorage and we were eager to catch up with Russell's news. He had named his boat well for he truly is a free spirit, a good-looking Californian who reminded me of Robert Redford. His thick blond hair was fashionably long, no grey that I could see, and when it flopped over his eyes he flicked it back with a casual gesture. His face was freckled by the Californian sun and his smile was warm and sincere. It was difficult to guess his age, perhaps forties or fifties, certainly young enough to go out for a night on the beer with Luke yet old enough to ask Janet and I to join him for dinner.

His long-term partner, Kya, stayed at home to look after her business, her children, and her dogs, while Russell, having sold his business, took off to explore the oceans of the world. He bought his 45-foot Dolphin catamaran in Brazil and sailed it up the South Atlantic to the Caribbean single-handed. Mostly he sails single-handed, but he is modest and unassuming about it. Although he has a general plan to cross the Pacific, the route he takes and where he ends up is always open to change. We will never be surprised when *Free Spirit* pulls up in the bay next to us. Janet and I first met Russell in a bar in Santa Cruz. He walked in, sat down at our table, and we hit it off from the beginning. We saw him again several times in the Marquesas and here he was again in the Tuamotus—this time with two friends from Hawaii.

All of us from *Free Spirit, Sora,* and *Moonraker* met up for a walk around the village that morning and we were surprised to meet a smartly dressed young woman wearing a black jacket and skirt that looked rather out of place. I asked her name. "Angel," she said. "It's my name, but I'm not!"

Angel explained that she owned a black pearl farm in Ahe and that she had come from Tahiti for a meeting. She asked us if we would like to visit the pearl farm the next day. The Tuamotus are famous for black pearls but we had no idea how they were farmed. Did the fishermen dive for them with a knife between their teeth? We eagerly accepted her invitation to visit the farm and find out.

That afternoon we all went back to the Tiareroa pass on *Free Spirit* so that we could drift dive the pass. Russell had learned this technique at the last island he visited and he wanted to introduce it to us. *Free Spirit* anchored just outside the pass and five of us slipped into the water wearing our masks and snorkels. We hung on to a long rope attached to a dinghy and drifted face down through the pass on the incoming tide. The strong current whooshed us through. Lying motionless on the water looking down on the coral was an amazing sensation. The coral appeared to be rolling along fifteen feet beneath us like a moving walkway. Wherever we looked there was an ever-changing kaleidoscope of brightly-coloured fish—red, yellow, purple, orange, and black, all quite oblivious to our presence. They were larger and brighter than any I had seen in the Caribbean. In fact, my comprehensive book of reef fish in the Caribbean failed to help me recognize many of the new species we saw. There were sharks, too, but by this time I was more comfortable with them, even looking for them, hoping to get up close for a good photograph. It was a wonderful new experience, and we were entranced by the natural beauty and remoteness of this lovely island. This is what sailors can only dream about as they read *Yachting Monthly* in the rush hour train back from London on a Friday night. And here we were, doing it.

We rose early for our trip to the pearl farm and there was much excited chatter as we motored the ten miles over to the other side of the atoll on *Free Spirit*. The informal arrangement was that Angel would see us arrive and come out to guide us in, and to our relief it all happened just as she said it would.

Angel and her brother operate this small family business from two sheds on stilts in very shallow water, and eight workers live in a few isolated huts on the shore. We were enthusiastically greeted with a warm welcome. Apparently we were the first yacht ever to visit them. They demonstrated the pearl production process for us in some detail and Angel, whose native tongue was French, explained the life cycle of the pearl to us in broken English.

Baby oysters are spawned locally or acquired partly grown from other atolls if the farm can't produce enough. They grow on lines that hang down in the sea, like mussels, and when they are mature, after about a year, they are harvested. The lines are marked by the orange buoys we had seen dotted all around the atoll. In the shed, a highly skilled operator performs the implant that will create the pearl. This is done by inserting a Chinese shell (which looks like a small yellow bead) into the oyster. A small section from the lining of a live oyster is delicately inserted next to the implant, and develops a film around the yellow bead that will eventually become a black pearl.

Luke and Max both had a go at doing this, and despite great concentration they killed the oysters in the process! As you might imagine you need a good eye and a steady hand and the training takes more than a year. The operator has to implant one hundred oysters an hour and must keep up his speed or they will die from being out of the water too long. This work used to be done by the Chinese and Japanese, but the Polynesians have now reclaimed it for their own employment.

The implanted oysters are tied to a long string, colour-coded to denote the month and year, and placed back in the water for two years. Then they are brought back to the shed to be opened. This is a really exciting moment, as the skilled operator is looking for the perfect black pearls, which will have great value. The pearls vary greatly in size and quality. Many are rejected because they are misshapen in some way or do not have a perfect colour; only twenty percent make it to market, and even these will be graded for quality, with very few making the top grade. The best will sell for about one hundred dollars. Luke looked at a perfect one and whispered quietly in Janet's ear, "Call me a philistine, but it looks like a ball bearing to me." When the first pearl has been taken from the oyster a new implant is made, and a second growth produced, but by the third year the quality will no longer be acceptable.

The pearls are sold in bulk through an agent in Tahiti and are sent to New Zealand where they are crafted into jewelry and marketed worldwide at a much higher price. There are some sixty pearl farms on Ahe alone and many other islands in the Tuamotus rely on this industry as their only source of income.

We were overwhelmed by the time and effort taken to show us the pearl-making process. The people here were genuinely friendly; they wanted to give us gifts and expected nothing back. They lead a simple life but seem to be happy. We left with gifts from our hosts, and some of us purchased pearls. Russell returned the hospitality with a bottle of rum and we gave them *Moonraker* T-shirts.

On the way back in the afternoon we stopped at the pass for some more drift diving. It was even better than the first time. A group of seven sharks appeared quite close up, white tips and grey tips about five or six feet long. They took no notice of us, and I was now relaxed about swimming with them.

Fifty miles from Ahe we came to Apataki, an even more remote atoll. We entered the wide and deep Tehere Pass at slack water at two in the afternoon and anchored just inside the pass so we could drift dive through it on the incoming tide. It was fun but not as special as the Tiareroa Pass. Nowhere else did we see such diversity of colourful fish, such vivid coral, or such clear water as we had in Ahe.

Apataki was discovered in 1722 by the Dutch navigator Jakob Roggeveen. It is an average size atoll measuring eighteen by fifteen miles in total. The lagoon has two navigable passes, the Tehere Pass in the north, which we came through, and the Pakaka Pass on the southwest, where the only village, Niutahi, has four hundred residents.

We motored around the inside of the reef to an anchorage at Parao. The sun burned down from a clear blue sky, with only a light breeze, too light to sail. But we would have motored anyway to have more control in uncharted waters strewn with coral heads.

In such a remote place it was a surprise to find another yacht anchored at Parao. The owners came across and sat in their dinghy chatting to us. They were a pleasant couple, about our age, but unlike us had been sailing in the Pacific for many years. They were truly ocean nomads. They told us that they thought this anchorage was so lovely that they had stayed for ten days. I looked around to see why. There was absolutely nothing there, just a narrow strip of land, lagoon on one side, ocean on the other, a sandy beach, and palm trees as far as I could see in any direction. Some armchair sailors might think that total solitude, silence, and days of doing nothing was idyllic, but it wasn't for me. I was beginning to understand myself better, and although I may have once thought that this was paradise, now I realized that I needed to be more active. Increasingly during this voyage I had the feeling that time was passing me by. I was sixty-seven years old. I had faced my own mortality in the hospital bed in Grasse. Time was beginning to run out and there were still other things that I wanted to do with my life.

The next day we moved a few miles around the inside of the atoll to an anchorage at Totoro. Our pilot book told us that we might meet Mr. Assam and his family there. Sure enough Mr. Assam came out in a boat and invited us to go ashore. He is Chinese, small and thin, but fit, wiry, and strong from years of hard physical work. His wife is Polynesian. She has a broad figure, a warm smile, and wore a bright yellow top and a straw hat decorated with beautiful strings of shells. They were wonderful people and extremely kind to us. Together we wandered around their small market garden, where, with love and hard work, they coax vegetables from the thin soil in a hostile environment and breed pigs and chickens. Their chicken farm is run on a commercial scale, and eggs are sold to the local village and neighbouring islands. We strolled around the farm with them, marveling at their endeavor and ingenuity. Afterwards we sat in the shade of a palm tree, with the sea lapping gently at our feet, drinking coconut milk from the shell, while they told us their story.

Mr. Assam's father came to the South Pacific from China but was evacuated from the Eastern Tuamotus in 1966 when the French commandeered the area for nuclear bomb testing, which, despite international protest, went on until 1996. He ended up in Tahiti, where he got married and had children. His son, who we were talking to now, grew up and became, like so many Chinese, a shopkeeper. He met his Polynesian wife there and they married and had two children who were educated in Tahiti. Twenty years ago he saw a business opportunity that he grasped with both hands. His wife owned land on Apataki, handed down by her family, and he had the idea of starting a pearl farm there. With his Chinese business acumen, sheer hard work, and the courage to overcome many obstacles—including a typhoon that destroyed their property—the business prospered. Now their own son, Alfred, had married and taken on the running of the pearl farm with his wife, Pauline, while Mr. and Mrs. Assam, now in their sixties, look after the vegetables and chickens. The family dynasty seems set to continue as Mr. Assam's twenty-one-year-old grandson, Tony, now works in the pearl farm, too.

They showed us a book with photographs and messages from yachts that had visited them. Imagine our surprise when we found we knew one of them! Nick Pochin had visited here on his round-the-world voyage in 2005. We had met Nick at the Southampton Boat Show in 2001. He had a Discovery 55, the same make of yacht we owned when we crossed the Atlantic in 2002. We added our own photographs of *Moonraker*, and noticed that there were visits from about ten yachts each year. To our surprise Mr. Assam told us that some visiting yachtsmen practically demand food and hospitality, so we were flattered when they asked us if we would like to join their family for dinner that evening.

When we came ashore with Luke and Max we found the total workforce of sixteen men sitting at a large outside table having dinner. The family sat at a separate table with us. Mr. Assam's daughter-in-law, Pauline, who spoke English very well, told me how difficult it was to get men who were prepared to take on the tough and lonely existence of working on a pearl farm in such a remote place. The Polynesian workers, mostly from Tahiti, are attracted by good wages and the opportunity to save all their money (accommodation and meals are provided), but Pauline told me that they can tell within a few weeks whether a worker is going stay the course or be homesick. Sometimes they return home because they miss even simple pleasures like going to a bar for the evening. Those that stay accept that this is a tough seven-day-a-week job with time off only for the evening meal and sleep.

After dinner, with the flickering lamp casting deep shadows, Pauline explained that while her husband is running the pearl farm she spends much of her time in Papeete, managing the business end, selling the pearls, arranging exports, and doing the accounts. Her two younger children are at school there, because of course there is no school on Apataki. Pauline reached out to us with engaging warmth, sincerity, and frankness, and we promised to go and see her when we arrived in Papeete.

The next day Pauline's husband, Alfred, took Luke, Max, and I out in a workboat with four of the men. They were young, lean, brown, fit, and strong, dressed only in swimming shorts. It is hard work, loading the boat with the long ropes and lines with the implanted oysters, heaving them overboard, laying them in straight lines and then placing the orange marker buoys. When that is done they haul in the ropes with mature oysters tied to them. If things go wrong, as they frequently do, the men have to dive down to release the ropes and are exposed to dangers, particularly tiger sharks, the biggest threat to their lives.

Before we left, Mr. and Mrs. Assam accepted our invitation to come on board *Moonraker* for breakfast. They brought with them leis, the traditional Polynesian flower garland given as a welcome or farewell. The flowers were picked from Mrs. Assam's garden very early that morning. They were concerned for our safety and wished us "bon voyage" for the rest of our passage. It was very touching. Mr. Assam gave us detailed instructions on how to navigate the dangers in the lagoon before reaching the pass. We didn't expect that they would pose any problems.

Our intention had been to anchor off the village of Niutahi until slack water later that night, when the incoming tide made it safe to go through the Pakaka Pass, but when we got close to the village, a strong wind was whipping the sea up into white horses, making anchoring unsafe. The pass itself looked dangerous, with the wind blowing in against the powerful outgoing tide, creating a treacherous turmoil. A yacht was moored up against the jetty in the pass but the conditions made it impossible to go alongside there. With no safe anchorage or place to moor up there was no alternative but to try to go out through the pass now, but once we entered we would be committed, with no possibility of turning back.

The tide was running out of the lagoon at over five knots with a massive volume of water sluicing out through the narrow channel, like water from a bath gurgling down the plug hole. In order to maintain steerage we had to motor fast, so we were being pushed out very quickly at around 10–11 knots, almost out of control. It was a frightening moment, but in a few minutes we were squeezed out of the lagoon like a pip from a lemon and emerged into the relative quiet and safety of the open ocean.

Our next port of call was Rangiroa, pronounced, *rung-ee-roh-ah,* and known locally as Rangi. It is the second largest atoll in the world. The lagoon is forty-five miles long and eighteen miles wide and could enclose the entire island of Tahiti. It is the largest and most populated of all the Tuamotus with over three thousand inhabitants. It is so large that if the wind blows strongly it becomes an inland sea, especially if the wind is from the southeast, which brings large waves to this otherwise calm blue lagoon in just a few minutes. We hoped we wouldn't be that unlucky with the weather.

Discovered in 1616 by Dutch navigators, Rangi remained relatively unchanged until a small airport was built in 1965. This led to the growth of tourism with daily flights arriving from Tahiti, but the character of the atoll did not seem to us to have been spoiled. Most of the tourists are backpackers, happy to live a simple life and embrace the local culture.

Our good friends Ian and Bev Miller made the long flight out from England to sail with us for two weeks. None of our other friends or family were able to make the long journey out to the Pacific, so it was a thrill to see them stepping off the interisland plane and walking across the tarmac at the tiny airport. We had thought about taking the dinghy round to the little dock at the airport, which would have been a novel and memorable way to meet them, but we thought they might get a soaking from the spray as we motored to windward in the choppy sea and opted instead for the convenience of a taxi.

That evening at the Hotel Kia Ora we saw a traditional Polynesian dancing display. The show was spectacular. The men were warrior-like and the women seemed so … well, so sexy. Their hip movements were mesmerizing and they had the most enchanting smiles. Here at last were the beautiful and seductive women I had been hoping to see in the South Pacific, the girls that turned the hearts and minds of Fletcher Christian and the Bounty mutineers. Janet and Bev were greeted with a lei hung around their necks by a well-muscled warrior. Perhaps the warriors were staking a claim, but whatever the reason Janet and Bev were flattered to be the only guests honoured in this way.

A trip in our dinghy to the Tiputa Pass didn't disappoint us and amazed our visitors. As usual we saw large and small fish of different colours, and this time even dolphins jumping right out of the water in the surf close to us. But the highlight in Rangiroa was swimming with sharks. A high-speed boat and guide took us to the Blue Lagoon. It is named for its graduated shades of blue, changing from pale turquoise in the shallow water to dark blue as it gets deeper. There were dozens of baby black tip reef sharks swimming around the water's edge and we waded among them. Even Janet, whose confidence was growing all the time, joined in. These small sharks were gathered there because it was a regular lunch spot and they knew they would be fed later. But the main event came after lunch. We went out to deeper water in the launch and anchored where large black-tipped reef sharks swam around our boat. The guide said, "You can get in with them now." There was silence. Nobody in our party of eight moved. Was he joking? A look at his face confirmed that he wasn't. Well, I thought, somebody has to be first, so I jumped in. When the others saw that I had not been eaten for lunch, they joined in.

The sharks were between four to six feet long, magnificent creatures, designed to swim with grace and power. They came very near to me, but never closer than six feet, and I felt completely safe and at ease. It was wonderful to be able to observe them so close up. Ian and Bev were spellbound and we regretted that none of us had an underwater camera.

When we had all climbed back into the boat the sharks got their reward—the remains of our barbequed fish, which created a feeding frenzy. The atmosphere was soured somewhat when the guide reached into the water, grabbed a shark by its fin, and pulled it on board, where it thrashed about helplessly. They do it so that tourists can get a closer look at a shark but we found it unnecessary and cruel. In fact I thought that the whole idea of feeding sharks in this way seemed to create an unhealthy association between humans and food that could lead to shark attacks.

On the way back, our guide, who was driving the boat, spotted a manta ray some way off and we slowly approached it. Then we saw that there were two, and when we stopped the boat alongside them they slowly performed somersaults, displaying their white underbelly as they turned head over heels. These huge creatures have a wingspan that can be up to twenty feet and yet their movements were controlled and graceful. They were like synchronized swimmers. It seemed hard to believe that they were not performing just for us. It was such a privilege to be as close to wildlife as we had been that day.

Luke Windle, shipmate and captain.

Haniteli and Lucy O Fa'anunu at Ene'io Botanical Garden, Vavau, Tonga.

Graham with Semisi, Road Runner, in Vavau, Tonga.

Dolphins are difficult to photograph, but Max got this one perfectly.

A marine iguana, Galapagos.

Janet with Yvonne Katapura, owner of Chez Yvonne and mayor of Hatiheu.

Ladies smartly dressed after church in Ha'afeva in the Ha'apai Group of Islands, Tonga.

*A special moment—Graham with former Miss World—,
Jennifer Holsten, in Grenada.*

Our very good friends, Trond and Lesley, from the yacht Coconut.

Graham enjoying a beer on Free Spirit with Russell Eddington.

Alan Bowes, the founder of whale watching in Tonga, and owner of the Mounu Island Resort.

John Samuels, the warden of the marine park, Suwarrow.

John Samuel's house where all were welcome - Suwarrow, Cook Islands.

Sea lions sleeping on the back of Moonraker in San Christobal, Galapagos.

Max with a giant tortoise in Santa Cruz, Galapagos.

A humpback whale rising out of the water.
You can see how close it is by the rails of the boat.

Colin, from Coconut,
getting to know more about the coconut crabs on Suwarrow.

A fish vendor at the covered market hall in Papeete, Tahiti.

*Mrs. Assam at her remote black pearl farm
on the atoll of Ahe, in the Tuamotus.*

Jean Renwick in her beautiful garden at Sunnyside House, Grenada.

William, president of the Hanaiapa Yacht Club, came for lunch on Moonraker when we visited Hiva Oa in the Marquesas.

The colourfully dressed women of San Blas looked as if they had stepped out of a page of National Geographic magazine.

Melanie in her art studio on Huahine in the Society Islands.

Moonraker, reaching with the big red spinnaker up.

*Luke and Max land a massive marlin.
It was well after dark by the time they got it onboard.*

A wild, wet and windswept reef, surprisingly flat and pink - Suwarrow, Cook Islands.

Graham, Janet, Luke and Max celebrating Luke's 27th birthday in Tahiti.

Humpback whales - Tonga.

Janet entering a bure, the tradional Fijian hut, on the island of Ovalau.

*Lepolo and Michael visiting us on Moonraker
in the Ha'apai Group, Tonga.*

*Mr and Mrs Assam come on board to bid us farewell
with the traditional 'leis' flower garlands.*

Paradise found! An idyllic setting - Suwarrow, Cook Islands.

Rough sea conditions in a gale.

Running fast with the wind behind us in a gale.

School children eager to show us their village - Nuapapu, Tonga.

The children always loved our yellow balloons - Vanua Levu, Fiji.

The local bus - island style! The Yasawa Islands, Fiji.

13

A Tragic Death

We had an unusually rough night sailing the two-hundred-mile passage from Rangiroa to Tahiti. It was a pity as it was the only long sail we would do with Ian and Bev on board. The wind was uncharacteristically from the south, and during the night we went from motoring with no sails to sailing hard on the wind with two reefs in the main. A big swell made the motion uncomfortable. It was not the trade wind sailing we had become accustomed to.

The rough seas and the swell gave Luke an opportunity to ask Ian's opinion on our creaking mast, a problem that had been plaguing us for months. In certain conditions the mast didn't just creak, it made a sharp crack. It had been a worry because being dismasted at sea is one of a sailor's worst nightmares. Ian and Luke discussed several possible reasons but didn't come up with an answer. Luke didn't think it was a serious problem but to be safe we decided to have a rigger look at it when we got to Tahiti.

Arriving in Tahiti was a major culture shock for us after months in small islands where the population was a few hundred or less. In Tahiti it was one hundred and seventy thousand—more than half of all of French Polynesia. The population explosion is comparatively recent. Under French government and with some influx from Chinese merchants and shopkeepers, the population was still less than five thousand at the beginning of the twentieth century, but grew slowly to twenty thousand by 1960. All that changed in the mid-sixties, when the Faa'a International Airport opened the island up to tourism, and port development facilitated the growth of commercial and passenger shipping. Today Papeete, the capital, where most of the people live, is a thriving modern city and you might think that you were in France if it was not for the lush green mountains and blue Pacific sea.

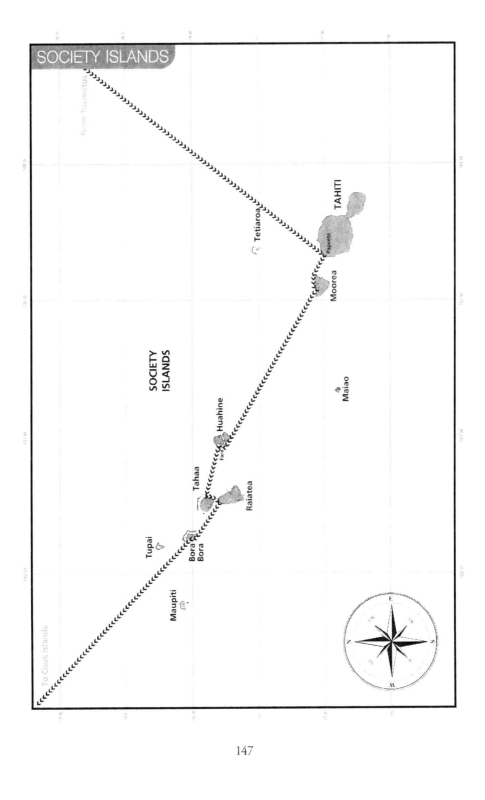

The outer islands rely on this bustling hub of French Polynesia for everything: markets for their exports, government, high school and university, hospitals, supplies of every kind, and even visits for major shopping trips. The roads are excellent, and we were surprised to see so many cars, mostly new and expensive. It seemed to be an affluent place and it came as a surprise after the poor islands we had just come from. The large Carrefour supermarket, close to the Marina Taina, had everything we could possibly want. Having spent months buying limited fruit and vegetables at stalls and small general stores, Janet was pleased to be shopping in a well-stocked modern supermarket.

A short taxi ride from the marina took us into the city and the Vaima Centre in the central shopping area. There we found modern shops of every description: men's and ladies fashion, music, leather goods, beachwear, cameras, jewelry, opticians, and sports equipment. It was fascinating because it was so different, but it was surprisingly expensive. Costs were up to double what one might expect to pay in England for the same goods. This is primarily due to high import taxes. But there is no income tax, which helps the locals manage the high cost of living, and they enjoy the same substantial benefits of the French health and welfare systems as mainland France.

Tina, our Polynesian guide for the day, took us on a tour of the island. Louis, the driver, was a French expat who had lived in Tahiti for twenty-five years. Between them they gave us an entertaining insight into life in Tahiti that was more interesting than any guidebook. Our first stop was the bustling market in the centre of Papeete. The covered marketplace was vast, as big as a football pitch and on two floors. We were dazzled by a riot of colour and bombarded by the cacophony of sounds of business being done. Exotic smells of spices filled the air. Competing cries of vendors echoed through the hall. The stalls were run by Polynesian women as colourful as their wares. Their floral dresses were yellow, orange, red, and blue, and on their heads were black straw hats or floral garlands. They sat patiently on stools waiting for their next customer and it was a pleasure to walk by, look, chat, smile, and not be hassled.

Their stalls were piled high with Chinese cabbage, potatoes, onions, lemons, limes, mandarins, oranges, melons, cucumbers, spring onions, tomatoes, mangoes, and bananas—a feast for eyes that had been starved of most types of fresh fruit and vegetables for months. Chunks of tuna were laid out on slabs with hundreds of smaller silver fish. Fresh beef, lamb, and chicken were piled high. You could even buy them on the hoof! Delicious smells drifted from the bakery stalls selling bread, cakes, patisserie, and pizzas. It mingled with the scent of fresh flowers and orchids. Wood carvings, basketware, hats, exquisite shell jewelry, and even the white bones of sharks' jaws were displayed on stalls, as were the ubiquitous black pearls.

It was here that Ian and Bev first noticed the transvestites. We had noticed men dressed as women everywhere and had been told that there was an old tradition in Polynesia that a family with no girls will bring up a boy as a girl. I asked Tina, our guide, if this was true. She laughed. "Wherever did you hear that? It's true that you see men here dressed up as women, but it's probably because of the free and easy Polynesian lifestyle. It's nothing new and there's no embarrassment."

The only main road in Tahiti circles the outside of the island and covers one hundred and twenty miles. Soaring volcanic mountains rise in the centre and the lower slopes are blanketed with forest. A green velvet carpet runs down to the turquoise sea. The whole island is protected by a necklace of white surf-strewn reefs, separating the deep blue of the ocean from the pale blue of the lagoon. It is an emerald surrounded by sapphires and diamonds. It is not hard to understand why the early explorers, Samuel Wallis, Louis de Bougainville and James Cook described Tahiti as a paradise two hundred and fifty years ago and how, in 1789, twenty years after Cook's visit, Lieutenant Bligh (who had served under Cook on the *Resolution*) and the crew of the *Bounty* fell under the spell of Tahiti and its nubile young women.

Bligh allowed the crew to live ashore to care for the potted breadfruit plants they were collecting to take to the West Indies, and they became accustomed to the ways of the Tahitians. Many of the seamen and some of the young midshipmen were tattooed in native fashion. Master's Mate and Acting Lieutenant, Fletcher Christian, married Maimiti, a Tahitian woman. Other warrant officers and seamen of the *Bounty* were also said to have formed "connections" with native women. Bligh was not surprised by his crew's reaction to the Tahitians.

> *The Women are handsome ... and have sufficient delicacy to make them admired and beloved. The chiefs have taken such a liking to our People that they have rather encouraged their stay among them than otherwise, and even made promises of large possessions. Under these and many other attendant circumstances equally desirable it is therefore now not to be Wondered at ... that a Set of Sailors led by Officers and void of connections ... should be governed by such*

> *powerful inducement ... to fix themselves in the midst of plenty in the finest Island in the World where they need not labour, and where the allurements of dissipation are more than equal to anything that can be conceived.*
>
> —A Narrative of the Mutiny: Lieutenant William Bligh, 1790.

Tahiti has been made famous not only by the great explorers, but also by great artists, none more so than Gauguin, who was captivated by Tahiti, where he found the inspiration for some of his greatest paintings. Tina had worked at the Gauguin Museum for four months so she suggested we go there. It was fascinating to read letters and records of the life and work of this sad, impoverished, disturbed, and unhappy genius, who had so little recognition in his own lifetime. But the museum was not as interesting as the one we had already seen in the Marquesas, probably because it did not have the benefit of the large collection of Gauguin paintings (albeit copies) that we enjoyed in Hiva Oa.

Although Polynesians are now Christians, they have a deep respect for the beliefs and traditions of their ancestors. This became very clear to us when Tina took us to a marae where a large tiki had been defaced with material objects like money and a watch, probably put there by tourists. She stood before it shaking and visibly upset. I asked her why. "She is a goddess. I can feel her power. She is unhappy." There was no doubting her sincerity and yet she didn't feel able to touch or remove the offending objects and we moved on. Polynesians may have been Christians since missionaries first arrived in Tahiti in 1797, but deep-rooted pagan beliefs remain imprinted on their psyche.

It's wonderful to watch Polynesians talking. They talk with their faces in the same way that the French talk with their hands, and they are very expressive. I was booking a ticket with Air Pacific, Fiji's international airline, when the pretty young girl serving me went over to discuss a problem about my trip with her supervisor. Of course I couldn't understand a word of what they were saying but I watched the conversation progress through the reactions on her face—at first questioning, then puzzled, then surprised, then concerned, and I became worried until I saw her face break into a smile. "Is there a problem?" I asked as she returned. "No," she replied with a beam.

After a few days in busy Tahiti we were ready to leave for the tranquility of the nearby island of Moorea. On the way there we heard the strange and haunting song of whales singing. It was a plaintiff sound of moans, howls, and cries. Nobody knows what it means, whether it is to communicate or to attract potential mates. The sounds seemed to be coming from underneath the boat, but although we watched carefully there was no sign of them. They were probably very deep and the whale song can travel a great distance.

We anchored in the beautiful Opunohu Bay, the same bay in which Captain Cook anchored on his first voyage to the Pacific.

> *Here was a paradise beyond compare. Eimeo (Moorea), stunned even the most travelled, the most blasé of the officers and men of the two sloops. Clear streams and a river poured into the bay, the slopes were a mass of flowers and flowering shrubs, fruit of every description was for the picking and the waters teemed with fish… although there were numerous and willing girls at Eimeo the happiness of Cook's men was made complete by the arrival of their women from Tahiti.*
>
> —Captain James Cook: A Biography *by Richard Hough (1997)*

Cook was welcomed and his men surely felt that they had discovered paradise, but Cook's discovery inevitably led the way for other European explorers, and the introduction of weapons and alcohol had a disastrous effect on the population of Moorea, which seriously declined during the nineteenth century, as indeed it did throughout the South Pacific.

* * *

From our anchorage in Opunohu Bay we could see thatched bungalows built out over the water, and where there were bungalows we knew there were bars that would be serving sundowners. It looked no distance at all in the dinghy, but soon we were trapped in dozens of coral heads and unable to use the outboard motor. "No problem," said Ian, "we'll just paddle into the beach and walk up to the hotel." There was a splendid thatched bar next to the pool, with a tempting list of exotic cocktails. The sun dropped to the horizon and a guitar player strummed a Polynesian melody. Another cocktail followed the first but, still in high spirits, we hadn't really thought about getting back in the dark. It couldn't really be a problem for four experienced sailors, could it?

It was dark when we finally found the dinghy. Bev and Janet paddled us out into the lagoon. Ian had the torch and was looking out for coral heads. We didn't seem to be moving. "Bev, you're not paddling hard enough," he shouted. Bev and Janet paddled harder, but after a few minutes Janet said in between giggles, "We're still not moving." The girls paddled even harder, but despite all the splashing it became clear that the dinghy still wasn't going anywhere—and then the penny dropped. The dinghy was stuck on top of a small coral head that we couldn't see from either side of the boat. We all collapsed in laughter. "What are we going to tell Luke?" said Janet. "We'll have to own up." Ian pushed us off and we paddled back to deeper water, still laughing at the thought of our dinghy stuck on top of a coral head as the tide dropped.

The nearby village of Papetoai was reputed to have a good restaurant but although we walked three miles down a quiet road we couldn't find it. But we did find John Michelle and his amazing home. He lives in the hull of a Polynesian catamaran that now has a thatched roof. Wide wooden steps lead up into the boat and sailcloth canopies provide cooling shade around the outside. Seats are covered with scattered cushions and ship's oil lamps provide light at night. The boat has been set down on a piece of land that is now an enchanting tropical garden. It would be hard to exaggerate the charm of his unique houseboat and the beautiful garden. He made us freshly squeezed fruit juices and we sat in his garden chatting about our sailing experiences, the suitability of different types of yacht, and the pleasures of sailing.

John Michelle is a wandering sailor who left Paris as a young man twenty-five years ago. After years of sailing in the Caribbean, he crossed the Pacific to French Polynesia and spent the last fifteen years in Moorea. Many would think that he had found paradise, but now he has put his property up for sale and is going back to sea. This time he plans to go to China. He has his eye on an old racing boat that will surf down the waves. "I want to go fast. I need nothing inside, just a bunk, a cooker, and a toilet. Everything else is extra weight." He shrugged with a "don't care" gesture. "Why do I need it?" He is a fascinating character, a true salty dog. Meeting people like him makes us feel privileged to belong to the sailing community.

* * *

Opunohu Bay is a popular stop for yachtsmen travelling through The Society Islands. We were one of twenty boats anchored there, including *Free Spirit* and *Coconut*. We had first seen *Coconut* when we were in Shelter Bay Marina in Panama. Luke and Max had got to know the owners there, but it wasn't until meeting them here that we really got to know Trond, Lesley, and their two children, Camilla and Colin. Three years ago Trond, a rugged blond Norwegian, gave up his work as an industrial psychologist and left Norway to sail to Australia with his family. I so admire young families like this that are sailing a small boat across the world's oceans whilst taking on the responsibilities of the children's welfare and education.

Trond invited us to go with them to an impromptu beach barbecue for the yachts in the anchorage. Every boat took food to share and a large wood fire was built on the beach from driftwood. It was a great opportunity to make new friends. The only trouble was that it was a dark night with no moonlight so it was impossible to see the person you were talking to. It was a Polynesian version of a masked ball! You talked to a person and next day had to try to match a face to a story, which could have embarrassing consequences!

At the barbeque we learned about a spot an hour's dinghy ride away where we could swim with stingrays, so the next day we set off in our dinghies to find them with our friends from *Free Spirit* and *Coconut*. The water was shallow and crystal clear, giving us a perfect view of the stingrays swimming around us. They were about three feet in diameter with a grey-black back and a white underbelly. The long tail has a barb that can sting, which is how it gets its name, but it will only do that if you stand on it. Two large eyes protrude from the top of the body. They swim effortlessly, just flicking the tips of their wings to surge forward. They look menacing, like miniature American stealth bombers, but in reality they were just like large puppies, rubbing up against our legs and allowing us to stroke their soft white underside. Six large black tip sharks circled around hoping to get some of the food we were giving to the rays. Janet came in the water, too, and now knows how to recognize the black tips and white tips, which are harmless.

Meeting local people is one of the things we enjoy best about blue-water cruising and we were not disappointed in Moorea. While out walking we heard music coming from a village and saw a large crowd gathering in a field. They told us that the ladies were about to rehearse for a Mother's Day intervillage Polynesian dancing competition. There must have been over fifty mothers and grandmothers taking part. The drums began their insistent and repetitive rhythm and the women's hips began to sway, some more easily than others, it has to be said, their arms and hands painting pictures in the air.

After the first session the best dancers were moved into positions where they could be easily seen and copied by the others. Because this was just a rehearsal they weren't wearing traditional grass skirts but they still made a colourful spectacle dressed in floral skirts of green, blue, red, and yellow. As the rehearsal progressed they lost their initial shyness, picked up the rhythm and got more into the mood, watched all the time by the critical eyes of the elder women who were organizing the dancing.

A group of spectators gathered around the band. Men had drums of different sizes and it seemed that everyone had brought a guitar or handmade banjo. The men were big and strong and many had covered their arms in the blue tattoos that have been traditional among the Polynesians for centuries. I moved in and out of the spectators and the band chatting to everyone. I must have looked the odd man out but no one seemed to mind me taking photographs and I was made to feel welcome.

The next morning we woke up to find that our two fishing rods had been stolen from their holders on the back of the boat. It came as a shock. We had seen a local canoeist among the yachts in the evening and we assumed that he had come back in the night and quietly made off with our rods. It was an isolated incident but it upset us. Someone on another yacht suggested that this was a characteristic of the ancient Polynesian culture: Possessions are there for all to share. It is true that that Captain Cook had problems in Moorea when two goats were stolen under his very nose and he "fell into a terrible rage the like of which none of his officers had witnessed before." But that was over two hundred years ago. This was probably just one bad individual, I thought, and it would be responsible to go to the police station to report it. I had taken a photograph of the canoeist the day before and, as he seemed to be taking a lot of interest in our boat, I thought he might be the villain. Feeling rather proud of myself, I showed the gendarme my digital photograph. He took my camera and studied the photograph carefully. "Ahhh," he sighed, as he looked up with a knowing smile. "That is the local fireman."

Back in Tahiti we said a sad farewell to Ian and Bev. We had appreciated them coming all the way out to the South Pacific, and we'd had a lot of laughs. The next five days were spent in the Marina Taina in Papeete, so that Luke could get a rigger to inspect the mast and have other work done. After the rigger's inspection, and having talked to the mast makers in New Zealand, Luke concluded that there was nothing wrong with the mast and that we could sail to New Zealand without any worries. The problem probably occurred when the mast was put back in the boat in Newport, but if the creaking continued, we would have another look at it in New Zealand.

While work was being done on the boat in the marina we took the opportunity to take a closer look at Papeete. *Lonely Planet* says, "Pulsating Papeete is not always the easiest pill to swallow ... sweaty concrete jungle bursting with bright lights and grimy edges oozing strange sounds and foreign smells."

It might be a town that holidaymakers might want to avoid, but for us it was a welcome change. We liked the hustle and bustle, the shops and the restaurants. It made me realize that I missed civilization—walking down the seafront boulevard, sitting in a French café with a cup of coffee, reading an English newspaper—we had missed these simple pleasures and enjoyed them again now.

Discovering good restaurants was another novelty. Our favourite was the Mango Café, where we went for a farewell lunch with Bev and Ian and returned twice more. It was the first smart restaurant we had been to since we left the BVI. The décor was Conran style, modern but much smaller. White was the predominant colour with scatter cushions providing bright splashes. Clever use of mirrors made the dining room seem much larger. The cooking was French, with a small but enticing menu that reassured us that everything was freshly prepared and cooked. Patrick Brunel, the owner, was an interesting and much-traveled French chef, manager, and entrepreneur. He also owns two specialist French bakeries in Tahiti and plans to open another restaurant. Patrick has worked in management for top hotel restaurants in France, Europe, Beverly Hills, and Tahiti, and has come late to owning his own business. He was obviously enjoying it and used his experience to get it all right. Interestingly, when I asked him what his biggest problem was, he replied, "Changes of government that produce radical swings and affect consumer's confidence," a sentiment that would probably be echoed by businessmen in any part of the world.

The Tahiti Sevens rugby tournament was taking place in Papeete while we were there, with teams from New Zealand, France, Samoa, Fiji, Tonga, the Cooks, Niue, and of course, Tahiti. Samoa overcame Fiji in the final to take the cup. The games were played over two evenings under floodlights to avoid the heat. We went to watch the quarterfinals, semifinal, and final.

A Tragic Death

The rugby was top class but fun and entertaining. The atmosphere was what you might expect anywhere in the world—young men enthusiastically supporting their team, drinking beer, and eating burgers. It was a total change from the way of life we had been leading on the boat, which did us all good.

Down by the waterfront we found an interesting craft festival in a large open-air arena. It caters for tourists, especially the hundreds that come in from the cruise ships, but on a quiet day it is an interesting experience. There are dozens of individual stalls selling a profusion of delicate shell jewelry, black pearls, brightly-coloured garments, basketware, hats, wood and stone carvings, all beautifully made by the stall holders. There was no pressure selling, the vendors were just happy to talk to us while we admired their work. I bought myself a necklace and Janet cried, "Oh no! You're not going Polynesian?"

"Maybe," I replied, "but at least I haven't been tattooed yet!"

Here, as everywhere in the world, taxi drivers are the font of all knowledge. I had an interesting chat with Popo, a taxi driver, who had lived in one of the outer islands before moving to Tahiti. I asked her about the changes she had seen in Tahiti in the last fifty years. The two things she immediately mentioned were the airport and television.

As an example she told me a story about the small island where she grew up. Her family and all the inhabitants went to a meeting called by the minister of their church to give their views on the proposal that there should be an airstrip. Some argued that it would be a good thing—that they would be able to be taken to hospital in Tahiti by plane instead of by boat, that they would not be so cut off. The minister listened carefully but concluded that in his view it would be a bad thing because he felt it would change their traditional way of life and, of course, it did.

Popo conceded that when the airport came to Tahiti in 1965 there was economic development, jobs, cars, and better homes. But, she said, people gave up their simple way of life, became busy, and cared less for the welfare of others. The Polynesian tradition of giving gifts and expecting nothing in exchange, of giving time and helping others was disappearing. Television depicted a new western lifestyle that was fashionable, that the young aspired to. It showed social behavior that was acceptable in TV fiction and gave permission for similar behavior that had previously been unacceptable. Young people soon moved out of the family home to lead independent lives, have babies, get married and get divorced.

When you look around at the affluence in Papeete no one can deny that the Tahitians are economically far better off than anyone else in the South Pacific, but like all good things it has come at a price.

* * *

Tahiti is by far the largest and most important island in the Society Islands, but the group also includes Moorea, Huahine, Taha'a, Bora Bora, and Ra'iatea. These islands have a romantic image but although they are beautiful islands, some say that they have been spoiled because the large jets that fly into Tahiti have made them more accessible. We were interested to see for ourselves what the effect of tourism had been.

On 29 June we left Tahiti with two reefs in the main and only the staysail bound for Huahine (who-ah-heeny). We had delayed sailing for a day because of strong squalls and rain. I am usually the cautious one when it comes to bad weather, but this time it was so horrible that even Luke had second thoughts. He called *Free Spirit* on the VHF radio. "It looks nasty. I'm staying put," Russell told us. But after a few hours the wind seemed to be easing and we decided to leave in the early evening. The wind was still shrieking in the rigging and driving sheets of heavy rain through the anchorage, but Luke reasoned that we would get shelter from the lee of Moorea in the night, and the forecast for the next day was for the wind to drop. These strong squalls and rain feature regularly in Cook's *Journal*. That's something that hasn't changed.

Luke was absolutely right. When we came under the lee of Moorea the strong wind dropped away and by the morning we were motoring for lack of wind. Huahine appeared as a low landmass, unlike the mountainous Tahiti, and it looked very green and covered in forest with no signs of habitation. We entered through the reef into sparkling emerald green water. This was the wide, deep Avamoa Pass, the pass that Cook came through when he discovered Huahine in 1769. Of course Cook had to work the entrance out for himself while we had the benefit of charts, but just as in Cook's day, our eyes were our best guide, clearly identifying the gap in the white surf breaking on the reef.

Captain Cook made several visits to Huahine between 1769 and 1773, and in 1777 he stayed for seven weeks. It was Cook who named the group of islands the Society Islands, "as they lay contiguous to one another." On his first visit, Cook arrived in the *Endeavour* on 16 July 1769, and was met by natives who were initially shy until they saw Tupia, a Polynesian man who was accompanying Cook. After that they came on board without fear. Among them was the king of the island, whose name was Oree. Cook exchanged names with him, and afterward they addressed each other in that way. Then gifts were exchanged, with Tupia giving gifts for their gods, and the natives giving Cook a hog and some coconuts for his God. Cook drily remarked in his log: "Thus they have certainly drawn us in to commit sacrilege, for the hog hath already received sentence of death and is to be dissected tomorrow." He set about surveying the island and completed it in three days.

The anchorage in the lagoon is close to Fare, the largest village. It has just one street, a supermarket that had an open front so that the cash desks were almost on the pavement, two Internet cafés, a tourist information office, and several souvenir shops. Tourists come here on a day trip by boat from the more popular neighboring islands like Bora Bora, but there were no hotels, only small bed-and-breakfast homes. Mostly the people we saw were locals going about their business, loading up their 4WD trucks with supplies, or hanging out at the only bar/café that sat at the end of the dock. There were no signs of rampant tourism ruining this island yet.

It is even free of the large cruise ships that ply the Society Islands. A concrete dock and reception area were built in Fare to land the passenger launches from cruise ships, but when the first captain anchored his ship he wasn't happy about the space he had to swing to on his anchor chain, and being fearful of the reef, declined to stay. Now the cruise ships anchor in splendid isolation in a deserted bay on the other side of the island, much to the chagrin of the local merchants in Fare, who are missing out on the tourism business.

Just past the café there is a small sandy beach enclosed by rocks. The surf was up following the strong winds and men in canoes and kids on boards were surfing the rollers. This was the first time we had seen canoes surfing. It looked quite dangerous. One man came surging in on a large breaking wave heading straight for a rocky breakwater and only saved himself at the last minute by throwing himself clear of the canoe, which went crashing into the rocks seconds later.

Canoes are a very big part of life in French Polynesia, but especially in Tahiti and the other Society Islands. We saw men out training most nights, and it looked very serious. It is probably the number one male participation sport. They race in several classes of canoe, one-man, two-man, five-man, and eight-man. The racing canoes are called proas and they have an outrigger on one side to balance the slender canoe. In a changing society we were pleased to see that this tradition has maintained its place in the Polynesian way of life.

We explored the island by car. (Luke came with us but Max was on holiday in England celebrating *his* father's sixtieth birthday.) Driving around it was easy to appreciate how Huahine is geographically different from other islands we had been to. It has many indented bays that stretch inland, giving the impression of water everywhere as we drove around the flat coastal perimeter road. We found a river with stone fish traps that were centuries old but still being used. A large stone-shaped funnel had been built in the river entrance. It ended with a V-shape, its point facing the sea. The fish were swept into the V on the outgoing tide and were speared or caught with nets. In a nearby stream we saw very large, very old sacred eels being fed by their guardian, who stood among them in shallow water. He knew what he was doing, though. A passerby tried to feed them and nearly had his fingers taken off.

Huahine is famous for vanilla, and grows much of the world's supply. We stopped to visit a small vanilla farm and met Francois, the estate manager. He was a dark-skinned, tough, wiry Polynesian with short-cropped hair and a huge toothy grin that lit up his face. A real man of the soil, he proudly showed us the crops he cultivated "all on my own." It was the first time we had seen vanilla being grown. The bushes are like vines, trained along wires. The plant has a white flower that becomes a pod that is dried out then sacked up. It is exported to be processed for use as flavouring for food. Francois told us that he also grows coconuts, hot chilies, papayas, noni, pineapple, grapefruit, bananas, soursop, and pawpaw, "all on my own," he said again proudly as he stretched his arms wide to indicate the size of his estate, which, in truth, did seem very large for one man to handle.

Janet was especially interested in the garden and had clearly made a friend. Francois asked for his photograph to be taken with her to add to the collection he has pinned on the wall in the one-room house where he lives alone. It must be very hard work, with long days, and lonely, too, but he seemed happy. We printed the photographs for Francois and posted them to him.

Driving on we passed a sign hidden in the bushes. Janet said, "Stop. I want to go in there." I hit the brakes and backed up the hundred metres to the entrance. Janet had seen an art studio, and by chance we had stumbled upon a local artist named Melanie. Her studio was a traditional thatched Polynesian hut with a roof of woven palm leaves. It hardly seemed waterproof enough to protect her paintings but she reassured us that it was, although it only lasts two or three years before it has to be remade. It is interesting to see how durable traditional building methods are in this part of the world. The huts may look flimsy but they have been built with local materials to withstand the prevailing weather conditions.

Melanie was a beautiful woman, probably in her early forties, with long red hair flowing over her shoulders. She told us that she is American by birth, but lived in Moorea until 1979 when she moved to France and Providence. She lived there for twenty years and was juried into the *Salon Nationale des Beaux Arts de Paris* for two years in succession. She returned to Polynesia in 1999 and has since had several exhibitions in the Society Islands and an artist residency at the Meridien in Bora Bora. Some of her work was displayed in the studio. Her paintings are bold and vivid: rolling green hills, calm aqua marine lagoons, sandy palm fringed shores, dark Polynesian women with long black hair, and warrior-like men. She mainly painted in oils but also liked to experiment with different materials. As we talked it was clear that we had met a serious artist who was held in high regard. A large original oil painting sells for around five thousand dollars. Examples of her paintings can be seen on her Web site: www.polynesiapaintings.com.

We were totally absorbed by Melanie, who lives the quintessential artists lifestyle—a bohemian with a complex personal history and no interest in material things. Outside the studio were her two broken-down cars, stuck together with duct tape but still working. The little Fiat Panda had big beautiful flowers painted on its rotting body! No doubt she could have a different lifestyle if she wished but she has been drawn under the spell of Polynesia, and like Gauguin and other artists that have gone before her she was in love with the people and the country she paints. It was stimulating to meet her. I wished we had time to get to know her better, but like so many other people we met, Melanie would remain in our memory long after our voyage ended.

That week we also met an interesting American couple who were on vacation. We had motored slowly down inside the reef protecting Huahine and found a sandy bay and a small resort with thatched "over-water" chalets. They are built on stilts above the water and guests have the luxury of stepping down into an endless infinity pool, the sea. No sooner had we got the anchor down than a couple in a kayak paddled out to say hello, curious to see our yacht and hear about our way of life. We invited them on board and they introduced themselves as Tom and Jennel Hiroch. Tom looked like Robert De Niro, and had an engaging smile and boyish enthusiasm that made him look younger than his sixty-one years. Mind you, a beautiful wife twenty years younger and a six-year-old daughter probably helped keep him young, too. They live on Malibu Beach, where he is a dentist to rich and famous clients. He obviously loves his work and has the lifestyle to go with his successful career.

When he said he was a dentist I opened my mouth and said, "Oh good, can you have a look at this little problem?" I was joking but to my surprise he took me seriously and asked, "What's the problem?" "Just two broken teeth and two missing fillings," I jokingly replied. It was true, actually, but it wasn't causing any pain and because of the lack of facilities I had planned to wait until we got home before going to the dentist.

But Tom insisted on having a look and reassured me that the teeth would hold up until I could get proper attention. Slightly embarrassed, because I hadn't meant to ask for advice, I thanked him. "Don't worry," he said jokingly, "now I can write off my vacation to tax." They kindly invited us ashore for dinner with them that evening at their hotel, the Te Tiare Beach Resort, Huahine's one true luxury resort, which can only be reached by boat.

Tom has that "can-do" attitude that typifies the entrepreneurial spirit that prevails in America. He had invented and taken to market a unique product that uses a fibre-optic cable to beam light into the patient's mouth. His brother, a design engineer, developed the idea with him and together they established the patents and launched the product (www.isolitesystems.com).

We played volleyball on the beach with them and had dinner in glamorous surroundings as Tom's guests, along with the owners of the resort. Next morning he and his wife came to have coffee with us onboard *Moonraker* and showed us some unusual black-and-white and sepia photographs Tom had taken of our boat. He warmly invited me to Malibu for dental treatment. How could I say no?

* * *

From Huahine we sailed on to Taha'a. The leaden sky brought prolonged heavy showers of tropical intensity. We anchored outside a small boatyard with wireless Internet access and sat inside the boat, snug and dry, delighted to have our laptops and access to the outside world while the rain drummed down on the cabin roof incessantly.

A Tragic Death

The weather had been awful since Ian and Bev left ten days earlier, with very strong winds followed by squally weather. Black clouds crept up and let rip with wind and rain, but then quickly moved on. In between we had cloudy days and then a few with blue sky and sunshine. Then we would think, "That's it, the bad weather has all cleared through now," only to be disappointed the next day. I suppose we shouldn't have been surprised. When you see the lush vegetation covering the islands in a blanket of green you just know there has to be a lot of rain. But that's not what they tell you in the holiday brochures, and we felt very sorry for an Italian honeymoon couple, who confessed gloomily that the temperature in Rome was 100 F. Here it was a cool 70 F, but hey, if you are on honeymoon, does the weather matter?

The Society Islands are volcanic, and although there are reefs surrounding the islands, the volume of water flowing in and out is far less than in the coral atolls. The passes are wider so entering and leaving is less time-critical than in the Tuamotus. We motored up inside the reef on the west coast of Taha'a (which is almost connected to Ra'iatea) to snorkel the Paipai Pass. It was very wide, about three hundred feet, with only a gentle incoming tide. The drift dive took Luke and I about twenty minutes and we had never seen so many fish. There were thousands, swimming so close together that you could hardly see the coral beneath them. This huge mass of brightly-coloured striped fish spread like a carpet in every direction. At dinner that night we talked about this amazing sight and reminisced about the time that Russell had introduced us to drift diving in Ahe.

The next day we arose early to motor the short distance from Taha'a to Ra'iatea to meet Max, who was returning from England. At eight in the morning we anchored outside the small marina at Ra'iatea. Luke collected Max from the nearby airport and they arrived back huddled in foul weather gear. As the rain was so heavy, we decided to stay anchored where we were. Five hours later the marina manager came over in his outrigger canoe. "Can you move please?" he asked politely in French. "You are too close to the end of the runway. You can tie up to that red mooring buoy closer in."

It was still pouring but Luke and Max immediately set about raising the anchor. A few minutes later Max put his head down into the saloon. "Janet, can you spare a moment?" She went on deck to find a police patrol boat alongside with two very irate gendarmes. They spoke no English but were waving their arms angrily at us and pointing to the runway. Janet explained in French that we were already getting the anchor up to move to the mooring buoy the marina manager had shown us, but they were not satisfied.

Why hadn't we answered the VHF radio? Hadn't we seen them waving at us? Why had we anchored there? "Desolé, monsieur," Janet said as sweetly as she could. We moved out of the way and onto the mooring buoy but the gendarmes were still angry and the situation seemed to be getting more heated. "The captain must come to the gendarmerie in town immediately," one of them commanded, and Luke had no alternative but to comply.

Now he was getting worried. He checked the chart and found that there were no anchoring restrictions. He could not see any signs nearby restricting anchoring, or instructions to call the control tower or police. Were our papers in order? He had cleared out of Polynesia in Tahiti, but our agent had told him that it was permissible to stop here in Ra'iatea, still in Polynesia, but on the way through. Perhaps this was the reason? Or worse, perhaps they suspected us of carrying illegal drugs or firearms? Even though we thought we had done nothing wrong we knew they could make life very difficult for us.

After a short discussion we decided that it would be best if Luke went to the gendarmerie on his own, without Janet as a translator, because if Luke couldn't speak French and the gendarmes couldn't speak English, a stalemate was the most likely outcome, and no arguments would be possible.

They didn't take Luke with them but asked him to follow them in our dinghy. If they wanted him to get a good soaking before he got there, they must have been very satisfied. Hours went by and we heard nothing from Luke. The rain continued to come down in sheets and we became gloomier. We had heard terrible stories about yachts falling foul of the law in remote parts. If some law had been broken or if we were suspected of a serious crime, what might happen? As time went by and evening drew on we became increasingly worried that Luke might be spending the night in jail. What would we do if he were arrested? Could the boat be impounded? At the very least it seemed that there would be fines to pay. Would we need to contact the British consulate in Tahiti for help?

The silence was broken by the sound of an aircraft taking off, flying over the spot where we had been anchored a few hours before. "Well, that one would have missed us by at least a hundred feet," Max quipped. It eased the tension and we all laughed. After several hours we heard the familiar sound of our outboard motor approaching and rushed on deck,

A Tragic Death

so glad to see Luke back, and not in handcuffs. We sat him down with a stiff drink and listened to his story.

He told us that he had been kept waiting for a long time but when he was finally allowed to present the ship's papers, the gendarme appeared unable to understand them or to have any interest in them. He wanted to know who the owner was, and wanted to see the lady who spoke French. Dutifully protecting his owner from whatever fate awaited, Luke pointed to the ship's papers to show him that the owner was a corporation in the Cayman Islands. He left the room for an hour and when he returned there was more gesticulating and frustration, but eventually the gendarme screwed up his face and allowed Luke to leave. It seemed that our tactic of, "Sorry, I don't understand," had paid off.

On reflection we guessed the gendarme must have been criticized by the airport control tower who had probably told him we had been anchored in the flight path all morning, and that he hadn't been doing his job properly. He got kicked so he kicked us. Ah, well. We had avoided having several feet shaved off our mast and a major diplomatic incident!

* * *

Ra'iatea is known by Polynesians as the sacred island because of its famous Marae Taputapuatea. We had seen marae throughout Polynesia, but this was a royal marae, which had influence over all of Polynesia. It is on Cape Matahira, a flat area at the northern end of the island. Close by is the Te Ava Moa (sacred) Pass where chiefs in their great ocean-going canoes entered the lagoon. They came from as far away as New Zealand and Samoa to pledge their obedience to the king.

Although the site looks ancient, most of it only dates back to the seventeenth century. It has great significance in the Polynesian religion. It has been suggested that the large blocks of coral that form much of the structure of the marae were taken straight from the reef shelf by lighting fires at low tide to shatter the big chunks of chalk stone. All we could see now was a large rectangular floor of black rock and coral, which was the court area, and then a raised platform, or ahu, that formed the altar. The ahu is surrounded by a wall. Drawings show how rooms within the court would have been built with wood and a thatched roof. Much of the original structure has been destroyed or stolen—the missionaries did not want to preserve pagan places of worship and often smashed the temples to use the materials to build their own churches. The walls of the royal marae remain, though.

Next to the royal marae is the family marae of the high lineage Hauviri, to whom this land belonged. The cavities of the marae are decorated with the skulls of warriors killed in battle. Important ceremonies took place there to appease the anger of Oro, the god of war, including human sacrifices. To please the gods a young man would agree to sacrifice his life, happy in the belief that he would join the gods and in the knowledge that his family would rise in status as a result of his sacrifice. The community would gather here for births, deaths, and family events, and at important sites like this, village meetings, sacrifices, and wider religious ceremonies were practiced.

These marae are the last visible remains of ancient Tahitian culture. From carbon-dating techniques it is thought that the earliest were constructed in the twelfth century. However, the chiefs were at the peak of their powers in the fourteenth to eighteenth centuries until European influence and missionaries eroded their authority. Little is known about the people except what we have learned from the first European explorers, especially Captain Cook, who in 1769 stood at this very spot. A large board depicts Cook at the royal marae witnessing a human sacrifice. Drawings showed the thatched boat sheds where giant canoes were kept. They had two hulls with masts and sails to make long ocean passages and they were large enough to carry live animals to sustain the travellers on their voyages. Our guide told us that Polynesians used these giant canoes to sail to the Easter Islands, Hawaii, and the Marquesas, and even as far as New Zealand. It is believed that the sacred mountain here in Ra'iatea is the New Zealand Maoris' spiritual home, and that their spirits return to this place.

These migrations are covered in mystery, as are the visits to this marae by kings from faraway lands. Everything that touched the marae was cloaked in secrecy and the stones have never given up their story. I wondered why so little was known about ancient Polynesia. It must be because their society was very primitive compared to the Greeks and Romans. Why that is remains a much deeper anthropological question. At its simplest level there was no writing and so there were no records, nothing to leave behind but stones.

Pondering these thoughts, we stood for a long time staring at the blackened stones, caught up in their grandeur and the sacred atmosphere.

It is a place that moved us and opened our minds for the first time to the hidden ancient history of the Polynesians.

* * *

From Ra'iatea we moved on to the most famous of the Society Islands, Bora Bora, for a long time known as a playground for the rich and famous. Cruising along the coast we saw groups of thatched huts, but these weren't villages, they were luxury resorts, with their signature thatched cottages standing on stilts over the water. We anchored in a small bay close to Bloody Mary's, a restaurant that is a world-famous watering hole for international celebrities. Their names have been carved into a board outside the entrance to the restaurant—Rod Stewart, Harrison Ford, John Denver, Diana Ross, Jane Fonda, Marlon Brando, Jimmy Buffett, David Lean, Ringo Star, Juliet Mills, Billy Idol, Rowan Atkinson, Meg Ryan, Goldie Hawn, Patrick Swayze, Senator John McCain, to name but a few.

It's not difficult to see why celebrities like to come here. They like to be seen where other stars go, and it has a casual but exclusive ambience and a level of service that suggests that discretion is guaranteed. The restaurant is surrounded by beautiful gardens and has a high thatched roof. Inside, the floor is deep sand and the tables are made from rough-hewn but highly varnished wood. But despite the deliberately casual Polynesian style, the food, the staff, and the service tell you that this restaurant is a cut well above the average and certainly very different from anything we had seen elsewhere in Polynesia. Even the way that dinner was ordered was different. Having been shown to our table, we were invited to go to a large chiller cabinet where the maitre d' showed us the meat and fish available, explained where it came from, and told us how it would be cooked. It was certainly a more interesting way to order food than looking at a menu.

After dinner, I asked the manager how they selected which celebrities would be put on the board. "Do they phone up in advance to say that they're coming because they're worried that they might not be recognized? Or do they actually ask to have their name included and risk the embarrassment of refusal?"

"It's not a problem," the manager explained. "A committee sits each month to decide which, if any, of our visiting guests should be immortalized. But we sometimes have a problem with minor stars from TV soap operas who do ask for their name to be included."

"How do you deal with the ones that don't merit a feature?" I asked.

The manager smiled. "Oh, it's quite simple. I just tell them it isn't my decision. I ask for their name and say it will be put to the committee."

There was quite a gathering of yachts in the bay at Bloody Mary's and among them were *Coconut* and *Free Spirit*. We had last seen Trond and Lesley, from *Coconut*, in Moorea, and we invited their young children, Colin and Camilla, to come wakeboarding and water skiing. They were excited about coming, but an hour later Trond called up on the VHF. "Do you mind if we delay? *Magic Roundabout* has just called up on the radio to say that he will be here soon and the children just can't wait to see Tom."

Tom was a very close friend of Trond and his family. They met two years earlier in Spain and Tom then crossed the Atlantic on *Coconut* and was so taken with long-distance sailing that he returned to England to do it again on his own boat. Trond and Lesley had been in Antigua while Lesley recovered from back surgery, so Tom was able to catch up with them on his new boat, *Magic Roundabout*. They had been cruising in company ever since. Tom was only twenty-three, and both his parents had died when he was young, so he was brought up by his grandparents and his elder sister. I think he adopted Trond as a surrogate father, and the children adopted Tom as their honorary uncle.

Later, when Tom had safely anchored, we all walked on the beach together. I chatted to Tom while Colin and Camilla had fun with water sports in the dinghy with Luke and Max. They had met Tom in Panama, but we had only met him briefly when he had come to get fresh water from us in the Galapagos, and again in Moorea when he came to our boat to collect Luke and Max to go diving. Now we had the chance to talk and he told me how he had sailed single-handed from England across the Atlantic on *Magic Roundabout*, a Sweden Yachts 340. This was no mean achievement. Crossing the Pacific he had a friend, Mark, to crew for him but Mark had left and now Tiree, his girlfriend, who he had met in Antigua, had joined the boat to sail down to New Zealand with him. She was a little apprehensive about how she would take to life at sea in a small boat. As we stood chatting at the water's edge I felt strangely ill at ease.

That evening many of the yacht crews met in the bar at Bloody Mary's. The atmosphere was convivial and everyone mingled and made introductions. Tom was with Max and two young Australians, Mark and Juliet on *Savaro*, and we went over to chat to them. Tom wanted to know how we were enjoying sailing our dream at the other end of the age scale. He was unusual for a person so young in that he seemed to be genuinely interested in other people, whatever their age.

A Tragic Death

The next day, Saturday 14 July, we sailed around to the other side of the island to snorkel at a spot where we had been told we might see manta rays. Russell and his crew, Ami, came from *Free Spirit*. It was a perfect day, blue sky, warm sunshine, and a light breeze, with no omens of the tragedy to come.

The first sign of alarm came when we had a call on the VHF radio from Lesley on *Coconut* asking if we knew where Tom was. She said that they were worried because he'd gone snorkeling but hadn't returned. Luke and Max were unable to shed any light on where he might have gone. Because Tom was single and young my first thoughts were that he had simply gone off without telling anyone, as I know from personal experience young people sometimes do. I confided in Russell that we had had scares like this with our own children, and told him about the time when our daughter, Julia, at the age of sixteen, had gone missing for a whole night when she was staying with her grandmother. She turned up right as rain the next day, having spent the night on a boat moored in the River Hamble, explaining that she couldn't get back and that there was no phone. I remembered what a terribly worrying time that had been.

We were on our way back to Bloody Mary's bay when we heard another call on the radio that was more alarming. It was an "All ships" call, asking all yachts in the area to keep a lookout for Tom. Trond was making the call and he gave a full description of Tom. It was clear that it was now being treated as a serious incident. We were all very subdued, alone with our thoughts, trying to imagine what could have happened.

As we motored close to the main pass, a favourite dive spot, Luke asked Max to get in the dinghy and see if Tom had gone there, or if there were any divers there who might have seen him. We waited in silence until Max came back to say that there was nobody there. As we continued motoring back the worst possible thing, the unthinkable, happened. We heard Lesley's distraught voice on the VHF radio calling her husband. He was out searching in their dinghy but had a portable VHF radio. Her voice was choking with emotion but she just managed to get her message to him before breaking down.

"Trond, I have got some terrible news … Tom has been found dead, hanging on our anchor chain. Come back."

Nobody spoke. We arrived at the anchorage in silence and looked across at *Coconut* and *Magic Roundabout* and the activity taking place. We didn't know what to do. It didn't seem that we could be of any help at this moment. The radio continued to be our only source of information as the tragedy unfolded. A doctor who had gone on board *Coconut* was on the radio to the Tahiti coast guards, who had been monitoring the incident.

"We have located the missing person."

"Is he okay?"

"Negative. We want you to arrange to come and take the body away now."

A police rescue launch arrived soon after and we watched Tom's body being taken on board. No one knew what to say. We were all deeply shaken, but Luke and Max were in shock. They were close friends of Tom, and like all young people they believed in their own immortality. It was very hard for them to come to terms with what had happened. Ironically, it was Tom who had been teaching Luke and Max to free dive. He was a very experienced diver and I am sure they must have been asking themselves, "How could this happen?"

Trond came to see us an hour later. We were all glad as it hadn't seemed right for us to go over to them so soon. He amazed me with the way he lightened the atmosphere right away by just talking about the incident, explaining what probably happened.

At about ten in the morning Tom told his girlfriend, Tiree, that he was going to "get lunch"—by free diving for fish with his spear gun in the anchorage. Conditions were ideal for making a fast descent using an anchor chain, because in the light winds the chain went straight down. Ironically he chose the anchor chain of his best friends on *Coconut*.

He would have reached the eighty feet to the bottom quite quickly and was probably hanging on to the chain waiting for a fish to come by, but lost track of time, drifting into a euphoric state and blacking out. Air in the body is compressed at that depth and has neutral buoyancy, so he would have just sunk to the bottom.

He was discovered by two fellow yachtsmen who were doctors and also scuba divers. Trond had been organizing a search above the surface around a wide area but the yachtsmen started looking in the most logical place first and quickly found him. He had no marks of any struggle, so he had not been trapped and he had a peaceful smile on his face.

The same questions kept repeating themselves as poor Trond struggled to come to terms with the enormity of the tragedy. "Could I have done more to help?" "How could it happen to such an experienced diver, who took safety very seriously?" "Why was he diving on his own when he usually went with me or Luke or Max?"

Everyone gathered on our boat, and we talked and it helped. Colin and Camilla were wonderful in the way they were coping, and in a strange way they helped the rest of us. Looking at our long sad faces, and uncomfortable with the silences, Colin asked, "Does anyone know any jokes?" At first I was shocked; it seemed inappropriate. But then I realized that for a young child with no inhibitions this was his way of coping. He relieved the pent-up tension by making us laugh as he and Camilla went through their repertoire of jokes, including funny faces and actions. It seemed bizarre, but no one rehearses how they are going to react or behave after the tragic death of a loved one.

As twilight came we had stiff drinks and gradually the rum numbed the pain for those closest to Tom. "You just have to get through today," I told Trond. "Tomorrow you can start thinking about what has to be done."

Trond arranged a simple farewell service for Tom the next day, Sunday. The police found two Protestant ministers, one who spoke in French, the other in Tahitian. It seemed that every blue-water yacht in Bora Bora had turned up at the dock at Bloody Mary's. There must have been seventy people standing silently listening to Trond as he introduced the service. He began by thanking everyone for coming to say goodbye to Tom, and explained what had happened, as most people had no idea. He then went on to tell how they knew Tom and how the whole family had come to love him. He talked about Tom's zest for life, his love of adventure, but also of his kind and considerate personality that had endeared him to their family and everyone who met him.

It must have been very, very difficult for him to do, but with pauses and deep breaths he carried it off with great feeling and dignity. It was very moving. He asked if anyone else wanted to say a few words about Tom. I thought that perhaps Luke or Max would. I think they wanted to but were too overcome with emotion. To my surprise Colin and Camilla stepped forward and bravely added their own words about their friend Tom. It hardly seemed possible that two children so young could stand up in public at such an emotional time and speak in such a mature way. I didn't know Tom well enough to speak then, but looking back I wished that I had said something to express the support of everyone there for Trond and his family, who bore the weight of the tragedy on their shoulders.

Tiree remained bravely silent in her grief throughout the service. She had so recently joined Tom on *Magic Roundabout* to build a long-term relationship and it had been shattered almost before it began. Now she would have to rethink where her life would go.

Flowers were laid on the water and as they drifted away we all comforted ourselves with the thought that Tom had died in a place that he would have wanted, doing what he loved, and that he had lived a full life in his twenty-three years. But the truth was that this was a young life, full of promise, that had been tragically cut short.

The next day I felt strongly that I wanted to move on, to leave Bora Bora. We couldn't, of course, because Trond had many practical arrangements to make to put Tom's affairs in order and we felt we could at least provide moral support and help to "babysit" the children while they were busy. Luke was pleased to be able to do what he knew best: prepare *Magic Roundabout* for a delivery crew to take her to New Zealand.

Trond too was eager to leave Bora Bora behind. "Everything seemed so meaningless after we lost Tom," he said. Tom's death had changed the lives of the people close to him.

When we had done all we could to support Trond and Lesley we started to make plans for our departure. Luke spread out a large chart across the saloon table and drew lines in pencil showing the options for visiting the Cook Islands.

The Cook Islands are widely spread out, in some cases with hundreds of miles between them, so it wasn't going to be possible to visit them all. The first option, which most of the yachts seem to have favoured, was to head south to the main island and the capital, Rarotonga. The second was to sail on the direct course for Samoa, visiting only one deserted island, Suwarrow, which was inhabited only by a park warden in the summer months. The third option was to sail north to the island of Penrhyn.

We had concerns about the first option, because the pilot books led us to believe that the harbor at Rarotonga was too small and shallow for our yacht, and that anchoring outside would be impossible because deep water ran right up to the shore. The second option might be disappointing because we would not meet any of the Cook Islanders, so we opted for the third, the little-visited and very remote island of Penrhyn.

We left Bora Bora with a black cloud hanging over us. The events here had changed us, and they had a much greater effect on Max and Luke. There was a different atmosphere on the boat as we set sail for the Cook Islands.

14

The Isolated Islands

It is six hundred miles from Bora Bora to Penrhyn, which would take us three days. We set out with the expectation of strong winds, and were glad we hadn't left the day before, as some boats did—we heard on the radio that they had winds up to forty-five knots. But it had blown through and we had a very pleasant sailing breeze at first, but later the wind fell light and variable and we motored. A big swell was running so it was uncomfortable, and as usual on our first night out we did not sleep well.

The wind continued to be light and from behind us so we motored all of the next day. It was tedious and uneventful but we comforted ourselves with the thought that it was better than the nasty weather experienced by those who had left earlier. The monotony was broken only by sighting a ship about five miles away, the first we had seen, and by Max catching a large wahoo, about thirty pounds and five feet long. It filled the freezer, so no sooner had we put to sea than the boys had to stop fishing again.

There was plenty of time to study *Lonely Planet*. Penrhyn gets its name from a British ship, *Lady Penrhyn*, which called there in 1788. She was one of the original convict ships returning from Australia. The island had a reputation for a Maori population so fierce that early visitors did not dare to land or let the locals on their boats. We hoped it had changed by now! It is extremely remote.

We probably motored most of the six hundred miles. With hindsight perhaps we should have steered twenty degrees off course to put the light wind on our beam, which would have given us enough apparent wind to sail. It would have taken a day longer but been more pleasant.

We arrived off Penrhyn on Saturday afternoon with plenty of daylight left to go through the pass and into the lagoon. But with full cloud cover and occasional heavy squalls that wiped out visibility, we decided to wait. The lagoon has no navigation buoys and there are coral heads everywhere, so if we got through the pass safely we would have to rely on visually finding our way up the channel to the anchorage by the village. We needed the sun so that we could look down into the clear water to see the coral heads. It was too risky, so we found a spot shallow enough to anchor outside the reef and waited for tomorrow and hoped for sunshine.

From where we were anchored I could see the pass. It was very narrow, only just a bit wider than the length of our boat, and there were waves breaking on either side. It was a bit daunting. The lagoon itself looked vast, but we knew from Warwick Clay's pilot book that the many coral heads would make it difficult to navigate. There were no other yachts. It felt very lonely.

In the early evening a small boat rowed out toward us loaded down with people. We watched them approach curiously. Despite the fearsome reputation that this island had in the past they looked friendly enough!

Our visitors were a Polynesian family dressed in T-shirts and shorts. It was pouring with rain and the group of three adults and two children were huddled beneath brightly-coloured but battered umbrellas. The man stood up in the boat and introduced himself as Pa. Although he was the father of the family I think that Pa really was his first name, that it didn't mean "Dad." He explained that he was the government officer from the agriculture department and reminded us that tomorrow was Sunday and that strict observance of the Sabbath meant that we would be unable to enter the lagoon to clear customs, health, and agriculture until Monday, when representatives would come on board and clear us in. It was disappointing but there was nothing we could do but wait another day. It seemed ironic that such a small and remote country should be so very bureaucratic.

But Pa explained all this in a very friendly way and as it was raining so hard we asked the family to come on board. Pa, emboldened by his official role, had no hesitation in stepping into the cockpit, but despite my pleadings, his wife, two children, and a friend would not join us. I think they were curious but terribly shy. They just sat there partly sheltered by their umbrellas, softly singing songs that sounded more Maori than Polynesian. Whether it was to welcome us or to cheer themselves up I couldn't tell, but it was a strange sight. Finally I did coax the two children onboard by offering them Coca-Cola, but they took the drinks quickly and scurried back onto to their small boat. We felt terrible that they should be sitting out in the rain but what else could we do?

They were all inquisitive, none more so than Pa, who did not suffer from his family's shyness. He told us that we were only the fourteenth yacht to visit Penrhyn this year, so the arrival of any yacht was obviously quite an event for their small community, and probably explained the reticence of his wife and children. He asked to look inside the boat. "Is that a plant you have there?" he enquired, spotting Janet's artificial flowers in a vase on the table. I assumed he was asking in his official capacity, so we politely showed him that it was not a live plant crawling with pests.

Having got the business out of the way he uncovered a wicker basket that contained several dozen birds' eggs, which he told us they had just collected from a small island in the lagoon. They were probably gulls' eggs, but I was unable to find out what kind. "Big ones that fly," was all I could get out of him. The eggs were about half the size of a hen's egg, and had pretty brown speckles. Later, I tried one boiled and it tasted very good, although it had a stronger taste than a hen's egg and was almost all strong yellow yolk with very little white. I wondered if we should pay for them but Pa assured us that they were gifts. By now we realized that we would be expected to reciprocate, and Janet offered *Moonraker* T-shirts for the family, which they liked.

Pa came out again to meet us on Monday morning and guided us through the narrow channel between the coral heads. We anchored outside the village of Omaka and he brought out the other officials who would clear us into the Cook Islands. He took us ashore and introduced us to some families and we racked our brains wondering what to use for bartering, as we had come ill-prepared for this social custom. It was easy in Captain Cook's day; you just gave nails for sex—in fact you only needed one nail! I had brought whisky for this purpose—barter not sex—but I was worried that in a religious community they might not approve of alcohol.

I was rather taken aback when Pa asked me if we had a spare VHF radio as it's quite an expensive piece of equipment. "No, I'm sorry, Pa. I don't think we have a spare," I replied. He explained that he wanted one so that he could contact his base in an emergency when he was out fishing. Luke pulled me to one side. "Actually, Graham, we do have a spare. There are two that don't work, but all they need is a new aerial, and a piece of wire would probably do the trick." I gave Pa the news and he grinned. We knew he had it rigged up because he called us on the radio a couple of hours later. In fact we would get a call from him several times a day. It was just like kids at Christmas and it gave us pleasure, too.

The VHF radio crackled into life again and we were surprised to hear Russell's voice. *Free Spirit* was only ten miles away on the other side of the atoll and Russell had heard us talking to Pa on the radio. He was thrilled to hear that we were so close and promised to come over to see us the next day.

Penrhyn is as remote as any Pacific island we are ever likely to visit. You probably won't even find it on any map you look at, and it is well off the beaten track of most cruising yachts. It is eight hundred nautical miles from Rarotonga, the capital of the Cook Islands, and two hundred forty miles from Manihiki, the nearest island. Its original Maori name is Tongareva, and it was first discovered by settlers from the Samoan islands who were traveling east toward Tahiti around 1000 BC.

Early accounts tell of fierce and erratic behavior by the natives, but that had all changed by 1853 when *Chatham*, an American ship, was wrecked on the reef. The survivors were welcomed and cared for until they were rescued a year later. The islanders trust and kindness was betrayed in 1862, when they were grossly abused by corrupt and greedy outsiders. Four Polynesian "teachers" introduced by western missionaries literally "sold" their congregation to Peruvian slavers for five dollars per head. The population was reduced from around seven hundred to just eighty-eight, and none of the slaves ever returned.

The Cooks became a British territory but were then governed by New Zealand until they too gave up responsibility for the islands, which became independent. But New Zealand left a valuable legacy: entitlement to their passport. Consequently Cook Islanders are able to travel there to live and work. They earn good money, and most of it is sent home to support families left behind.

The four hundred islanders on Penrhyn have a way of life that has changed very little over the last hundred years. A supply ship comes once a month and a small aircraft may come weekly if the freight to be carried warrants it. There are two villages, Omaka and Tetautua, a much smaller village on "the other side," as they quaintly call each other across the lagoon. Omaka seemed run down and desperately impoverished. Most of the inhabitants have been to the capital, Rarotonga, and many even to New Zealand if they have family there. They have seen the things that money can buy in the developed world and they covet them. There are a dozen or so trucks and cars, although they are hardly needed as there is nowhere to drive to. Some brought back DVD players from New Zealand. They like what they see about life in the movies and often asked us for DVDs.

The Isolated Islands

Following independence and years of financial mismanagement the government of the Cook Islands is desperately in debt, and there is little social welfare or investment. The pearl farm industry in Penrhyn had collapsed due to poor conditions and low market prices. Perhaps there was not the business acumen or work ethic that we saw in the Tuamotus. There had traditionally been a strong copra market, but they are unable to compete with French Polynesia because of the French government subsidy. Clams were the new hope, but that too seems uneconomic.

Sitting on the verandah of his house overlooking a beautiful white sand beach we talked to Pa about the economy. He told us of his plan to build thatched bungalows there to attract tourists. It seemed a good idea, but he went on to say that it couldn't work because the weekly air service from Rarotonga, was often cancelled. There is a hospital, but it looked almost derelict. A solitary nurse was the only medical help on the island. I asked Pa what would happen if a villager had a heart attack or a serious accident. "He would die," he replied pragmatically.

The government does provide some help to the community. It supplied two generators that produce electricity for a limited period each day. Alpepe is the island's mechanic and his job is to keep them running, but when we met him he was busy with a broken car and two outboard engines. "They all bring their problems to me," he said with a smile. "Do they pay you?" I asked. "No," he replied, "they don't have to as I get paid a salary by the government."

On the "other side," in Tetautua, the people seemed happier. They were just as poor and lived in simpler housing—often just a wooden shack with a tin roof, and usually only one room. There were no cars, just a few mopeds. But here everyone asked us to come into their houses as we strolled down the dusty track that is the main street. The community was more independent and less concerned with the lack of help from government. In one of the houses we talked to Joseph, a leader in the village, and he told me that a delegation from Tetautua had been to New Zealand to raise money from the Cook Islanders living there. "We raised two hundred grand [NZ$] and bought a new tractor and trailer, a truck, and a boat," he said proudly.

There was no paid work other than government jobs, but that is how it has been for centuries, and they seem to get by. They are almost self-sufficient. Fish, coconuts, breadfruit and papaya are plentiful. They keep pigs and chickens. No one is going to starve. The rain is regular enough to fill their water butts. But they need money to buy petrol for their boats and they need food staples, flour and rice. An air fare to Rarotonga costs NZ $800, and one of the women has to go there to sell the straw hats that the ladies have woven.

As we walked down the dusty path between the houses people stopped us to chat. The teacher showed us her school and invited us into her home. We talked about the way of life in Tetautua. Her husband sat in a chair on the verandah ignoring us. Later she explained that he was mentally ill and his behavior was erratic and violent. She had to make him sleep in the schoolhouse at night. Her children, except for the youngest, had left home to stay with relations on "the other side" to get away from him. It was a very sad story and helped us to appreciate that even here in paradise there are social problems. There was no welfare system or medical help, no counseling or institutions for the sick. This wonderful lady was living in a nightmare from which there was no escape.

The pilot books talked about trading with the locals but we didn't know what to expect. Would we be haggling over whether a live chicken was a fair swap for a DVD? In fact, it doesn't work that way at all. The people were so friendly and generous they just wanted to offer hospitality and give gifts to visitors. It was their way. We were always being offered coconuts to drink from the shell and given papayas, woven pearl fans, shells, bird's eggs, and even a live chicken.

Gift giving, not bartering, is entrenched in the culture and gifts were naturally expected in return. It was true that they would ask if you had some of the things they needed. Russell gave them a section of anchor chain, some bolts, and even a DVD player he didn't want. We gave whatever we could, but wished we had come better prepared with practical gifts for both adults and children. We did have a big stock of balloons and they were a great success, bringing excitement and laughter to the young children who flocked around us.

The local policeman, Henry, asked if we had a spare hand torch. On the boat we have small torches that are recharged simply by shaking them. I gave one to Henry and couldn't resist doing an impression of Del Boy from *Only Fools and Horses*.

"Henry," I said, "this is the best torch you are ever going to have in your life. It doesn't need batteries. When it runs out you just give it a little shake like this." I demonstrated, shaking it up and down like a sauce bottle. His wife, who was sitting on the ground weaving, pricked up her ears. "How long do you have to shake it for?"

"As long as it needs, my love," I said, smiling like Del Boy.

Henry came up to me the next day, his face beaming. He told me that they had used it last night and were very pleased. "I want to give you something," he said, and handed me a large and very beautiful cowry shell. It summed up the gift-giving culture that we were beginning to understand.

I have rarely seen more friendly people. They are deeply religious and strongly attached to the family ethic. Although they are poor in material possessions it did not seem like third world living. They had plentiful food and shelter and enjoyed their close-knit and self-supporting community. Can we in western society learn from this? Although it seems an idyllic existence, the truth is that most of us are too entrenched in the economic model that drives our society to be able to give it up—not just the material possessions, but also the cultural, social, and business fabric that make up western culture. I watched the villagers sitting around, having completed their simple daily tasks of getting food, cooking, and cleaning. Although I could see that they were happy I found it difficult to understand how they could enjoy doing nothing for most of the day. I knew that I would be deeply unfulfilled by this way of life.

Perhaps it is sad though, that even in these remote Cook Islands, society is changing. Visits are made to relatives in New Zealand. Material possessions are brought back. People want to improve their homes and their standard of living. Children are educated and emigrate to find work as nurses or mechanics or engineers. Whatever we may think of the "rat race" and being "wage slaves," the economic attraction of western society seems irresistible, and these islands will surely be very different in fifty years time.

It was in Penrhyn that the pressures of four of us living together in a confined space for so long began to surface. I had some issues with Max that had been bothering me on the passage from the Society Islands, and on a boat even small issues can become big problems if they're not discussed and resolved quickly. Janet didn't have the same concerns as I did, but she could see that I was getting upset and agreed that it made sense for me to talk to Luke about it. It was almost impossible to have a confidential conversation on the boat so Luke and I created a reason to go ashore on the day we left. We walked through the village and out to the airstrip and had a long chat. It was very helpful and cathartic for us both. The tragedy of Tom's death in Bora Bora still hung over us and continued to affect the boys deeply, and it became apparent that there had been a misunderstanding between Max and myself. Luke understood the problem, explained Max's point of view, and agreed to talk to him. Over the next few days our relations seemed to be back on an even keel.

I mention this small incident because it was only a symptom of a larger malaise in me. I had been feeling ill at ease. Although I was enjoying the wonderful experiences, I had begun to feel that there was more to life than sailing. I was feeling guilty about being on what seemed like a permanent holiday. There were other important things I wanted to do before I died. Mostly I had these feelings on the long sea passages, and I hadn't discussed them with Janet, although I suspected that she was intuitively aware of my feelings.

On 28 July we were at sea again, making the three-hundred-mile passage from Penrhyn to Suwarrow, an uninhabited atoll with only a resident park warden living there to protect wildlife. The lagoon would provide a good, sheltered anchorage, so we planned to stop there for two or three days to see the wildlife in the national park before continuing the seven-hundred-mile passage to Tonga.

Although there were strong winds and big seas it was no problem as the wind was behind us. What was more difficult was coping with the squalls. There were two the first day and they doubled the wind strength in a very short time. We could see them coming, though, and at night they were visible on the radar. Fortunately there were none that night. It was our first night at sea again, so as usual we didn't sleep well. It didn't help that large seas made the boat roll, knocking the wind out of the sails. At seven in the morning a threatening squall came through on my watch but I was able to handle it without reducing sail. It was our forty-fourth wedding anniversary, and there wasn't much opportunity to celebrate, but I promised Janet a celebration dinner when we got to Tonga, although I had no idea what type of restaurant we were likely to find.

The wind dropped on the last day. Luke and Max put the spinnaker away and we expected to motor the last one hundred and forty miles, but after an hour we unexpectedly got a 15–20- knot breeze on the beam that allowed us to sail through the night comfortably and fast. We timed our arrival perfectly, sighting Suwarrow at nine in the morning. Entering the narrow pass presented no problems and as we motored round the corner of Anchorage Island we saw six other yachts anchored there. We recognized five, of them including once again *Coconut* and *Free Spirit*.

Suwarrow is wild, rugged, and very remote. The only people who live there are John Samuels, the warden of the Suwarrow National Park, his wife, Veronica, and their four small children. The family is dropped off by a cargo ship in May, along with all the supplies they need for six months. They should be collected again sometime in October, but the first year they were there the ship forgot to come and they had to be taken off by a passing yacht in November!

Suwarrow is one of the finest anchorages of the Pacific, a ring of tiny islands, the largest no more than half a mile long and three hundred feet wide, linked by a rugged drying reef that shelters a central lagoon covering an area of around twelve miles by eight miles. The atoll's official name, Suvarov, comes from the Russian ship *Suvarov*, which discovered the island in 1814, but the Cook Islanders call it Suwarrow.

Its low-lying reefs are no protection from cyclones and the waves that sweep right over the atoll. The American author Robert Dean Frisbie, who spent several years there in the 1940s, had to lash his children to the trunks of trees to prevent them from drowning when a severe cyclone struck the island. He wrote a book about his experiences called *The Island of Desire*.

Anchorage Island, the islet where we anchored, was described by Robert Louis Stevenson's wife, Fanny, as the most romantic island in the world. Although it wasn't the inspiration for his most famous book, it really is a "treasure island." In the mid-nineteenth century, a ship's crew unearthed a box full of coins, and a few decades later, New Zealander Henry Mair discovered a horde of eighteenth century silver pieces of eight, hidden in a turtle nest. He became involved in a fight and most of the coins are still lying somewhere beneath the sands of Suwarrow. We didn't find them!

The island was made most famous by Tom Neale in his book, *An Island to Oneself*, which described his Robinson Crusoe life there in three periods between 1952 and 1977. It is a fascinating story of a man and his wish to prove to himself that he could live independently of the trappings of society and survive with only his own company. He married Sarah Haua in 1955, and had children, but she never came to Suwarrow. John Samuels told me that he had once met Sarah in Rarotonga, and that she had been deeply upset that she was not mentioned in the book, and indeed Neale clearly gave the impression that he was a bachelor. In 1977 Tom Neale was found by a passing yacht, suffering from stomach cancer. He was taken to Rarotonga and died there eight months later. A stone monument on the beach commemorates his experience on Suwarrow. It reads: *Tom Neale, 1952–1977, lived his dream on this island.*

The Chart drawn by Tom Neale

Now Suwarrow is a national park. John Samuels is a well-educated Polynesian man, strong and muscular, with smooth brown skin and wiry black hair tinged with grey, a caring face, and enquiring eyes. He had been a policeman in Rarotonga but grew disillusioned with the life and saw an advertisement for his present job. He was ready for a change and although he didn't know much about it he applied, and to his surprise it was offered to him on the spot. The only condition was that he had to leave the next day!

John and his family live in a small wooden house on stilts that has one room upstairs for sleeping and a ground floor area, open on three sides, for living and cooking. He has an old generator, which had been mended by a yachtsman recently, a deep freeze that is broken and cannot be fixed, and a single-sideband radio that is his only contact with the outside word.

The previous incumbent was called Papa John. His title was caretaker, which described his role, but conservation had no part in it. John Samuels took a different view. Although it was not part of his job description (he didn't have one), he instinctively felt that a more active role in protecting wild life was a key part of why he was there. On his first day he met a yacht arriving from Rarotonga. "Papa John told us we would enjoy catching and skinning birds to eat," they hailed. "No, you won't," he said. "Why not?" they asked. "Because I'm in charge here now and it's not allowed."

With the authority of his government department he created a set of written rules for visiting yachts that are designed with nature conservancy in mind. No scuba diving. No spearfishing. No taking the female giant coconut crabs to eat. No lobster catching. No birds' eggs taken.

It sounds draconian but he enforces the rules in a very relaxed way, and encourages visiting yachtsmen to enjoy the park and follow the code, gently restraining them when they stray. He takes them on nature walks across the reef and to the outer islands, where the birds nest. Yachtsmen appreciate the guided tour, and he can keep an eye on what they are up to. He only does this once a week so he doesn't disturb the birds too frequently

John has no technical training for the job but has an intuitive feeling about what is best for the island. He told me he turned down a request for a monthly ecotour from Rarotonga because it would create a precedent, become more frequent, and disturb the wild nature of "his island."

For generations the men on the northern Cook islands have taken the birds, the eggs, the turtles, and the coconut crabs to eat. But John understands that this cannot continue unchecked and this is what makes him such a natural for this unique responsibility.

Although he lives a hermit-like life he is pleased to see cruising yachtsmen when they come ashore. In John Neale's day back in the sixties, only four or five yachts would pass by in a year. Last year it was over a hundred. All get a warm welcome. On our first night, along with the five other yachts in the anchorage, we were invited to join a potluck supper at his house. When he blew his conch shell it was the signal for us to come ashore bringing food and drink. John made the wood fire and grilled the fish and we sat around his large wooden table, making new friends and enjoying the convivial atmosphere. There was a wonderful spirit of friendship and camaraderie with sailors from Norway, South Africa, Australia, France, America, and England.

As we strolled back down through the palm trees and along the white sand beach to our dinghies, I realized what a special evening it had been. This was the essence of the blue-water cruising life that we had been seeking. This was our dream.

The sense of isolation strengthened our close community. The yacht *Savaro* with Mark and Juliet arrived with a broken boom. Jim on *Ruby Slippers*, an experienced and practical sailor who owns a boat yard in Seattle, and Trond on *Coconut*, immediately set about helping with repairs, gathering together rivets and a rivet gun, and at the same time made the rig more secure. A French yacht, *Fidel*, had a problem with its computer wiring, and Luke was able to fix it.

The next day John invited us all to join him for a nature walk out on the reef. At low tide the reef is a wild, wet, and windswept experience, a vast expanse of pink coral, almost flat so that we could walk across it, but still covered in rock pools filled with water where the sea had receded. The blue sky was splattered black with hundreds of sooty terns filling the air with their screeches as we approached. Their eggs were carelessly left on the shore and under bushes, but perfectly camouflaged among the white and brown pebbles where they lay. Young tropic birds were sitting fearlessly in their nests on the ground as I came close. In the air we saw frigate birds and masked boobies, and on the shoreline a curlew with its long curved beak. John had occasionally seen one before but didn't know what it was. I identified it from one of my bird books and left him a photocopy. There was no reference to them being seen in this part of the world, so this one was way off course.

As we moved from the reef to a small outer island Colin and Camilla found two coconut crabs. It was the first time we had seen them. They are half-crab and half-lobster, ferocious-looking creatures that live underground

The Isolated Islands

and climb up trees to knock down the coconuts that they then crush and eat. John let the children entice one of the crabs onto the end of a stick, where it clamped on. Colin could have carried it away like that and wondered how it could be so stupid as not to let go.

Out on the reef Luke found a two-foot sphere with an aerial, which had been washed up. After much discussion the consensus opinion was that this was a radio beacon used in drift net fishing. Large fishing boats set drift nets free and locate them again by radio signals from units like this. Luke being Luke, he had to take it apart to see how it worked.

The next morning Janet woke up and went on deck to find that our dinghy was missing. This was a shock because if the dinghy was gone we would have lost our primary shore transport, and it would be irreplaceable until we reached New Zealand. Our first thought was that the boys had not tied the dinghy on properly when they returned last night. "Bloody hell," I exploded. "How many times have we talked about that?"

When we sat down to think more calmly about what might have happened we discovered that neither Luke nor Max were on the boat. Although we were rather worried we assumed that they had stayed the night on one of the other yachts and the dinghy was with them. It was still only 6:30 so we decided to have a cup of tea and make a radio call to the other yachts in the bay a little later on if they had not returned.

Then we heard a radio call between two of the yachts in the lagoon mentioning the search for a dinghy and realized that it was our dinghy they were talking about, so we joined in the conversation and gradually discovered what had happened. After being ashore, Luke and Max had gone back to *Coconut* that night, but when they went to get in the dinghy to come home, it wasn't there. Although they had tied the painter to a cleat on *Coconut* the rope had worked free in the mysterious way that ropes do, and the dinghy had simply disappeared. The boys were mortified and wanted to find it before Janet and I realized it was missing. There was no possibility of searching in the night, so Trond promised that he would take them out to look for it at first light.

It was lucky that the dinghy was lost in the lagoon and not in the open sea, because the wind could only have blown it onto the reef on the other side of the lagoon. But the lagoon is five miles across, a huge search area. John and Veronica, who knew what had happened, volunteered to help and joined the search in their boat at dawn. Their local knowledge of wind and tide was vital in estimating where the dinghy might be and it was they who found it on the far side of the atoll. When I thanked John profusely, he said, "It's nothing. That's my job."

He allowed us to replace the precious petrol he had used in his outboard motor and give them food, which they needed to eke out their supplies, but they expected nothing. John Samuels is one of those special people who put a lot more into life than he takes out of it. It's a lesson we could all learn from.

15

Swimming with Whales

On 1 August we set our course to sail southwest and head directly for Vava'u, the northernmost group of islands in Tonga. It was perfect sailing weather, with a pleasant breeze of fifteen knots just aft of the beam, calm seas, and sunshine. It had always been our intention to make Samoa the next stop after Suwarrow, but the more we read the pilot books and *Lonely Planet* the more we realized that it might not be as interesting as we had expected. American Samoa, is centered at Pago Pago, a large commercial port that sounded as if it were best avoided. *The Pacific Crossing Guide* says it is "noisy, dirty and smelly, and offering nothing other than its low prices and the benefit of US territory." Although Western Samoa had the attraction of the house where Robert Louis Stevenson came to live, and eventually die, we thought that we would rather use the time available in Tonga and Fiji. They are extensive archipelagos that could take months to explore properly and we only had time for six weeks in each.

The five-day passage was mainly uneventful. On the second day Janet saw our first and only ship at three in the morning, a large ocean fishing boat lit up like a cruise ship. It passed about five miles away. Like the one before, it didn't show up on the AIS system. The autopilot flicked off again when I was on watch but it locked on again as soon as I re-engaged it so it wasn't a problem, but it was still frustrating to have this intermittent fault. Max was excited when he caught the first fish on this passage, a decent dorado weighing eleven kilos (twenty-five pounds). The team went to work, Luke busy filleting and Janet vacuum-packing in meal-size packs.

On our fourth day out the wind began to build and contrary to the forecast it increased to twenty knots and continued to strengthen and veer during the night. During my 4:00 AM watch it increased to twenty-five

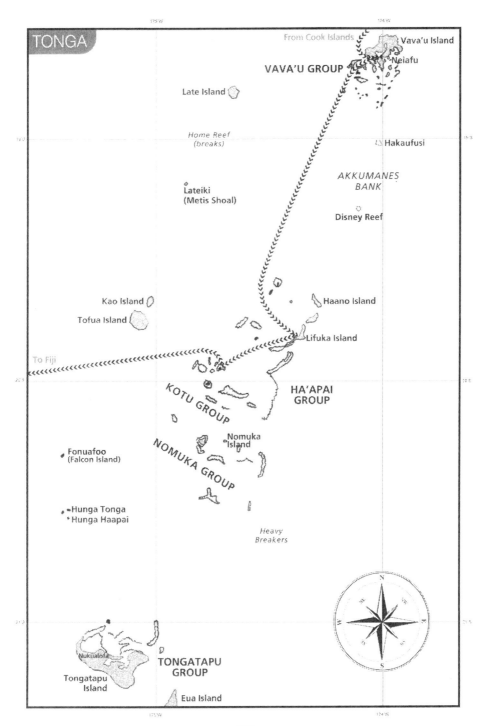

knots. As we had full sail up I kept bearing away to lower the apparent wind speed. This was our normal tactic when there was a temporary strengthening in the wind. I thought that perhaps it would settle down again as forecast so that I could get back on course, but an hour went by and it didn't. We needed to reef the mainsail. I was worried because I was now 30 degrees off course. I thought about it. We needed two people to reef the mainsail, but at night in a strong wind and big sea I probably needed to wake both Max and Luke. Luke had only been down for an hour and I was loathe to disturb him. I was also very aware that if I did go down to wake him it would mean leaving the wheel, and I was afraid the autopilot might click off again, causing an accidental gybe, as it did when Luke was at the chart table. Although the odds against that happening were minimal, the more I thought about it the more I didn't like the idea of leaving the wheel.

I tried to persuade myself that the wind would drop, but if anything it was increasing. Now I was sailing almost dead downwind and the boat was really being overpowered. It took a lot of concentration but it wasn't long until the end of my watch. As soon as Max came up I said, "We need to reef." He called Luke right away and they put two reefs in the mainsail, and we came back up on a reach. The boat was immediately more comfortable and we resumed our course. In the two hours I had been on watch we had come off course and had been sailing on the limit of what was safe with full sail. I had made a mistake in not calling Luke at the beginning. I was annoyed with myself and vowed to be less hesitant to call crew up to reef during the night in future.

On Sunday 5 August we crossed the International Date Line, so it was suddenly Monday 6 August. We had lost a day in our lives! This is why Tonga likes to call itself "The place where time begins." The next day, Luke sighted Tonga at dawn and shortly afterward he saw the magnificent sight of a humpback whale that came up to spout just a few boat lengths away. I was asleep but hoped we would see them again, because according to our pilot books it was the season when humpback whales migrate to Tonga to breed.

When I came on deck at eight that morning I was surprised to see high cliffs on the horizon. It was a very different landscape from the flat coral islands fringed with palm trees that we had become used to. As we made our way between the cliffs it reminded me of entering a river estuary in the west of England, Dartmouth perhaps, and we watched, fascinated, as the green hills and fields slipped by and we made our way into the totally sheltered anchorage at Neiafu. We tied up alongside the commercial wharf at 9:35 AM to clear customs. We had logged 740 miles and taken one hour less than four days, averaging 7.8 knots. In our best twenty-four-hour period we did 215 miles and in our slowest 162 miles.

The Kingdom of Tonga, the sole remaining Polynesian kingdom, is made up of 170 islands, of which 134 are uninhabited. The population is only 112,000. It was first settled in ancient times, perhaps as long ago as 2500 BC, by migrants from Southeast Asia. Although Dutch navigators discovered the islands in 1616, it wasn't until Captain Cook came in 1773 and 1777 that there was any European knowledge of Tonga, which Cook called "The Friendly Islands." Cook and his men traded metals and weapons for food and water, bark, cloth, and other primitive curiosities, which were later marveled over in European society drawing rooms.

Neiafu, where we docked, is the capital of Vava'u, the northern group of islands. The small town overlooking the harbor was full of activity, with waterfront bars, restaurants, a market for fresh food and fish, and shops selling most things we needed. Perhaps the most tempting was the bakery with its smell of freshly baked bread, croissants, and pastries. It was all such a contrast to the Cook Islands we had left behind! Wandering down the main street it wasn't at all obvious which shops sold what. If we wanted liquor, for instance, we discovered we had to go to the furniture shop. But the most bizarre location was for frozen meat. After making enquiries we were given directions to a house up a side road, but when we walked into the yard we saw only broken cars. A lady came out to greet us with a cheery smile. "Yes, you are in the right place," she said and took us out to a shed filled with freezers. The meat was from New Zealand and good quality, so we took advantage of the opportunity to stock up the freezer.

There were several interesting bars and cafés on the hill overlooking the harbour. While we were having lunch there we met an Australian couple, Greg and Debbie Cockle, who became good friends. They owned a yacht called *Volare*, a Catalina 42, which Greg had bought in California and was sailing back to Australia with Debbie. I liked him and we spent a lot of time with them in the four weeks that we were in Vava'u. We had similar backgrounds, both of us having started our business lives selling advertising space. Greg had gone on to be the advertising manager of Telstra, Australia's telecommunications giant, and then moved from being a client to being head of an international advertising agency in Southeast Asia. He had taken a sabbatical during that time to sail through Southeast Asia, but now he was semiretired and sailing across the Pacific.

The Moorings yacht charter company has a base in Vava'u. It is an unusual but perfect location for sailing holidays with dozens of beautiful islands and safe anchorages within a few hours sailing. The winds are usually pleasant 15-knot breezes and the sea is flat because of the protection the islands provide. Yacht charterers keep the town busy, and many small businesses have sprung up to support them. A steady flow of cruising yachts arrive from the Pacific and others come up from New Zealand and Australia. In total I must have counted over seventy yachts anchored or moored in this picturesque harbour.

One of the enterprising waterfront bars, the Mermaid, which also calls itself the Vava'u Yacht Club, organizes a yacht race around the harbour every Friday night. It was primarily aimed at the yacht charterers from the Moorings, but the cruising boats that are passing by are encouraged to join in and it is great spectator sport for the bar customers, who get a running commentary. We decided that *Moonraker* was too large to race in the confined spaces of the harbour so I was delighted when Greg invited me to race on *Volare*.

It was just a fun race, but put a skipper behind a wheel against seven other yachts and how the adrenaline starts to flow! We counted down the seconds to the start and were on the line for the gun but too far to leeward, so had to tack to make the windward mark and went round in fourth place. We made up places on the downwind leg, and moved up to second. Then we heard on the radio that the lead boat, a 50-foot racing yacht, had not checked in before the start and had to go back to the last mark as a penalty. Their skipper was a Kiwi and the normally quiet Greg, who was all fired up now, surprised me by shouting, "Aussie, Aussie, Aussie, Oi, Oi, Oi," as we passed them on their way back to the mark.

It looked as if we would now be in first place but a wind shift in the Kiwi's favour minimized their penalty. *Volare* crossed the line second but Greg was happy. He had done well. As soon as we got the sails down out came the cold "tinnies"—Fosters, of course. Later in the Vava'u Yacht Club a noisy crowd of "yachties" talked the race over again. It brought back happy memories of our own racing days a long time ago.

But despite the fun we were having I still felt unsettled. The problem was that Janet and I had not made a plan of what we would do after we got to New Zealand. I had only committed to crossing the Pacific. We had agreed that we would take stock when we got there and then decide what to do, but I thought Janet assumed that we would carry on sailing around the world. I had the feeling that she loved it so much she would like to go on doing it forever. I felt like the captain of *The Flying Dutchman*, the ghost ship that could never go home. I knew how much it meant to her but I now had serious doubts about how long I wanted to live the ocean nomad life. I had a strong sense that my time was running out. At sixty-seven it is not hard to calculate the years left—to estimate the average age of death as, say, eighty, take off the final years of being old and infirm, and come up with a sum that is the active years of life left—say ten in my case. There was so much I wanted to do, and the years fly by so quickly. I wanted to see if I could become a writer, an unfulfilled ambition since my school days, I wanted to design and build a dream house with Janet, I wanted to see if there was one last business idea in me, and I wanted to see more of our grandchildren growing up. So much to do and so little time to do it . . .

Sitting with Janet in a quiet open-air restaurant one balmy evening I sensed that the moment had come to bring the subject up. Feeling rather awkward, I began to explain. She took my hand and smiled. "I knew you felt like that," she said. "Don't worry about it." It was such a relief to get it off my chest. "But what will we do when we get to New Zealand?" I asked. She paused and said, "Why don't we ship the boat to the Mediterranean? We can have it there by early summer next year and have all the family and grandchildren on the boat for their summer holidays. We could cruise in Turkey, Greece, and Croatia, places we have never been to, and then put *Moonraker* up for sale at the end of next year." I was dumbstruck. It was such a simple solution. Now that we had discussed the problem, and we had a plan that Janet was happy with, I felt that a weight had been lifted from my shoulders. I had a spring in my step as we strolled down the street.

* * *

We thought that the best way to see the island of Vava'u was to have a guided taxi tour and we were lucky enough to find Semisi to be our guide. He was young, well educated, and spoke very good English. Because he had a German wife he had spent time in Europe. I think this gave him a better perspective of his homeland, and as we drove around the island he not only pointed out the sites of interest, he also gave us insight into the political and cultural history of Tonga.

Perhaps what was most interesting was that, although we appreciated that Tonga was a monarchy, we had not realized that it was essentially still a feudal system, rather like that which prevailed in England in the Middle

Ages, with the king and the nobles ruling the country. Some aspects of this semi-serfdom were abolished by King George Tupou I in 1845. He gave his country a constitution and representative parliamentary government based in some respects on the British model, and established a system of land tenure, whereby every Tongan male upon reaching the age of sixteen was entitled to rent an "api" of eight acres (a plot of bush land) and a village allotment of about half an acre to build his home. But the king and the nobles still rule the country and trouble was brewing.

When the British think of Tonga, those of a certain age will remember Queen Salote, who attended Queen Elizabeth's coronation in 1953. Hundreds of thousands of loyal British subjects had bought televisions for the coronation and were mesmerized by the ample body of Queen Salote travelling in an open carriage. Sitting next to her was a diminutive sultan. Noel Coward is reputed to have famously quipped that her travelling companion was "her lunch." It was a rainy day and Queen Elizabeth travelled through the streets of London in a covered carriage, but Queen Salote remained bareheaded to show Tongan respect in the presence of someone of higher rank. Through that gesture she won the hearts of the British people and they mourned her passing in 1965.

Since then, the Tongan royal family has had a chequered record. Queen Salote was succeeded by her son, King Taufa'ahau Tupou IV. He developed a reputation for corrupt, get-rich-quick schemes, and lost many millions of the country's money, and to this day Tonga lurches from one economic crisis to the next. Although it gained full sovereignty from Britain in 1970 and was admitted to the Commonwealth, the king was reluctant to embark on domestic political reform and this led to unrest.

The pro-democracy movement (THRDM) that had begun in the 1970s had been gradually gaining influence, initially through strike action, but in 2006 there were violent riots in the capital Nuku'alofa. Many buildings were burned down in a demonstration against the new king, George Tupou V, who had continued to deny the people democracy.

Semisi himself had mixed feelings about all this. Although he felt a traditional loyalty to the king, as a young man who had travelled in Europe he felt that the absolute power of the king and the nobles was wrong, and that the people should have majority representation in parliament. He explained that the single legislature was composed of the cabinet, nine nobles, and nine elected people's representatives. The cabinet consisted of the prime minister and other ministers who were appointed for life, and all but two of them were nobles.

On the other hand he wasn't happy about the violent demonstrations. "That would never happen here in Vava'u," he said. As a result, the new king postponed his coronation following advice that it could only inflame matters further. Interestingly, while writing this book, I read in the *Daily Telegraph* that the coronation has now taken place. King George Tupou V, at the age of sixty, was formally crowned King of Tonga on 1 August 2008. *The Telegraph* reported: "The ceremony was carried out with great pomp and circumstance, the king resplendent in crisp white stockings and shiny black shoes, sitting on a huge golden throne in front of a thousand guests, including the Duke and Duchess of Gloucester, Crown Prince Naruhito of Japan, and the Maori King of New Zealand." He was anointed by the archbishop of Polynesia because Tongans are prohibited from coming into physical contact with the monarch. Although the ceremony was carried out in traditional splendor I was interested to read that earlier in the week the king had pledged to divest himself of most of his feudal powers, dragging Tonga's constitution into the twenty-first century and allowing commoners to elect a majority of MPs for the first time. I think Semisi must have been pleased.[24]

We learned much about the traditions, culture, and lifestyle of the Tongan people from him. For most of the last century Tonga has been inward-looking and somewhat isolated from developments elsewhere in the world. Tongans as a whole have tended to cling to many of their old traditions, including respect for the nobility. However, the actions of the pro-democracy movement, better education, outside media influence, technology, and travel have slowly begun to change how Tongans see their lifestyle and society. Although Tongan society has traditionally been devoid of materialism, these advances are changing that. As Semisi rather bluntly put it, "A young Tongan man is happy if he has a flash car and a full belly."

But driving around with Semisi it still looked a very backward and isolated country. Nine out of ten adults are large and overweight as a result of a poor diet and lack of exercise. Free-range pigs run everywhere (Janet said she would remember Tonga as the "land of pigs") and fatty pork and root crops cooked in oil make up the staple diet. But Tongans have a deep sense of hospitality and are generous with their food and belongings, and welcomed us into their homes. Family is the core of Tongan life, with

---

24 *On 11 November 2009, the BBC reported that a powerful committee had recommended that the power of the monarchy be largely dismantled in favour of a fully elected parliament, and that King George Tupou V was likely to support its proposals.*

adopted children, cousins, and other relatives living together with parents and grandparents. Everything is shared, from food to sleeping arrangements. Household jobs are distributed according to gender. Men tend the umu (the underground oven), grow the food, catch the fish, and do manual work. The women clean, wash clothes, cook the food, and take care of the children. Most Tongans have their own house and the family plot of land, which makes them largely self-sufficient.

Semisi pointed out the island's prison, although we wouldn't have known it because all we could see were bungalows and well-tended gardens. "But there aren't any fences to keep them in," I said, puzzled. "It's not necessary," he replied. "They've got nowhere to escape to, and in any case everyone knows who they are, so it would be pointless."

As we came to a school we saw children playing a rugby match. I asked Semisi to stop the car so that we could watch. The boys were probably under fourteen but played with skill and enthusiasm. Running with the ball came naturally. They were wearing rugby shirts and shorts but I noticed that they had no boots on, although they kicked the ball well enough. "Why don't they wear boots?" I asked. He explained, "They don't wear shoes in everyday life so it feels very unnatural to put boots on to play rugby." I lingered for a while, watching their boyish exuberance, and thought what a great international equalizer sport is.

Semisi suggested that we spend a day visiting the Ene'io Botanical Garden. It was created by Haniteli O Fa'anunu and officially opened on 22 August 2006, by Her Royal Highness Princess Salote Pilolevu Tuita. The land had been in Haniteli's family for many years, but the garden is a retirement project for which he is well qualified, having been the minister for agriculture and fisheries. As a senior government minister from a leading family he was obviously well connected. I saw a photograph of him shaking hands with the pope. He had always had a great interest in trees, and had planted many hundreds of specimens throughout the garden, which he sees as a legacy for Tonga. Lucy, his young second wife is a charming university-educated woman who grew up in Nuku'alofa.

Together they are working hard to create a garden of distinction that will also be a cultural centre where visitors can see Tongans working at their crafts in a traditional setting. It is only open to large parties by appointment, but with Semisi's introduction, Haniteli and Lucy welcomed us at the gate as if we were royal visitors, draping flower garlands around our necks in a warm welcome that epitomized the hospitality and friendship of the Tongan people, whatever their station in life.

As we strolled along the paths in the cool dappled shade of a canopy of trees, we came upon men and women working at their traditional trades—weaving, wood carving, and mat making. In Tonga, craftwork is not a hobby for those who are artistically inclined; it has an important economic and cultural role in the community. Traditionally, Tongan wealth is measured in terms of tapa, the name commonly used to describe Pacific bark cloth and mats. The ladies were making the tapa cloth from the branches of Chinese paper mulberry trees, and then decorating it with animals and flowers using a stencil in earthy red, brown, and black colours. Weaving is equally important and pandanus mats are the most highly regarded examples of Tongan weaving, and are often made for weddings as well as everyday wear by men and women. Weavers also make floor coverings, baskets, belts, hats, and trays.

A beautiful white sand beach fringes the garden, and we watched women walking into the sea with pandanus leaves, which are left to soak for a fortnight in carefully marked zones and later retrieved to wash out the salt and dry in the sun. When they are dry the women work each leaf between their fingertips to make them more malleable, then they are cut into fine threadlike strips that are woven into taovala, the fine mats they wear around the waist.

We sat on the balcony of Haniteli's house watching the women walking back from the sea and commented on how fat many of the women were. Lucy smiled. "You should understand that in Tongan society fat women are prized by men and held in high regard because it can be seen by all that they can afford to eat well. A thin woman is pitied as someone who is not well looked after." She told us that even though she was from a well-to-do and well-educated family, her parents were concerned that, since her recent marriage, she had lost a great deal of weight to become what we would call "a more fashionable shape." Her parents worry that her husband is not feeding her properly!

A Tongan feast is something that visitors are urged not to miss and Haniteli and his wife were giving one that night for thirty tourists. It took place on the balcony of their house overlooking the exquisite Ene'io beach. Although it was a "paid for" event, Haniteli and his wife were perfect hosts and gave us our first insight into Tongan traditions. Suckling pig was the highlight of the feast, and we drank cold local beer as we watched the pigs roasted on spits in front of us. Freshly caught local fish had been cooked as well, along with rice and root vegetables. After dinner we were treated to a display of traditional Tongan dancing by women and children who worked on the estate. Dancing in Tonga is different from the dancing we had seen in the Society Islands, with its mesmerizing swaying of the hips. In Tonga, the female dancers move more subtly, with the emphasis on the arms and hands. Women and young children expressed themselves with feeling, their dances telling traditional stories of the history and culture of Tonga.

Captain Cook was impressed by Tongan dancing, too. A Tongan chief asked him and his men to entertain them and so they performed a poorly executed series of military exercises that ended with gunfire. The Tongans must have been nonplussed but returned the gesture with a polished traditional dance performance. Cook noted in his diaries, "This far exceeded anything we had done to amuse them." He tasted kava and witnessed many local rites, as we had just done. He enjoyed the food too. In Nomuka he ate fish cooked in coconut cream for the Ha'apai chief, Finau, and was so impressed that he ordered his own chef to cook fish the Tongan way.

A few days later we sailed down to the resort at Mounu Island. Greg and Debbie, our new friends on *Volare* who we met in Vava'u, had successfully bid for a free dinner there at a charity auction, so we went along to join them. It was good to be sailing again after spending time in Neiafu. Initially we went the required ten miles off shore to jettison our black tank (toilet waste), something we don't have to worry about out on the ocean. Then we tacked back against the wind to Mounu Island. The sun shone out of a blue sky with puffy cumulus clouds and the brisk breeze on my face felt good. The sea was flat, protected by the many islands, making for fast sailing. This was quite different from long ocean passages. I was using the wheel to steer and not the autopilot and I could feel the power of the boat through the rudder. Luke and Max stood by the sheets to make a quick tack as we came close to an island where the water became shallow. Then as the boat heeled to the breeze on the new tack they trimmed the sails for maximum speed. With frequent tacking we picked our way through the islands until we reached the Mounu Island Resort and dropped the anchor in crystal clear water.

Mounu is a very small private island resort with sparkling white beaches fringed with palm trees, a picture perfect pacific island (www.mounuisland.com). There are just four cottages for guests and a small clubhouse/restaurant. After pulling the dinghy up through the surf on the beach we looked wet and bedraggled as we stepped up onto the wooden deck. We needn't have worried that we would be out of place. The eight resort guests sitting at the large solid wooden tables overlooking the beach were also barefoot, dressed in faded jeans and sun-bleached shirts and blouses.

The dinner was splendid and we sat out in the soft warm evening air swapping yarns with Greg and Debbie. Later we were delighted to meet the owner, Alan Bowe, who came to sit at our table. You couldn't ever miss Alan. He is a larger than life character, a sixty-three-year-old weather-beaten sea salt with a huge bushy white beard (like Uncle Albert in *Only Fools and Horses*). But appearances can be deceptive. Alan was an advertising whiz kid who had his own agency in New Zealand and sold out to Saatchi & Saatchi when he was only forty. He sailed a charter boat in the South Pacific for a few years and then one day, when he was watching humpback whales in Tonga, he jumped in the water with them to see what it would be like!

From that small beginning the whale-watching business in Tonga was spawned. Now there are thirteen licensed operators, and Tonga is world famous for swimming with whales. Alan has cornered a niche in the market, catering to an up-market clientele who come to his exclusive desert island hideaway to see whales. Television companies from all over the world are taken out by Alan to film these amazing creatures. The week after our visit a crew from the BBC was coming for two weeks.

As the wine-mellowed evening drew on, we were absorbed by Alan's tales of how he had had to adapt to do business in Tonga. He fell in love with Mounu Island when he first saw it and wanted to obtain a fifty-year lease (foreigners are not allowed to buy land). It was crown land and it would be difficult to get permission, so he bought the finest pig he could find. It cost him five hundred paanga (Tonga dollars) but he spared no expense and personally delivered it to the then governor of Vava'u, the official who granted leases. The lease document was signed that day.

Next he had to get permission to build his resort. He knew what he had to do so he bought two big wahoo and sent them down to the capital on Tongatapu, by plane, asking his agent to meet the aircraft and deliver the fish to the then-minister of lands. She phoned him and was very upset.

"Alan, the fish weren't on the plane."

"What do you mean they weren't on the plane?"

"They said they couldn't take them."

"You mean they did take them!" Alan remarked dryly.

Undeterred, he caught two huge yellowfin tuna and took them on the plane himself and delivered them personally to the minister of lands who beamed with delight as he was going to a royal feast for the Tongan queen's seventieth birthday that night and was able to take them as his gift. Permission was granted!

The new king was not popular with all his subjects and in November 2006, after the riots, Alan saw an opportunity and sought an audience with the king. "Your majesty, your image is not good with the people. You are seen as a taker and not a giver. I know how you can change that." (Good advertising psychology: Identify the client's weakness and then tell him how you can correct it.) "I would like you to grant me the world media rights to your coronation. I will negotiate substantial fees from the world's media networks for the rights to film it. There are so few ruling monarchies left in the world that I believe it will attract much media interest. We will set up an educational charity in your name and the money will be used to provide computers for every school, and your people will be grateful and see you as a giver."

World media rights granted! Once an advertising man, always an advertising man. What an interesting person.[25]

Away from the main island of Vava'u there are many small islands in the Vava'u Group that are only accessible to yachts. We went ashore on an island called Nuapapu, where we had our first taste of village life in the outer islands. The island had two villages. When we arrived at the first, Mataka, it seemed very quiet, which puzzled us, but then we found out that the men were all out fishing and the women were in a communal hut weaving. One of the women, Sara, came to greet us and showed us her simple home and their umu, the hole in the ground where they make a fire to heat stones to cook on twice a day. She introduced us to Fa'aka, who spoke English and took us round the village. It was not good manners to wander uninvited and unaccompanied through a village and it was customary Tongan hospitality for the women to show visitors around. Fa'aka had been educated in Nuku'alofa to the age of eighteen, but had married a local fisherman and come back here to live. It was fortunate that she spoke English quite well because the locals don't and you miss so much if you can't communicate. Most of the villagers here left school at eleven with only the most basic education. As we strolled around she pointed out a small hut that has the only telephone in the village. If there was a phone call the nearest passerby answered it and then shouted out a name and the message got passed down the village to the person being called to the phone!

---

25 *The king chose to establish a trust with the funds generated ($400,000) to combat diabetes, which is a huge problem in the kingdom.*

Fa'aka took us to the communal hut where the women sat on the floor weaving, and we watched them making the mats they sell. Then the fun started. One of them started singing and soon they all joined in the traditional Polynesian melody. Another lady began a song and this one involved clapping so I joined in. When one lady started dancing (they were all large middle-aged ladies, by the way) I joined in with a bit of a dance of my own. They loved this! One woman got up and came over to get me to dance with her. All of them were in fits of laughter now, but I didn't understand why. I thought they were laughing at my dancing. We had several more dances and then Fa'aka explained what they were singing and why they were laughing. They were making up the words of the song as they went along:

"If I dance with you will you give me ten paanga for washing powder?"

So of course I gave my new friend ten paanga and then there was another song and dance. As you can probably guess the words this time were something like:

"Thank you so much! Now I can go and do my washing!"

They were all laughing again. We had so much fun.

Well, this was such a success, and they could see that I was a good sport, so they told Fa'aka that we had been invited to their traditional Tongan feast on Saturday, in five days time. She said that it was a special annual event and the ladies would dress me in traditional Tongan costume and want to dance with me! We were thrilled to be invited and promised to return along with Luke and Max.

That afternoon we took the dinghy and motored around to the next village. As soon as we got out of the dinghy we were overwhelmed by a crowd of young boys aged between five and ten, who had just come out of school, looking smart in clean white shirts and blue shorts. They took our hands and bombarded us with questions.

"What is your name?"

"You take boy to boat."

"Come to school."

"Play football."

They seemed so sincere and so friendly that we were touched by their unqualified friendship.

"You got lolly?" they asked. Lolly meant sweets. Sadly we had used up all our kiddy presents in the last village, so we had nothing to give them but it didn't seem to matter.

"You come see school."

They reached out for our hands and pulled us along the narrow path through the woods, full of chatter and excitement. It was very touching. At the school we met their teacher. She has sixteen boys and one girl, her daughter, in the school. They all work in one large room and she told us she finds it very hard teaching a mixed-age group. There is only one textbook for the whole class so that lessons have to be written out on the blackboard each day. It must be hard work but the standard of education seemed quite high. We looked through the exercise books at the standard of writing of the eight-year-olds. It seemed similar to what we would have expected in England. Here, as in most of Polynesia, education has the highest priority, and despite the lack of resources there is a real will to succeed among teachers, children, and parents.

One little boy, who seemed to have adopted me, stared into my face with his big brown eyes and implored me to come to meet his grandmother. He took me by the hand and led me to her hut. She was very old. Her thin white hair was neatly brushed back, and she was bent almost double by arthritis. But she seemed pleased that her grandson was introducing her to his new friend. She spoke no English, which was a great pity because we were unable to converse at all, but we watched her loving grandson together and she smiled as I ruffled his hair.

When we got back to the school the boys wanted me to play football with them on the grass in front of the schoolhouse. They were excited and exuberant, just like boys anywhere, and it was fun to be with them. They all wanted to come back to the boat, but Janet was concerned that it might get out of hand. I thought that was a pity but I didn't argue and went back to the boat on my own to find some small gifts while Janet waited at the broken stone wharf with the boys. When I returned with coloured pencils, one paanga and a Coke for each boy they screamed with delight.

Our experiences in these two villages showed us the true nature of the Tongan people—open, friendly, and warm. They are very poor, and that upset us, but they live happily as they have for generations. But as the standard of education rises, children's aspirations will rise, too, and then no doubt they will look for a more prosperous life overseas. Already half the GDP of Tonga comes from Tongans overseas sending money home, and that can only increase. What future then for these South Pacific islands?

* * *

"Look now, right behind us." We spun round and just twenty feet behind our small inflatable rib[26] a huge black whale rose up out of the water. No one said anything. We just watched in awe. Then it dove and we didn't see it again. Janet and I were on a full-day whale-watching trip. Paul, our professional guide, was an experienced diver and marine biologist who we'd hoped would find whales and give us an understanding of their behavior. We weren't going to be disappointed.

Soon we saw our second whale and sped over to it. "That's a good sign," Paul told us. "It's logging." This meant that the whale was lying still in the water, like a log, indicating that it was happy for us to have "an encounter." But then this whale dove, too, and by timing the intervals it was down, Paul decided it didn't want to play.

We searched around for a while but didn't see any more. Paul explained that whale watching is a waiting game. I was so thrilled to have seen these two whales close up that I didn't really mind if nothing else happened.

But it did. Whales began to appear in several places in the distance and we saw the telltale spouts of water. Then black humps appeared as they broke the surface. Paul watched for signs that one was interested in us. If they dove, or just kept swimming, he left them alone.

Then Paul shouted, "Over there!" We spun round to see the amazing sight of a whale breaching—jumping high out of the water, showing its white underside and big flippers before crashing back into the water again. A second whale treated us to a breaching display and incredibly we managed to capture both these moments on camera.

When we did find one that lay still in the water Paul asked, "Who wants to swim with it?" Only four swimmers are allowed in the water at one time so I was first to volunteer. (I was very glad I did, as we were not to have another opportunity to swim with them again that day.) I put on my wet suit, snorkel, mask and fins, slipped quietly into the water, and swam toward the whale. I swam up really close, about fifteen feet away, and saw its big eye watching me. I wasn't at all frightened because I was with a professional I trusted. I remember thinking, "This is something I will never forget." But when I got closer it flicked its tail, dived vertically, and disappeared into the deep.

It was hard to imagine that the day could get more exciting, but it did. After a long period of waiting we moved to another area, and Paul spotted a group of whales making the water boil as they thrashed around.

---

26 *A rib is an inflatable boat with a rigid bottom that allows it to motor at high speed.*

By chance we had latched onto a "heat run." The female was being pursued by six males eager to be chosen as her mate. It involves a "rumble," a lot of jostling as the males tried to push each other out of the way. Everyone was enthralled. Even Paul was enjoying it. The pod cruised along in a line, swimming very fast, and we kept our distance about hundred and fifty feet away from them. Now, unlike earlier, they were oblivious to us, concentrating only on the female. We continued in this way for two hours as they dived with their flukes (tails) high in the air, or pushed up out of the water, showing their heads, upper bodies, and fins. It was truly fascinating and words can hardly describe our feelings. Reluctantly we had to break off after two hours to make our way home again. It seems trite to say, "It was the experience of a lifetime," but that's how we felt.

I learned a lot about humpback whales that day. They are the most active and playful of all whales and live in either the Arctic or Antarctica, migrating to the Pacific in August to breed and calve. A humpback can grow to fifty feet long and weigh forty to forty-five tons. Their food is krill (small shrimps) and they eat four tons a day when they are in Antarctica, but they eat nothing when they breed in the South Pacific. A pregnancy lasts eleven months, so a female will mate in Tonga one year and return to the same place to calve the following year. Humpbacks from Antarctica have white underbellies and those from the Arctic are dark, and the two never mix. Each year about two or three hundred humpbacks come to Tongan waters from Antarctica to breed, while Arctic whales migrate elsewhere in the South Pacific.

There were once three hundred thousand humpbacks in the ocean but hunting has depleted their number. It is estimated that there are only ten thousand left. They are an endangered species protected by the International Whaling Commission (IWC) but despite this the Japanese would still be killing them if it were not for the efforts of Greenpeace. IWC delegates have voiced concern at Japan's attempts to reintroduce and increase commercial and scientific whaling, and in June 2005 the bid by Japan and other countries that the existing IWC moratorium be lifted was defeated by only a narrow margin.

Tongans themselves have hunted whales for centuries, consuming whale meat and using whalebone in numerous traditional ways. Until a royal decree in 1979, around ten humpbacks were caught every year. Today, however, much of Tonga's tourist industry depends on protecting them. Whale watching is big business in July and August each year. However, there are some who question whether swimming with whales is safe or ecologically sound. Our experience was that it was extremely well regulated and only carried out by licensed operators who had experienced marine biologists on every boat and followed strict rules of engagement.

We were so thrilled by our experience that we decided to make another trip. I was hoping that this time I would have the opportunity to spend more time swimming with them, because now I was convinced that this *was* the experience of a lifetime, and it wouldn't come round again. This time we went out on a boat owned by Alan Bowe from Mounu Island, and our guide was Valerie, a charming young French marine biologist.

We saw whales early on, but our first three attempts to get in the water with them failed when the whale dove as we began to swim toward it. It was obvious that these huge creatures are really very shy and to get an "up close" encounter is not easy.

Our captain, who knew where to look, headed out to open sea, but it was an hour before we spotted a whale some way off. It was immediately interesting because it kept slapping its fluke on the top of the water over and over again. It is not understood why they do this—perhaps they are trying to get pests off their body, or perhaps they are just having fun—but it is fascinating. The whale allowed us to take the boat up close, about three hundred feet away. The captain stopped the engine and we watched.

The whale seemed to become more curious and came right up to our boat, lifting its head out of the water as if it were trying to look at us. Then it swam upside down along the side of the boat and dove underneath. It was incredibly close. At times it seemed that it was touching the boat, although I don't think it actually did, and this carried on for at least half an hour.

The photographs I took are a lifelong reminder of this incredible experience. In some you can see the back of the boat with the head of the whale right behind it as it rose slowly out of the water. What the photographs don't tell you is what the atmosphere was like on the boat. There was no sense of fear. These big creatures are so gentle and yet agile, and in no way threatening. It seemed as if it was showing off for us and we loved it. Everyone was caught up in the excitement and there was a contagious feeling of happiness. We felt as if we were forming an affinity with the whale. Valerie told us that a display like this is a "once-in-a-season" event and for her it seemed to be a spiritual experience.

After half an hour we were allowed to get into the water with the whale. Valerie had been concerned that if we had gone in earlier we might have frightened it away. I was in the sea in a flash, not wanting to miss

Swimming with Whales

anything, but I needn't have worried. The whale was still friendly and curious.

Under the crystal clear blue water I entered another world. It was totally silent. The noise and babble of excitement from the boat had vanished. I saw the whale, just thirty feet from me, in no way inhibited by our presence in the water. Indeed it seemed to me that he relished it, performing the most graceful underwater ballet, rolling over to show us his white underside, diving down vertically and then rolling on his back to come up again. At one point he swam straight toward me, coming up from below so close that I felt sure he would touch me, but he didn't. Janet was watching from the boat and she thought he was going to come up with me on his back!

Finally he came into a vertical position, flippers thrown open in a crucifix gesture, head some ten feet out of the water. He held that pose for a minute or so as if taking a curtain call. By looking above and below the water I could see the whale from top to tail, a part of him in two worlds, divided by the shiny surface of the sea. It was a sublime experience to watch this forty-five-ton creature perform this ballet so gracefully and so delicately in front of an audience of four human beings.

The encounter exceeded anything I could have imagined. It was the most wonderful wildlife experience of my life. It engendered unfamiliar emotions, an ethereal feeling and a sense of affinity with the whale that I can't explain. The creature was so spontaneously friendly, so trusting! A terrifying vision flashed through my mind—the sea darkened by blood as this trusting whale approached a Japanese whaling ship, only to be cruelly harpooned. It was a chilling feeling and I wished I could warn the whale to beware of humans.

no song either
no humpback hum
just hopeless radio talkback
and the voices of politicians
drowning out the blood sounds
of another fifty whales
dying this summer
that man made song
the sound of dying
safe journey marine queen
the blue tapou of our ocean islands
may your song outlive ours.

—Karlo Mila: Safe Journey

* * *

We returned to the village of Mataka for the annual village feast day on Saturday afternoon and were warmly greeted on the broken stone wharf by Fa'aka and her husband, Ben. We had no idea what to expect and it was to be a day full of surprises.

Fa'aka explained to us that the feast was an annual event to raise money for the church, and senior ministers from the Church of Tonga had come from as far away as the capital in Nuku'alofa, over a hundred miles away. After an hour of buildup, with drum beating and tin bashing, the ministers arrived by boat. We were then invited into a hut to witness the kava ceremony. Kava is a traditional drink, a slightly narcotic brew made from the kava root. It looks like dirty dish water and I was told that it makes your face numb, but I assume it gives you a good feeling. On this occasion the men drank the kava in a formal ceremony. Only the village leaders and the ministers were included, all sitting cross-legged on a mud floor covered by coconut matting. After many prayers, one person dispensed the drink from a giant bowl into a half coconut shell and passed it to another, who carried the shell to each waiting minister, who slowly raised it to his lips and solemnly drank.

We were relieved when we were told we did not have to drink the kava, so having witnessed the ceremony we left and waited for the church service. It began with a solemn address by the presiding minister and was followed by rousing hymn singing from the congregation. They sang in natural harmonies and the church resonated with haunting melodies. Children ran around inside playing with the yellow balloons we had distributed earlier, but nobody seemed to mind.

Then some bizarre scenes followed. A large lady dressed in a gold skirt and a black cap strode into church and addressed the audience while the minister was still speaking. We were perplexed. Was this some madwoman? Then she pulled out a mobile phone and play-acted trying to make a phone call but getting no reception. For our benefit, I think, she kept saying, "Hello, hello." Everyone was in hoots of laughter, but the service continued as though it weren't happening.

Another lady with tin cans and our yellow balloons tied to her skirt seemed to get into an argument with the first lady and stormed around the aisles trying to drag her husband up to the front. She pretended to take photographs of the congregation with an imaginary camera, which everyone thought was very funny.

A third woman appeared dressed all in black with a large homemade Tongan flag draped over her shoulder and carrying a rugby ball. She propped the ball up in the aisle as if to take a penalty kick, threatening that if her husband did not come with her, she would kick the ball causing goodness knows what chaos. So he got up from his seat, she picked up the ball, and they walked arm in arm up to the altar.

We watched mesmerized, although we were bemused about what it all meant. It had all the elements of a Whitehall farce and it was just as professional and funny, but in this case the vicar didn't take his trousers down. We didn't understand what was happening but we hooted with laughter. Fa'aka explained that they were showing how happy they were to be able to give away their money to the church.

Then the collection was taken by a man who looked like something from a Quentin Tarantino gangster movie. He had a black suit, black shades with gold trim, black shirt, and pink tie. If you looked inside his jacket you wouldn't have been surprised to see a gun. When he came calling you were going to give, and my goodness did they give. He went round five times but we didn't understand why. Up at the altar the ministers were busy counting up the notes, putting them into piles by denomination, and entering the amounts into an accounts book. It seemed rather mercenary.

With all this money-collecting going on, we were feeling uncomfortable that we had not contributed and had not even been approached by the black-suited collector. However, when we first came ashore and met Fa'aka we'd asked about making a contribution to the feast, and she told us that it would be greatly appreciated if each of us would give twenty dollars, which the ladies who invited us could add to their donation, which we did. I would have been much happier if the money had gone to them, but she insisted it was what the ladies wanted. Now I asked her again whether we should be giving money, but she insisted that it was not appropriate.

After the money was counted the service continued. By this time it was four in the afternoon and we were getting quite hungry, and apparently so were some of the congregation. One of the women who was play-acting marched up to the minister while he was preaching, dove onto the floor in front of him, and loudly remonstrated. I asked Fa'aka what she'd said. She told me, "This service is going on far too long. We are hungry and we want our feast." This also met with howls of laughter from the congregation. It seemed very irreverent, but I feel sure we must have misunderstood much of what was going on. I took out my camera but was immediately told that no photographs were allowed in the church, which of course we respected.

The service finally ended half an hour later and we walked to the community hut next door where the feast was laid out. We sat in the hut on the matted floor with our legs crossed, along with the ministers, the village elders, and their wives and children. This was only a small section of the community and it was obviously a VIP affair. I was disappointed not to see the ladies I had danced with and who had done all the cooking.

The food was spread out on the floor under a muslin cloth and after the speeches the cloth was removed to reveal a magnificent feast: suckling pig, lobster, grilled fish, raw fish, octopus, fish cooked in green taro leaves, sweet and sour sauces, yam, potato, salad, risotto, omelets, cakes, and much more that I can't remember. The locals used their fingers to eat directly from each dish but only Janet, Luke, Max, and I had been given a china plate and a plastic spoon.

As we tucked in the speeches continued, with all of us chanting "malo," which means thank you, at the appropriate moment. The minister made a welcoming speech in excellent English, saying how special it was for the village to have "polangi" (foreigners) with them for their feast. I made what I hoped was an appropriate reply in English and of course thanked the ladies who had cooked such a wonderful meal.

I assumed that the rest of the village would troop in for a second sitting, but instead they came to collect the massive amounts of food left and take it back to their own huts. There was no drinking and no dancing, which was a pity, and it saddened me that the ladies who had invited us were unable to join in the meal. Even here, where everyone is poor, it seems that it is not a classless society. Religion is the backbone of the Tongan community and their traditional life. They have so little money, yet they give so much to the church. I asked the minister what the money they collected was used for, thinking that perhaps it went to provide schools and hospitals. However he told me that it paid for the upkeep of churches and minister's salaries, accommodation, and travelling expenses. When I queried how they could afford to give so much, he told me a story about Gandhi and the power of giving and concluded, "They may be poor, but they like to give, too." It made me stop and think about the pleasure of giving and the gulf between the cultures of the developed and third world countries.

From the Vava'u Group we sailed south to the next group of islands, the Ha'apai Group, which are even more isolated and in many cases uninhabited. It was here, in April 1789, between the islands of Tofua and Nomuka, that Fletcher Christian and his men took part in the most famous mutiny in British naval history, taking command of *HMS Bounty* and putting Captain William Bligh and eighteen crew adrift in an open boat. They were given only one hundred and fifty pounds of biscuits, twenty pounds of salted meat, one hundred and twenty pounds of water, the ship's log, a compass, and a sextant. They came ashore on the nearby island of Tofua but were met by hostile islanders who killed the quartermaster and they fled for their lives. Bligh and his shipmates reached Timor in the Dutch East Indies on 14 June 1789, with a remarkable story of survival after sailing 3618 nautical miles, the longest ever ocean voyage in a small open boat.

The mutineers sailed the *Bounty* back to Tahiti, where they had earlier spent five months gathering breadfruit, and sixteen men decided to stay there and take their chances of being recaptured by the Royal Navy and hanged—which they were. Fletcher Christian sailed away in the *Bounty* with the eight remaining crew, plus six Tahitian men and eleven women. After a voyage searching for a safe haven they eventually settled on the Pitcairn Islands. Christian was killed there in a bloody internal fight in 1793, only four years after the mutiny, but his descendants still live there today. As I closed my eyes I could imagine Fletcher Christian, desperately torn in his loyalties, crying out "I am in hell, I am in hell," before finally ordering Bligh and his loyal crew into the ship's boat, here at this spot on the ocean where we were now.

On Friday 24 August we anchored at a small island called Ha'afeva. It was a surprise to find another yacht in this remote place. She was called *Blue Stocking,* a 42-foot American ketch, and the owner, Paul, called us up on the radio for a chat. We invited him over for a drink with his wife, Janet, and their son Fred. They had already been ashore and met some of the local people, and they told us that we were included in an invitation to go to church with them the next day and then have a meal with a family they had met.

Luke and Max went diving on Sunday so Janet and I walked up to the village with the folks from *Blue Stocking.* It was an hour's walk but with only one path we couldn't get lost. Lepolo, the girl who had invited them to church, met us halfway and took us to her village. It was in a picturesque location on a beach and protected by a reef. The village was very small, just one sandy street with a few houses down each side, no cars, and just a few bicycles, but five churches. We could hear lusty singing. It definitely felt like Sunday.

The Wesleyan service we attended was more familiar to us than others we had been to, with prayers, lessons, and hymns that had numbers set out on a board. Hymnbooks were provided but they were in Polynesian of course. As usual the singing was magnificent with uplifting harmonies, the women counterbalancing the men and everyone singing their hearts out. The female lay preacher welcomed us warmly in English during the service, saying that they were privileged to have us with them in their church. I took a hymnbook and tried to follow the words but my attempts to sing were rather pathetic, other than "Amen."

After the service we spoke to the minister. Her full-time job was nursing in Nuku'alofa, but she was filling in here until a replacement was found. She was a middle-aged woman in her forties, a broad figure but not fat, with black hair swept up tightly on her head. She was appropriately but smartly dressed in a black silk blouse and black jacket with her trousers covered by a taovala, the woven mat worn round the waist to ankle length. She spoke English well and kindly asked us if we would like to join her for lunch. We thanked her and explained that we had already been invited by Lepolo and her family. She helped to answer many of the questions we had about life in the village and why such a small community had so many churches, all with services at the same time. She explained that in this very religious country there were four principle Christian denominations, Wesleyan (the most popular), Roman Catholic, the Church of Jesus Christ of Latter-Day Saints (Mormons), and the Free Church of Tonga. That left room for Tongans who were Anglicans, Seventh-Day Adventists, and Jehovah's Witnesses, as well as a number of minority faiths. This religious freedom may ironically have come about as a result of the activities of the Wesleyan missionary Shirley Baker, a man who had a very strong influence over the king in the 1850s and became the premier. Together they formulated the laws to abolish serfdom and the sale of Tongan land to foreigners. But Baker's influence and royal patronage made him the object of jealousy in the Wesleyan Mission camp and they conspired to have him expelled from the church on charges of adultery. Baker's work continued undeterred. In 1879 the Wesleyan Church disassociated itself from him and he created the Free Church of Tonga. The king urged all Tongan Wesleyans to abandon their church and join Baker's new church. A holy war ensued and eventually the British consul stepped in and convinced the aging king that religious freedom was necessary. Perhaps this is why there is such a proliferation of churches in every village today?

We strolled down the street with Lepolo and she stopped to introduce us to the villagers as they came out of their respective churches, smartly dressed in their Sunday finery—a loose-fitting black jacket with a purple blouse and matching long skirt, a pale blue coat dress, a bright red jacket over a black skirt. A small girl wore a pristine white frock. They all covered their heads with woven straw hats.

Lepolo looked smartly dressed herself in a black jacket and skirt and chic sunglasses. She was only seventeen but turned out like this she looked older. Her skin was brown and her hair long and black. She had a good figure although there were already signs that she might become overweight as she got older. Like all Tongans she had poor teeth, even at this age; we saw no evidence of dental hygiene anywhere in Tonga. She seemed to be well educated and her English was good, with a confidence and maturity that I had not expected in this remote environment. Perhaps that came from living in Nuku'alofa with her elder sister, who had a good job with a bank. She had brought Lepolo there to get her away from the family and experience a different life, a modern life with a job and a salary. Lepolo had worked in a supermarket but to my surprise she said that she found the work hard and disliked the routine hours. She had returned to her village and a future that she could not explain to me. It puzzled me that, unlike her sister, she had rejected the modern lifestyle. The difference between my belief in the work ethic and the traditional Tongan way of life was something I had difficulty coming to terms with.

At the end of the street we came to the house where Lepolo lived with her family. I was surprised to find that it was just a shack, with old corrugated tin walls and a tin roof. On each side small holes had been cut to make windows with crude wooden shutters that could be propped open or closed when it rained. The one small room had a dirt floor and a wooden partition screening off the kitchen area, which contained utensils and a bowl for washing. There was no electricity, running water, or sanitation. The family slept communally in a similar hut next door and in a further hut various possessions were stored. The huts were in a yard with a low corrugated fence that enclosed the dozen or so pigs the family owned. In another section of the yard there was a vegetable patch.

Lepolo introduced us to her mother and father and her brother Peter, who was nineteen. He was thin and tough, but looked as if he was rather simple. We also met her adopted brother, Michael, who was thirteen, and two younger children, one of whom may have suffered from Down syndrome. Her mother seemed very happy to meet us and said that they were honoured that we had chosen to join their family for lunch. The meal was ready to eat when we arrived. Her mother and father had not attended church that morning because they had been preparing the food for us.

We five visitors sat around a small wooden table on plastic chairs while the food was brought from the umu in which it had been baked. Each of us was given a plate with meat and fish wrapped in large green taro leaves. I asked if they had caught the fish themselves because we had seen some tins of fish and meat on shelves high on the wall. Then we realized that tinned foods were seen by them as an expensive foreign luxury, and that they had been given to us as a special treat, while they ate the local fresh fish. The family stood around us eating their food off the taro leaves with their fingers while the rest of us used assorted china plates and plastic forks. Lepolo told us that Sunday was a special meal and that every other day they ate only root vegetables and coconuts. The most wonderful thing was that, although we were conscious of their poverty, they were not. The mother beamed all the time and it was obvious that they were very happy to be the family chosen to entertain us. It was a very humbling experience.

After the meal they gave us papaya to take away and Lepolo, Peter, and Michael took us to their api to collect coconuts, a staple in their diet. Michael shinned up the tree and cut them down for us. He was a lovely boy and later we went out to a large grassy space near their house where we had fun throwing, kicking, and catching a rugby ball. I was chastised when a young woman politely told me that it was not appropriate to be playing with a ball on Sunday. I remembered that Sunday is a day when nothing should be done except resting, eating, and going to church. I apologized and we walked quietly back.

As we wandered up the street Michael told me about life in his village. When he finished, he turned to me with an enquiring look on his face and asked, "What is it like in your village?"

What is life like in your village? I was dumbfounded by the question. It was obvious that he had no concept of the world outside. In his mind everyone lived in a village. How could I answer a question like that? I quickly gathered my thoughts and tried to keep it simple in terms that he would understand. I told him that we too lived on an island in the sun with palm trees and beaches, but that we had many shops, cars, and television. But how could you have answered his question if you lived in a city and had a job in banking?

I was very saddened when I heard that he was not attending school. He was illegitimate and had been adopted by this family, but because he had no birth certificate he was not allowed to go to school. It made me very angry. How can any society or government permit that!

I was profoundly affected and thought about ways that we could help with his education, but I soon realized that none of these ideas made any sense. He was happy living with a loving family. I would be imposing my western values on his Polynesian culture. I had already seen plenty of examples of how my ideology was out of tune with theirs. But I wished then, and still do, that I could have done something to help.

When the children walked back with us to our dinghy I offered them money, which they wouldn't take, but Janet made up a large bag of canned food which they seemed happy to accept. It seemed to be an appropriate way of saying thank you after our lunchtime experience with canned food. They enjoyed the high-speed ride in the dinghy and were clearly impressed by the powerful engine, which was bigger than any they had seen before. I was interested to observe their reactions when they looked around *Moonraker* but they made very few comments. It was rather wonderful that they were not impressed or overawed in any way. It was clear that material possessions didn't matter to them. In any case a yacht was not something that they could comprehend. To them it was a ship like other ships that sail the oceans. They have no benchmark to compare it to. But they were thrilled by my digital camera and its instant results, and asked if we could send them prints of the pictures of them. We sent them a packet of photographs in the hope that the supply ship that comes to the island once a month would bring mail and that somehow it would find its way to Lepolo.

16

Aground on a Reef

We arrived in Fiji on 1 September, entering the harbour at Levuka on the island of Ovalau after nightfall. We should have arrived earlier but our dinner was interrupted by a large yellowfin tuna on the end of the line insisting that we pull him in. It was dark and we didn't fish at night, but the lines had been left out and Luke and Max were not going to give up the chance of the much-prized tuna, the first yellowfin they had caught. Landing a fish at night was a challenge they enjoyed. The fishing on the passage down from Tonga had been bountiful with a large sailfish (another beautiful fish I felt sad about catching), two dorado, and the tuna.

It was pitch dark when we passed through a six-hundred-foot gap in the reef to enter the lagoon. The charts cannot be trusted in this part of the world but fortunately this is a port for fishing boats and had leading lights to guide us in through the pass. Having found the two lights on the shore we waited until they were in line and safely followed them in and dropped anchor in the lagoon.

The passage from Tonga was unremarkable other than for the fishing and the fact that we reached 180 degrees of longitude west, exactly halfway round the world from London. Now we were at 178 degrees east on the way back! It had taken us through part of the Fiji archipelago. It covers an enormous area, 1.3 million square kilometers of which less than 1.5 per cent is land. Scattered throughout are three hundred islands, the largest being Viti Levu and Vanua Levu. Thanks to our GPS we had no problem avoiding the islands as we sailed through Fijian waters. We were at sea for only two nights but for some reason we were tired after the second night and glad to tuck in behind the reef at Levuka and enjoy a good night's sleep.

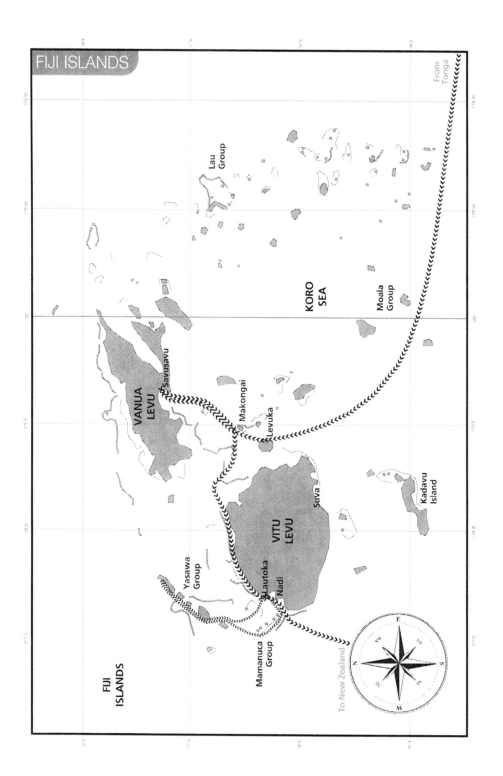

The Islands Time Forgot

The next morning we woke to find Ovalau under a blanket of rain clouds and strong winds. *Lonely Planet* says that the east coast of Fiji, where we were, has a lot of rain, but that the west coast is usually dry. No doubt this is due to easterly winds dropping rain onto the mountain ranges that run through the middle of the two main islands. Despite the rain, our first impressions of Fiji were very favourable. The customs officer came on board early on our first morning to clear us in. This was a convenience we were unused to. Even better, he was the most friendly, welcoming, and helpful customs officer I have ever encountered anywhere in the world. I asked him for the name and e-mail address of his senior officer and told him that I would be writing to say how much we appreciated the way we were treated. I did, and received a nice reply thanking me.

The original inhabitants of Fiji called their island Viti. They came from Southeast Asia around 1220 BC. By around 1000 AD, Tongan invasions began and continued sporadically until the arrival of Europeans. The name "Fiji" is attributed to Captain Cook. He asked the Tongans what the name of the islands to the west of them was. He heard "Feejee," the Tongan pronunciation of Viti, and so Fiji it became in 1774 when he arrived on the island of Vatoa in the Lau group.

Only a few years later, in 1789, Captain Bligh passed through a channel between the two main islands in his small open boat after the mutiny on the Bounty. He was unable to land and they were lucky to escape with their lives after being chased by cannibals. Even today this channel is known as "Bligh Water."

To understand Fiji today it is necessary to know something of its modern history. I hadn't done my homework and when we first arrived it caused me some embarrassment. I naively asked Babu, a taxi driver from the Indian community in Savusavu, "Did your parents come from India?"

"No," he replied, "but my great-great-grandparents did." When I asked why, he replied, "They had no choice. They were indentured labourers brought here by the British to work in the sugar plantations."

I squirmed in my seat. I had not read enough about Fiji to know about the indentured labour scheme, and I resolved to learn more about the history of Fijian society before asking any more embarrassing questions.

Fiji was pronounced a British crown colony in October 1874, at Levuka, where we were now. The British developed a strategy that remains fundamental in Fiji, but which is a major obstacle today in harmonizing the indigenous Fijians and the immigrant Indo Fijians. The British quite reasonably believed that if the chiefs who ruled the islands could be persuaded to collaborate with them, then Fiji would be more easily, cheaply, and peacefully governed. The colonial government therefore protected Fijian land rights by forbidding sales of land to foreigners, and today 83% of the land is still owned by indigenous Fijians. This policy successfully maintained peace.

The colonial government also passed laws prohibiting the employment of indigenous Fijians as plantation labourers. This was very popular, as Fijians, like other South Pacific islanders, were reluctant to take full-time work for wages, preferring a self-sufficient lifestyle. The climate and soil in Fiji was very suited to plantations producing cotton, copra, and sugar cane, but these required a large pool of cheap labour. So in 1878 the British negotiated with the Indian colonial government for labourers to come to Fiji on five-year contracts. They began arriving in Fiji at the rate of about two thousand a year and despite overcrowded accommodation, little regard for different caste or religion, and much hardship, most decided to stay. In truth, it was very difficult for them to return to India, but through hard work they improved their situation. By the early 1900s antislavery groups in Britain called for the abolition of the indentured labour system. By 1919, when indenture was officially ended, there were 60,537 indentured Indian labourers in Fiji.

The stage was now set for a long-standing conflict between the indigenous Fijians and the Indo-Fijians. The colonial government discouraged interaction between them. Indians, who were unable to buy Fijian land, began opening small businesses and took out long-term leases as independent farmers. The first half of the twentieth century saw economic dominance by Indians, who ran most of the shops, transport, and farms. Nevertheless the political structure meant that the Indians had the money but the Fijians had the land and the power. The 1960s saw a movement toward Fiji self-government and on 10 October 1970, Fiji became an independent country. In establishing independence, however, the structural problems in the racially divided country were neglected. Indian dissatisfaction continued to grow and greater unity among workers led to the formation of the Fiji Labour Party (FLP), which gained power in 1987 in a coalition government. This set the scene for a series of military coups that have continued to the present day and that gave increased power to the Great Council of Chiefs, the traditional ruling structure of the indigenous Fijians responsible for appointing judges and ruling on legislation relating to land ownership. The power struggle in Fiji is between the Great Council of

Chiefs, backed by the military, and democratic government, which would give more power to the Indo-Fijians.

It is impossible to be in Fiji and not be aware of the political issues. Newspapers devote much space to it and encompass a wide range of views. Most people we met were happy to talk about it, although at no time did we feel any racial tension on the streets or sense any hostility between the races.

Levuka, our first port of call, was a key part of the early development of Fiji. A small whaling settlement had been established in the 1830s and it soon became the main port in the South Pacific for traders and warships. In the 1840s there was a large influx of settlers and the town became a lawless and greedy outpost. It became the capital of Fiji when it was colonized by the British in 1874. Now it is the centre of the Pacific fishing industry, with big factory fishing boats from Japan, Russia, and China bringing their catch to the large fish-processing factory here, which employs several thousand people. It sounds as if it might be a terrible place but we liked it and didn't notice any smell from the fish factory. The main street was awash with black pools of rainwater as we dodged in and out of brightly-coloured Indian shops, which were bustling with business. Just outside the town there were several attractive buildings from the colonial era that are still used as government administration offices. They look splendid with well-maintained white wood cladding, wide balconies with ornate white balustrades, and green tin roofs.

Our customs officer had most helpfully arranged for his cousin to take us round the island in his big 4WD. He didn't think a taxi would be comfortable enough for us! The car slithered around the wet mud road at speed. It felt like the motor sport rally in the Welsh forests! The driver brought his sister, who spoke good English, and she gave us helpful insights into life on Ovalau, an island where there is almost no tourist influence. Everyone here knows everyone else, and as we drove round the island we frequently stopped so that she could introduce us to friends who took us into their traditional thatched homes, which typically have a tall, sharply-pitched roof and a main supporting wooden beam that runs the length of the roof. We chatted to them, with our guide translating, and she really helped us to learn about life in the villages. All the people we met were indigenous Fijians, many wearing rugby shirts from several different countries in anticipation of the forthcoming Rugby World Cup.

This is a rugby-mad country and on Saturday afternoon I went to watch a cup game. Ovalau were playing a town from the mainland. They played attacking rugby despite the mud bath conditions and deserved their 22–11 win. It was pouring with rain and no one else wanted to come so I had gone on my own, wearing my full foul weather sailing gear, which must have looked odd. The persistent rain made it feel just like England! The crowd, made up of Indians and indigenous Fijians, huddled under large multicoloured umbrellas. We chatted about the game and they were very friendly and quite different from the natives of Tonga. They were not so large, looked fitter, seemed better educated, and appeared to enjoy a more sophisticated lifestyle.

From Ovalau we sailed north to Savusavu, the main town on the second biggest island, Vanua Levu, which means big island. It was still wet and windy, so we had two reefs in the mainsail and just the staysail. When we arrived we saw many boats we knew, including *Coconut* and *Soul's Calling,* and around twenty of us, undeterred by the heavy rain, went ashore to have dinner at the Copra Shed restaurant. Everyone ordered curry—it's what you eat there! Dolly runs the Copra Shed with her team of smiling Indians. They were so completely different from the indigenous Fijians we had just met in Levuka. The rain couldn't dampen our spirits, and the room buzzed with chatter from our group as we moved around to talk to each other, exchanging news about who had been where, and done what, renewing acquaintances with old friends, eagerly making new ones, and generally enjoying the warm affinity of the sailing community.

Savusavu is a popular anchorage with yachtsmen. It is not unusual to find fifty yachts anchored in this sheltered inlet, which looks like a river estuary although it is actually sheltered by an island and connected to the sea at both ends. The town became prominent because it was the centre for North American-owned copra plantations during the colonial era, and although there was no longer big money in copra, there was still plenty of evidence of the copra trade being carried on. Savusavu was enjoying a property boom, with land changing hands at ever-increasing prices and plantations being subdivided to create smaller plots for development. Although it has become a bustling place, with lively bars and restaurants, and is set among a background of rolling green hills, the town is not especially pleasant and it is hard to understand why it is so attractive to property developers. Perhaps, as in other parts of the world, the appeal is in the views over the harbour, where yachts lie peacefully at anchor. A sad consequence of this land boom has been that some Fijian landowners won't renew their leases on Indian sugarcane farms in the hopes that their land might be developed for tourism, and this increases Indian insecurity.

* * *

We met many interesting characters who got washed up on the shores of South Pacific islands, never to leave them. In Savusavu we met Curly, who came here thirty-eight years ago as part of the New Zealand Special Forces and worked as an instructor, teaching jungle warfare to the SAS and their Aussie and Kiwi counterparts. He liked it and stayed.

Now he has a small business catering to the needs of the cruising yachtsmen. We were awakened by his voice bringing us the cruiser's network on the VHF radio early each morning. "Good morning Savusavu," he boomed out in the style of Robin Williams in the movie *Good Morning, Vietnam*, before giving us information about the weather, safety warnings, local shopping, and entertainment.

Curly also put on lectures twice a week that contain gems of local information. Luke and I went to one at which he talked about the dangers of relying on the yacht's GPS position (very accurate) in conjunction with old charts (very inaccurate). This is an area that is strewn with reefs that spell disaster for visiting yachts every year and Curly gave several cautionary examples of recent shipwrecks. His advice was to use the GPS position with great caution and rely on visual bearings on land, depth soundings, and colour of water to confirm the yacht's position. His lecture on cruising Fiji was delivered with such enthusiasm that we wished we had time to visit all the places he talked about, but it would have taken a full season.

Afterwards I sat with him in the bar and over a few beers he told me an extraordinary story. Some years ago his wife disappeared with no warning. He has never seen or heard from her since. As far as he knew they had no problems and she was not unhappy. He had been unable to trace her, although he thinks his children in New Zealand may know her whereabouts. It's a strange world.

Michael was another unusual and interesting character we met in Savusavu. Janet and I were having lunch in Bula-Re, a waterside café in town, when a man who had been sitting on his own drinking a beer came over. Michael was English and, recognizing our accents, asked if he could join us for a chat. We learned that he was married to a Fijian woman and they had been living in the bush for the last seven years. They lived in a simple way in a small corrugated iron house in the mountains. It had no electricity or water supply. They had kerosene lamps for light, although he confessed to having bought a generator six weeks ago. Water came from the nearby stream. He had no car, just a motorbike, and he and his wife came into town once a week to do the shopping and then took a taxi back. He grew his own produce on the land and sold what they didn't need in town.

You might think that he had "gone native," but he was well dressed in a clean safari shirt and shorts, and he seemed very healthy and fit for his sixty-six years. But intellectual stimulation is a problem for a man who was once a university lecturer and in later life a software developer. He was learning a musical instrument, and had formed the Savusavu Philosophers Club. Unfortunately there were only three members and now one of those had left.

I was surprised to hear that he missed England, especially the changing seasons, the village green, cricket, and the pub. He had been back to England three times in the last seven years and had thought about going there to live. The problem was that he is twenty years older than his wife, and almost certain to die first, so if they lived in England she would be left alone in a strange land with no family or friends, which he did not think would be fair.

We talked about rugby and the upcoming Rugby World Cup (he played rugby until he was forty-seven), cricket, Fiji politics, and all those things that men who are strangers find to talk about in the pub. We drank a little more beer than we should have at lunchtime, but we both enjoyed it. Then I said my goodbyes and left. We were ships that pass in the night.

Dario and Sabina, a young Swiss couple, were in Savusavu on their yacht *Top To Top,* and through the medium of Curly's cruiser's net they invited their fellow yachtsmen to a lecture one evening. We didn't know what to expect and were all in for a big surprise. Gathered in the bar at the Copra Shed they told us their incredible story, illustrated by remarkable photographs.

In 2002 they set out to sail to all the major continents and climb the seven highest mountains with zero carbon emissions by using wind power to sail, bicycles to cover the land, and their legs to climb the mountains. It was their way of doing something about climate change and the need to raise awareness of global warming and pollution. They take their message into schools wherever they go, talk about what they are doing, and explain how children can help. So far, twenty thousand children have been exposed to their message. After the talk they organize a "cleanup campaign" with the children, walking around the town or on the beach to pick up litter, and in this way children become aware of the problem and how they can make a difference.

As yachtsmen, we were particularly fascinated by the challenges they had overcome—appalling storms and major gear failures often in remote parts of the world, but they took it all in their stride. They sailed to the Antarctic to climb Mount Vinson, its highest mountain but were defeated by winds that created massive pack ice which prevented them from getting ashore to make the trek to the mountain. Undeterred, they are resolved to try again.

Along the way they have had two babies and carried on as usual, so now there are two young children to manage as well as their project! They have no money. Dario was a mountain guide and Sabina was a nurse. They had been loaned a boat for the project and have had some minor sponsorship that gives them an annual budget of $20,000.

They are a couple filled with the spirit of adventure and the courage and ability to overcome any adversity. Their sailing and mountain-climbing achievements alone are incredible and yet they are largely unknown. I wondered why they had not been more successful in communicating their mission to the outside world, generating more sponsorship, and using the world's media to tell their story about global warming, pollution, and how children can help. Perhaps it's because a project like this needs to be better financed, more ambitious in its business objectives, and more hard-nosed in its approach to raising money and working the media. It's unfair to be critical, though, because Dario and Sabina had no background in the business world. They are, after all, idealists, happy doing what they love, and the two of them have already achieved a great deal. But we felt that this project deserved to have much greater worldwide exposure than it has received so far. Their Web site is www.toptotop.org. We would encourage anyone to visit it to learn more about their project.

* * *

After a week of continuous rain and drizzle with thick grey clouds hanging over the hills and mountains surrounding Savusavu, Janet and I decided to escape and take a trip to the western side of Vanua Levu, where we hoped it might be dry. The road took us up through a series of hairpin bends into the mountains, where we gazed down on deep valleys covered in thick green foliage uninterrupted by any sign of human habitation. The spectacular views were obscured by a grey blanket that hung over the water, with the tops of hills rising above the misty clouds like islands pushing up through the sea.

Babu, our Indian taxi driver, took us first to the Waisali Rainforest Reserve, a protected area and biodiversity project. The foliage was beautiful, with many different specimens of trees, orchids, and fauna creating a painter's palette in shades of green. We had hoped to see the rare Fiji tree frog and birds such as the orange dove, but were disappointed to find out that they only appeared at night.

In an enterprising community project the local villagers had built a gravel path through the forest, with wooden rails in dangerous places, which made walking through the forest easy. In a valley the recent heavy rains had broken through a dam and swept away the bridge, but we were able to cross the stream by stepping on boulders to reach the other side. We were the only visitors, and had the forest and the park ranger who guided us to ourselves.

As we drove down the mountains on the other side of the island it felt as though we were entering another country. The tall grass was brown, the land was flat and arable, tethered cows grazed in the fields, and a truck was watering the road to keep the dust down. We passed a large sugarcane plantation and I stopped to take photographs of the men cutting the cane with their large machetes. They waved a welcome and shouted "bula" (hello) and signaled for me to go over to see them. I asked them to demonstrate how they cut the cane, and they let me have a go, which caused much laughter. Finally we dropped down to the coast and into the town of Labasa.

Labasa is the largest town on Vanua Levu, the only one really, as other than Savusavu there are only villages. The population is predominantly Indian. Although it is a large town, it is dominated by one long street teeming with people and the hurly-burly of business, where shops sell modern consumer goods, trainers, sports clothes, computers, cameras, TVs, and DVDs. It all seemed quite strange to us. We sensed that we had left the third world behind and were moving back toward civilization. The economy of Vanua Levu is based on the sugar industry and the sugar mill is just outside of town. We drove out to see it, passing a long line of stationary trucks, perhaps several hundred, loaded up with sugarcane that they were taking to the mill. An Indian farmer/driver told us that this was a normal queue, which can be up to six hundred trucks long and take five hours to reach the weighing station. The farmers get six hundred Fiji dollars for a truckload of raw sugarcane (about two hundred pounds sterling). It didn't sound much to me for all the labour and time involved, but he seemed to accept it.

Walking around town we came upon a colourful Hindu temple, the most vivid reminder yet of the Indian society in Labasa. To our surprise the priest came out and invited us to come inside. Although he did not speak English well he was extremely friendly, explaining the Hindu religious life to us as we walked around the temple. We chatted about our children and grandchildren—a subject that we found was of mutual interest everywhere we went, regardless of nationality, religion, or station in life.

Labasa has an abundance of Indian and Chinese restaurants and their delicious aromas wafted out onto the main street, stimulating our appetite. Babu recommended a busy restaurant where the food was particularly good. All around us businessmen and women were tucking into huge bowls of steaming Indian and Chinese food. We decided on a large plate of chicken chop suey, which cost five dollars Fiji, less than two pounds sterling. *Lonely Planet* says that Labasa "has nothing for the tourist," but we felt that we had tasted an interesting slice of real life in Labasa.

* * *

On Saturday 10 September we left Savusavu for the small island of Makogai. We were glad to escape the incessant rain that had spoiled most of our time there. It was an exhilarating fifty-mile sail. A flat sea, fifteen knots of wind, and warm sunshine made the sailing such fun that we steered by hand instead of using the autopilot as we usually did. If only sailing was always like this. As *Coconut* was going the same way we did a crew swap for the day, with Lesley, Camilla, and Colin coming with us, and Max going on *Coconut*. Lesley's back was painful again and she found the sea motion easier on *Moonraker* and lay down in the saloon. In addition to her sailing duties she managed the children's education, all the time suffering back pain, and bore it without complaint.

Makogai is well known as a former leper colony. Leprosy has been a dreaded disease since ancient times, and it was only in 1891 that a law was passed in Fiji to stop lepers from being clubbed to death—to put them out of their misery! In 1911 a leprosy hospital was established on Makogai, and eventually lepers from all the South Pacific islands were sent there and the island was given over exclusively to them. The hospital was staffed by dedicated nuns led by Sister Mary Agnes who arrived in 1916 and stayed until 1950 when she retired at the age of eighty. Her enlightened policies, encouraged by doctors, helped the patients to live in small villages according to their ethnic background, and lead as normal lives as possible. A technical school was established teaching carpentry, bricklaying, plastering, plumbing, engineering, and boat-building. For the women there was singing, cooking, sewing, knitting, and art. (This enlightened policy was also described in Victoria Hislop's beautiful but heart wrenching novel, *The Island*. Her story is about Spinalonga, an island off the north coast of Crete, which was Greece's main leper colony from 1903 until 1957.)

In 1911 Makogai had forty patients and this number grew to 744 by 1941. When lepers came here they knew there was no hope of return. But in 1948 a drug was discovered that cured leprosy, Sulphone. The improvements were dramatic. By 1957 there were only 620 patients and by 1966 only 150 and they were moved to a modern hospital in Suva. Although by this time 1224 had died and were buried on Makogai, thanks to the miracle of Sulphone, 2155 patients were cured to return home again.

As we landed and walked up the rotting wooden jetty I thought of the lepers who had trodden these planks on arrival, mothers taken from their children, husbands from their wives, children from their families. What must their thoughts have been?

On stepping ashore we were invited to Sevusevu, a traditional kava gift ceremony. We presented a gift of kava roots to the chief, and drank kava with him in a ritual in which he welcomed us to the island and gave us permission to explore.

A group of us walked for an hour to the other side of this beautiful island to attend the Sunday morning service in the small wooden church used by the eighty-two people who live there. The minister beamed at our unexpected little group at the back of the church. "It's a wonderful day, isn't it?" he asked.

It was, I thought, and how wonderful it was that so many who came here with horror and despair in their hearts were, in the end, able to go home to their loved ones. Quite unexpectedly I was shaken from my dreaming when the minister smiled and asked if one of us would like to come up to make an address. I was taken by surprise and looked around our friends, but they didn't respond, so I was glad to step up and tell his congregation what a privilege it was to share this glorious Sunday morning with them.

After our short stay on Makogai we sailed over to the mainland of Viti Levu where we had to clear customs at Lautoka. It is the second largest city in Fiji and is called "Sugar City." It smelled like it, too. It is a large commercial port and the docks are next to the sugar mill so that the crushed sugar liquid can be loaded directly for shipping to a refinery. There are no facilities for yachts so we had to take our dinghy into the fish docks to go ashore. It was very smelly! The town had good shops but was quite dirty, and we were glad to get away as soon as we could.

Having cleared into Viti Levu, we made for our real destination, Musket Cove, a nearby resort on a small island, which unlike most resorts welcomes cruising yachts. A large number were expected to gather there for the weeklong fun regatta organized each year by the resort owner.

The entry to Musket Cove was difficult because the reefs were not easy to see with the prevailing cloud cover. The following night a yacht tried to enter in the dark and went aground. We were ashore at the time but heard the distress call on our portable VHF radio and Luke and I went out into the darkness in our dinghy to provide assistance. About six other small boats came out to help. The yacht crew sensibly raised full sail to heel the boat over, Trond took a halyard to keep the mast pulled over, and the rest of us pushed our dinghies hard against the stern of the stricken yacht with the outboard motors going flat out. Inch by inch the yacht moved forward, gradually sliding into deeper water where the relieved crew was able to anchor. It was a calmly and professionally conducted emergency operation.

The Musket Cove Regatta is an annual gathering point for many of the yachts that have crossed the Pacific, so it was a happy reunion. But from here we would be going our separate ways, either making the final leg down to New Zealand, or continuing west to Vanuatu and New Caledonia before sailing down to the east coast of Australia. Janet and I planned to leave from Fiji and fly home for Christmas with our family, leaving Luke to take the boat down to New Zealand with extra crew.

Meanwhile we looked forward to enjoying the regatta, having fun and socializing with friends old and new. It would make quite a change from the quiet isolated life we had been leading for the last six months. The regatta turned out to be terrific fun, with lovely weather, good racing, and lots of activity off the water for the sixty yachts that took part. Yachts that had crossed the Pacific were joined by many Kiwis and Aussies who come up to Fiji for the season, so the event had an international flavour. On the opening night the citizens of the twelve countries represented sang their national anthems with gusto. Perhaps surprisingly, the largest contingent was not Aussie or Kiwi but from the U.S. There were only ten Brits, including our four, in the whole gathering.

Although rather grandly titled a regatta, it was essentially a fun event that catered to families with children. There were three "races." Race 1 was pirate's day with a race to a nearby island, which was to be invaded. The costumes were realistic and imaginative considering the limited resources available. Some yachts came up with outlandish ideas, such as a dead body hanging from the bowsprit! Water bombs, water cannon, and flour bombs filled the air as rival yachts bombarded each other. The children loved it, of course, but as we had no children on board we stayed out of the way.

Race 2 was a short seven-mile hop to Namotu, a small private island and resort that allows this yacht invasion for one day each year. There was only a light wind so we motored most of the way, thus disqualifying ourselves from the race, but once we got there we found a beautiful island. The barbeque lunch in an idyllic setting made it easy for everyone to mingle and share their experiences of sailing in the South Pacific. Down on the beach it was "let your hair down" time with distinctly adult games, a beer-drinking competition, won by the Aussies of course, and a wet T-shirt competition, which engendered an amazingly competitive spirit from some lovely ladies—the word "uninhibited" comes to mind—egged on by a cheering audience of macho men. A rather good-looking older gentleman revealed an astonishing amount of hair to win the hairy chest contest and the tug of war was fiercely contested. It was the perfect antidote for many days alone at sea.

Race 3 was the Malolo "Round the Island" race. This one was definitely being taken seriously and only twenty of the fastest boats were at the start line. As soon as the gun went it was clear that this was full-on racing. We were blessed by the best wind we had all week, about 15–20 knots on a bright sunny day, which made for perfect racing conditions. On the short upwind leg we were overcanvassed with the full mainsail, but it would have taken us a couple of minutes to come up on the wind to reef, so we dumped the mainsail in the gusts and hung on. What made this race different from others I have done is that it all took place inside the reef that surrounds the island. At times we were only a couple of boat lengths from the coral reef, with other yachts only a boat's length away on our other side, so we were at really close quarters with very little room to maneuver—definitely conditions to make the adrenaline flow. We worked our way up through the fleet after a cautious start. The race was won by a large catamaran, designed and built by the Australian owner, which did eighteen knots on a reach, lifting its hull! Second was a dedicated 65-foot racing boat helmed by a well-known New Zealand sailor who has raced with Russell Coutts in the America's Cup. He had won this regatta for the last five years so he must have been disappointed to have to take second place. We were third.

On nonrace days there was Hobie Cat racing organized as match racing—just two boats racing against each other. *Moonraker* and *Coconut* had three combined entries, Max and Camilla, Luke and Colin, and Trond and myself. To their chagrin Luke and Max were knocked out in the early rounds. Trond and I went out in the first round but we had a second chance in the plate competition for first-round losers and then made a comeback. With Trond steering we beat our good friends Greg and Debbie on *Volare* in an exciting and close run final in which the lead changed hands twice. The Le Mans-style starts were fun. At the gun the two boats were pushed into the water by helpers while the crew ran into the sea and dived onto the catamaran. Janet raised the largest cheer of the day when she lost her bikini top while climbing aboard.

With a golf competition, tennis, and beach Olympics there was never a dull moment. Each evening a different social event was arranged, usually based around the island beach bar where yacht crews could bring their own meat or fish for the barbecue, always a good opportunity to meet up with friends. A cross-dressing party with the theme "princes and princesses" attracted a lot of attention. Each couple that came before the judges had the audience in new shrieks of laughter. Max and Luke, who had raided Janet's wardrobe, made a handsome couple, causing quite a stir. The whole event had the feeling of an end-of-term party as everyone made plans for the final stage of their Pacific crossing. The regatta ended with a prize-giving dinner, which was the time for us all to say our farewells. We tried not to say goodbye, but we knew we would probably never see many of these good friends again.

Finally we made the break from Musket Cove and said a sad goodbye to the *Coconuts,* Trond, Lesley, Camilla, and Colin. We had seen them so many times since we left Panama! Now they were sailing on to Australia where they planned to sell their boat before returning to life in Norway. Trond has the happy ability to bridge age gaps and has been a good friend to us as well as to Luke and Max. Perhaps I am a father figure for him as he is for Luke. After three years sailing from Norway to Australia they were planning their new life. Trond had landed a new job, resuming his career in leadership development, but the children would probably find school something of a shock after so much time away. Lesley planned to go back to teaching. They would be sad to give up blue-water cruising, but life moves on and they were young enough to do it again.

From Musket Cove we motored the twenty miles to Robinson Crusoe Island just off the mainland of Viti Levu. That evening the heavens opened and there was a torrential rainstorm. With all the hatches closed it was intolerably hot, so we ran the generator, turned on the air conditioning, and watched movies on the DVD player. Next morning we awoke to an extraordinary scene. The blue lagoon we had anchored in wasn't blue anymore; it was a brown swirling turmoil. It looked as if we had anchored in the Orinoco River. When we went ashore we saw that the beautiful white sand beach of the day before had gone. It had been completely covered by broken branches and wood debris. The Orinoco River analogy wasn't so far from the truth. We were anchored only two miles from the mouth of Fiji's second longest river, and the rainstorm had released huge amounts of debris and soil that had been building up behind the many bridges that cross the path of the river and flushed it all out to sea.

Wayne, the Australian owner of the Robinson Crusoe Island Resort commiserated. "You couldn't see it on a worse day, mate." But it didn't matter. We walked around the tiny island, astonished by the temporary devastation caused by the storm. The only dwelling was the resort. It was very low-key, with small thatched cottages (bures) and a thatched bar and entertainment area. Apart from the backpackers on vacation Wayne's main source of income was from well-heeled tourists at the five-star hotels on the mainland. They came for day trips to enjoy a traditional Fijian meal cooked in the ground and a Fijian dancing show. As we sat in the shady bar with Wayne, drinking our beer, we watched about a hundred and fifty of them arrive, disembarking from the flat bottom boats that had brought them and waddling up the beach like penguins. "Just look at all those dollars coming up the beach. Don't ya just love it?" he cracked. Wayne looked after us well and made us members of his exclusive yacht club, the only members being world-girdling yachtsmen. We have the card to prove it and our membership number is ninety-two.

From Robinson Crusoe Island we headed for Port Denarau on Viti Levu, where we planned to rent a car and see something of mainland Fiji. The weather in Musket Cove had been perfect but now the heavy rain was relentless. We intended to take a four-day drive around the island but we drove straight past our first overnight stop to go on to Suva, the capital, thinking that the city is a better place to be if it is raining.

Suva, the biggest city in the South Pacific, was under a state of emergency when we arrived but everything seemed peaceful and we would never have known about it if we hadn't seen it on the Internet. The reason was the impending trial of ex-Prime Minister Qarase. Following a coup in December 2006 Fiji had been under the rule of Frank Bainimarama, who had appointed himself prime minister and head of the military. The elected government was ousted by armed soldiers who stormed parliament and escorted members of parliament from the Senate chamber. Elected Prime Minister Qarase was removed and accused of corruption and of taking Fiji down a path of doom. Now he was being brought to trial, a potentially explosive situation, and as a precaution the interim military government had introduced martial law in order to be able to deal with any agitation that might arise.

There were no signs of trouble or indeed any police or military presence on the streets other than a traditionally dressed police band playing as they paraded down the main street. We walked the streets at night. Everywhere the people could not have been friendlier. It made a mockery of the warning by the governments of Britain, New Zealand, and Australia, which told their citizens not to travel to Fiji because it wasn't safe. It was an insight into how politics works because it was clear that there was no danger to tourists whatsoever. There seems to be no animosity at all at street level between Indians and the Fijians. The ethnic problems occur in the power struggle at the top. When we talked to ordinary people they told us they just wanted stability from the government in order to be able to get on with their lives.

Sadly it was the ordinary people who suffered. The economy had been badly affected by events. The hotels were empty and so were the restaurants. We stayed for a night at a small luxury resort and conference centre with twenty-four rooms but only three guests. We felt so sorry for the owners and the welcoming staff who made their living from tourism.

Throughout our stay in Suva the weather conspired with politics to deal a double blow to tourism. The King's Road, the main road from Suva to the north, was closed because a bridge collapsed after torrential rain. A couple staying in our hotel were stranded when their flight to the Lau Group of islands was cancelled until further notice due to the weather. They were unable to join the wife's parents on their yacht.

With no other passable route north by car we amended our plans and stayed in Suva. Contrary to tourist books that say it is an overcrowded, dirty, and dangerous city with nothing to offer, we liked it. It was more modern than we expected, with sophisticated shops and restaurants and a smart six-screen cinema, which was an attraction to us as it was the first one we had been to in a year.

The Fiji Museum gave us a picture of the dramatic and bloody history of Fiji, a country where cannibals existed only one hundred and thirty years ago, and we learned much more about the archaeological, political, and cultural evolution of Fiji. Something that probably hasn't changed much is the market down by the docks, a large, colorful, noisy arena on two floors that sells a vast variety of fresh fruit and vegetables. No wonder the Fijians look fitter than the heavyweight Tongans!

In fact, Suva's shops and restaurants could rival those of many cities in Europe. It is a city that young people gravitate to, leaving behind the traditional society of the villages. It offers a total contrast, an individual life with the rewards of the material world—cars, bars, cafés, music, nightclubs, and western clothes, all available to anyone who can afford them. Television, dominated by western programming, changes the lifestyle of the young and affluent and encourages a new western culture. Suva is not the "picture-postcard" Fiji that holidaymakers flock to, but a place that any serious traveller could enjoy.

We drove back west along the Coral Coast on Saturday afternoon hoping to find better weather. The small luxury resort we stayed in on the way back had access to a magnificent championship golf course. Encouraged by a break in the dark clouds with blue sky peeping through, we went out to play nine holes in the afternoon. We had no golf gear with us, and I have an indelible image in my mind of both of us in heavy weather sailing jackets, trainers on our feet, tramping around a soaked and muddy golf course in the pouring rain, trying to swing a golf club.

Later, holed up in our comfortable hotel room while the rain hammered on the roof, we set the alarm for 3:00 AM to watch the Fiji versus Wales Rugby World Cup match on TV. It was worth it because Fiji won a close and exciting game. We were so pleased that the people in this rugby-mad country had something to cheer about. They have had much to endure as a result of the coup and the ensuing economic slump. Everyone we spoke to next day had got up to watch the game, and told us they were "so proud of our boys."

* * *

We sailed away from a rain-soaked Viti Levu and made our way out to the Yasawa Group of islands on the west coast, and to our relief the weather changed dramatically, just as the pilot book said it would, with clear blue skies, sunshine, and a pleasant breeze. When coming to Fiji it is worth remembering that "west is best."

The Yasawa Group is renowned as the jewel in the crown of Fiji: small islands with sandy palm-clad beaches, turquoise waters, and low hills covered in trees. There are many islands and small villages, usually with less than a hundred inhabitants living their traditional life—growing fruit and vegetables and fishing. The only intrusion into their quiet existence is from backpackers who seek the simple low-cost lifestyle, and stay in small traditional thatched resorts hidden beneath palm trees.

Although the islands of the Yasawa Group are close to the mainland, they have remained remote, and are governed by the same ancient traditions as the more distant outer islands. It was considered very bad manners to swim, walk on the beach, or go into the village without having the permission of the turaga-ni-koro (hereditary chief). This was granted through the Sevusevu ceremony we had first experienced in Makogai. I went ashore on the island of Waya and asked the first person I met if we could meet the turaga-ni-koro for Sevusevu. He ran off but came back five minutes later to say that we would be granted an audience with the chief in two hours.

I was excited. This was a scene I had imagined in my boyhood dreams. We all observed the correct protocol for the Sevusevu ceremony—properly dressed with shirt and trousers, Janet modestly covered up, no hats or sunglasses, and carrying with us our gift of kava for the chief.

As we walked into the village it was clear that we were expected and welcome. Women lined up on either side of the path to the chief's hut to show us handicrafts that they had made and were for sale. The chief met us and welcomed us into his hut. We sat cross-legged in a circle in front of him, making sure that our heads were below his and that our feet did not point toward him. I presented our package of kava roots, which he received graciously, and he invited us to drink kava with him. The men accepted the offer but when Janet wrinkled her nose he laughed and said it was quite acceptable for her to drink tea. When the bilo (half coconut) is passed to you it is polite to clap once to accept it, say bula, drink it down in one go, and then clap three times in appreciation. The chief said prayers, and on completion told us that we were now welcome visitors to the village, and that he would do whatever he could to help make our stay enjoyable.

Then, as is the tradition at this ceremony, we talked about many things. He spoke English quite well and was pleased to answer our questions about the lifestyle in the outer islands of Fiji and how it was changing.

He himself had left the island to go to the mainland in his late twenties and left his brother to fill his hereditary role as chief. On his return twenty years later, he had once again taken up his responsibilities as head of the village. His main duty as the community leader was ensuring that the laws were obeyed and that proper social behavior was observed. I asked him if there were any clashes between the law of the land and their traditional law. He told me that the police from the mainland were happy to turn a blind eye to what happened in the islands, provided that a civil, law-abiding society prevailed. He gave an example of a case in which a man had raped a woman, but had been dealt with according to their own laws rather than the civil law. The man was not beaten or stoned. He was made to atone for his crime by meeting the woman, to understand her grief, and by being ostracized from the social life of the village for a long time. We felt we had made a very good friend and when it seemed that it was time for us to leave we walked back through the village, talking to the ladies and buying some of their craftwork.

As we were in remote islands we hadn't expected to find a TV to watch the Rugby World Cup but were pleased that some of the backpacker resorts had satellite TV. Everyone had been watching Fiji play. In one small village the local resort made their satellite receiver available to the village and put it on top of a hill under an awning to get reception. The villagers climbed the hill each night to watch the games.

Most matches started at either 1:00 AM or 3:00 AM Fiji time, with only a few at the reasonable hour of 7:00 AM. It played hell with our sleep patterns but what a joy it was for us English exiles to watch England beating Australia! Janet watched Fiji take on the eventual winners, South Africa, only just losing after a very close and exciting game. What made the occasion special for her was watching the game with the locals in the village. To get there, Luke and Janet had to paddle the dinghy through coral-strewn shallow water at low tide at two in the morning (sadly I was too exhausted from previous late nights to get up). They were met on the beach by one of the local boys, who took them up to the large hut in the village where they had a communal TV. The hut was packed with as many as two hundred people, those in the front lying down flat so those at the back could see the screen. The hut was made of corrugated iron, and so the screams and shrieks made an incredible din, creating a supercharged atmosphere. Luke and Janet, the only white faces in the whole crowd, were warmly welcomed. Fiji lost but it was a memorable night.

The Islands Time Forgot

With only a few days to go before leaving the remote Yasawa Islands, our thoughts turned to our flight to England and then home. It was exciting as we hadn't seen our family for over a year, but we were sad, too, because our dream of crossing the Pacific was coming to an end. We had visited so many different countries, experienced so many different cultures, and met so many friendly people. They had invited us into their simple homes to share everything they had with us. It had been a rewarding, enlightening, and humbling experience that we would never forget.

Sailing back to Port Denarau we had our worst incident of the whole voyage. Ironically it was on the last day before Janet and I flew back to London. We were very relaxed, motoring the last thirty-five miles in light winds and a flat sea. We were fifteen miles offshore, a long way from any danger. Luke, Janet, and I were all in the cockpit, having just finished lunch. Janet offered to take over the watch from Luke. At the same time we received a VHF radio call from Greg and Debbie on *Volare,* who were nearby and on their way to Australia. We were excited to hear from them and were all engrossed in the radio conversation. There was an earsplitting crash. The boat came to a violent halt.

It happened so quickly. It was all a blur. For a second I thought, "What's that," and in the next moment I knew. We were aground on a reef. I glanced at the depth sounder and saw 0.1 metres under the keel. At the same time I heard Janet cry out in distress, "Oh, no! Graham! Graham!"

I quickly turned to where she had been sitting in the starboard helm seat. She was slumped on the deck between the wheel and the seat. There was blood all over her face. I gently lifted her up. Nothing seemed broken but she was very shocked. I carefully helped her below and lay her down on the bed. When I came back up Luke was taking stock of the situation. At first he thought the steering wasn't responding, but the autopilot was still on and when he switched to manual it was okay. The rudder was working normally and we were not firmly aground so Luke let the wind blow us off into nearby deep water. He went over the side with his scuba gear to inspect the keel and the rudder. Everything seemed to be normal. The only damage was the loss of some fairing around the bulb at the bottom of the keel. Then he made a full inspection of the inside of the boat. To my relief he found no damage or leaks. We continued on our way—shocked, shaken, and silent.

Janet was much better when we arrived in Port Denarau. No bones were broken, and her bloody nose was still straight although she was upset that she would have a swollen and bruised face when we returned to

England. But we had got off very lightly. Having navigated safely through reefs all the time we were in Fiji, in open sea and with no apparent danger, we had let our guard down. This small isolated reef did not show on the electronic chart we were using, but it did when we subsequently looked on a smaller scale. We were in the middle of a watch change and we were distracted by a radio call. No one was looking out. It was a lesson to learn from.

We flew out of Fiji the next day and Luke found extra crew for the passage down to Auckland. He would have a couple of months to take holiday and get work done on the boat before we returned to cruise in New Zealand. I had made the contractual arrangements to ship *Moonraker* from Auckland to Palma in April and we were already making plans to cruise in the Mediterranean in the summer of 2008.

As the plane lifted off the runway we gazed down on the Pacific Ocean and reflected on the people who go blue-water sailing and how different they were. They encompassed a wide range in age, experience, ambitions, boats, budgets, dreams, time scales, and future plans—but we all shared a love of sailing and adventure.

Yes, we came across died-in-the-wool ocean nomads, but they were a minority—people like Nick and Janet, Australians on *Yawarra*, a 40-foot steel sloop, who were returning home after twelve years cruising. Couples like this have traditional, simple, inexpensive boats. They can imagine no other life. Their goal is not to circumnavigate but to explore any countries and regions in the world that take their fancy.

More often we met families with young children who were fulfilling a dream to explore the world, typically as a two-or-three year project, like Trond and Lesley on *Coconut*, Edmond and Yossi on *Surcouf*, and Sean and Jennifer on *Soul's Calling*. They had all achieved their dream. We admired them enormously for their independence and courage.

Occasionally there were single-handers, choosing to sail alone because of circumstances or their inclination. Russell on *Free Spirit* set off to cross the Pacific on his own at the age of fifty-four because his partner and children couldn't come and this was the only way he could realize his dream. Others were more eccentric, like Warren, a seventy-five-year-old American we met at Musket Cove. He had spent his whole life racing, delivering, and cruising yachts. He built his yacht, *Flash Girl*, twenty years ago, and sailed brilliantly to take fourth place in the Musket Cove race. He told me he hopes for six or so more years roaming the oceans before he dies. Warren was truly an old man of the sea.

The youngest couple we met, on the smallest boat, and certainly with the smallest budget, had a 26-foot yacht called *Dream Girl*. The American boy, Ben, and Lisa, his English "dream girl," from Essex, were both under twenty-five and their boat was bought for just two thousand dollars. Not surprisingly, the largest group who go blue-water sailing were retired couples like Greg and Debbie on *Volare,* sailing their boat home, on their own, from California to Sydney.

But although our circumstances were different we shared a common bond. We had learned about values that are important—supporting each other in times of need, helping islanders when we could, respecting our partners and creating a stronger relationship, appreciating nature, wildlife, and our beautiful planet, but perhaps above all, learning that happiness is measured not in money, but in experiences, wisdom, and relationships.

Trond and I had often talked about the need for "purpose" in life. He explained that in an organization, purpose is rocket fuel. It directs efforts and energies in one direction. It kills conflicts and squabbles and eliminates the need for detailed control. And so it is with blue-water cruising. Couples and families need a purpose in their life, and nowhere is this more true than in the close confines of life together on a small boat for months and years.

Planning and carrying out such an ambitious project had given us all a sense of purpose. Married couples living on boats often run into relationship problems but the couples that we met in the Pacific had strengthened their relationships. Through a shared sense of purpose they had developed a profound respect for each other and for the different roles they had to play on board. As Janet said to me, "We need each other more on the boat than we do at home." We would all go home enriched by the experience.

17

Epilogue

We left the boat in Fiji and returned home for Christmas while Luke sailed *Moonraker* down to New Zealand. In January we flew out to Auckland and cruised the beautiful east coast of the North Island. It was lovely. In March we shipped *Moonraker* to the Mediterranean on a cargo ship, and then spent a full six-month season in the summer of 2008 in the eastern Mediterranean. It was wonderful to have children and grandchildren out for holidays and friends to stay. We were fascinated by the historic sites we visited in Turkey and Greece: Croatia with its endless offshore islands was a yachting paradise; southern Italy, Sicily, and Sardinia were places that I had always wanted to see. But the experience did not compare with the South Pacific. We knew that nothing ever would. We returned to Palma, Mallorca, in the late autumn and put the boat up for sale.

Janet was sad not to have continued sailing around the world. She truly loved the life more than I did, but after our heart-to-heart chat in Tonga she understood my feelings and they hadn't changed. I didn't fancy sailing in the Far and Middle East with its risks of piracy, religious extremism, crowds, and pollution. I wanted to do other things in my life now.

We have so many fond memories. We will never forget the friendly people we met in the most remote islands, their culture and their way of life. It was a humbling experience that has given us a better sense of values that matter. The wildlife experiences were magnificent, and swimming with whales in Tonga was awe-inspiring.

For two years we lived together with Luke and Max. Being a successful team was probably the biggest challenge of the adventure, and we stayed together and are still good friends. Luke has studied for, and passed, a higher level of commercial yachting qualifications and delivered yachts again while looking for a suitable position. He phoned me recently to say that he had landed a job as first officer on *Adele,* a 180-foot sailing yacht with a crew of eight, which will be sailing from Australia to Europe. Max has settled in Australia. He works as a graphic designer in an advertising agency in Sydney, and by a happy twist of fate lives with Tiree, who had lost Tom in Bora Bora. He sails socially on weekends in Sydney Harbour.

We have kept in touch with the friends we made. Trond has set up his own consultancy company in Norway and has found a good work/lifestyle balance. He told me, "I have been lucky that I have been able to convince some of my clients that leadership skills can be learned in the mountains—skiing, trekking, and sleeping in a log cabin." Lesley is teaching and they both work part-time so they are able to spend time with their children and each other. Colin and Camilla have come out top of their class at school, so three years away sailing and home schooling have done them no harm. Unable to sell their boat in Australia they shipped *Coconut* back to Norway. They were so glad they did and lovingly sail her on weekends and summer cruises. They dream of setting off for the Pacific again when the children have grown up.

Tom's sister, Alice, asked Trond what she should do about *Magic Roundabout.* He had heard about a charity called Ocean Watch that enables cruising yachts to carry out humanitarian and environmental projects. They bring qualified medical personnel to far-lying areas in the Pacific, organize reef watch groups, help in cleaning up beaches, and train islanders in waste management. Trond proposed the idea of donating *Magic Roundabout* to them and Alice was delighted to agree, knowing that Tom would have been very pleased.

Sean and Jennifer were unable to sell *Soul's Calling* in Australia and shipped the yacht back to the BVI, where it is available for charter and their own holidays. At home in Colorado their life is back in the fast lane, running their business.

Greg and Debbie sailed *Volare* into Sydney Harbour. Greg works part time selling boats for Catalina Yachts (what better salesman could there be?) and when he is not, they are racing and cruising in *Volare.* In his spare time he appears on the Australian yachting lecture circuit. Debbie is catching up with grandchildren.

Edmond and Yossi on *Surcouf* reached Australia safely but then had to change their plan to sail around the world and returned to Belgium to manage a business that was foundering without them. *Surcouf* was shipped back to the Mediterranean.

Epilogue

Bart and Dorothy, their friends on *Bauvier*, arrived in New Zealand soon after *Moonraker*, but decided not to continue circumnavigating to reach Belgium. Instead they spent a year in Australia before sailing on through Indonesia, Singapore, and Malaysia. On reaching Thailand, they made the decision that their childrens' schooling needs dictated that they head home and they are shipping their boat to the Mediterranean. Their voyage has been a great achievement, as they were inexperienced yachtsmen when they began. Yossi's cousins reached New Zealand and decided to settle there.

Russell sailed his boat from Fiji down to New Zealand. It shouldn't have been a surprise for us to see *Free Spirit* moored near us in the marina in Auckland Harbour. Kya joined him and they enjoyed five months together cruising New Zealand and the east coast of Australia. They were expecting a baby boy, and Russell said, "We will have a little larger crew than before, which will be fun." The last time I spoke to him *Free Spirit* was in Thailand and Kya and his one-year-old son are now permanent members of the crew.

As for us, we bought a large plot of land on a remote beach in the Cayman Islands and are building a traditional West Indian style plantation house and creating a tropical garden. What is most exciting is that, motivated by a greater awareness of the environment and the threats to our beautiful planet, our house will be totally powered by renewable energy. We will even produce our own water supply. We hope that our small example will encourage others to follow. The project has given us both a new sense of purpose "It's rocket fuel," as Trond would say.

Acknowledgements

I often wondered why acknowledgements in a book were necessary. I had no idea how much work goes into the making of a book and how much help the author needs. A special thank you to the early readers, Janet Morse, Julia Kandiah, and Chris Johnson, who took on the unenviable and enormous task of reading the first and very rough draft, providing direction and much needed encouragement. Trond Asdam, who read a later manuscript, saved me embarrassment by making many technical and factual corrections. My editor, Jane Cavolina, initially helped me make sense of the structure and style and then edited the manuscript, making an enormous contribution by polishing the text whilst still keeping it as my own work. Luke Windle checked the content of the sailing and technical aspects. Peter Kandiah offered his lawyer's eye for detail for an initial proofreading and Jane Cavolina has picked up the last of my endless mistakes and factual errors in her final proof reading. Thank you, too, to the many friends who offered advice on the title, which I agonized over, and Vic Bennie, Russell Bray, and Ken Spedding, who gave much insight into the front and back cover. Julia Goulden patiently offered many suggestions for cover designs before we selected the final version. Melanie Cumber Rodham made a difference with graphic design. I would also like to thank all those people we met who responded with support and more corrections, particularly, Jean Renwick, Jennifer Holsten, Alan Bowes, Melanie Dupre, Wayne, Rock, Simisi, Haniteli and Lucy O'Fa'Anunu and Tom Hirosch. To those lovely people we met but who I have been unable to contact I hope I have given a fair and accurate view of our meetings. Above all, a huge thank you to my wife, Janet, without whose help in all technical matters, I simply could not have produced this book.

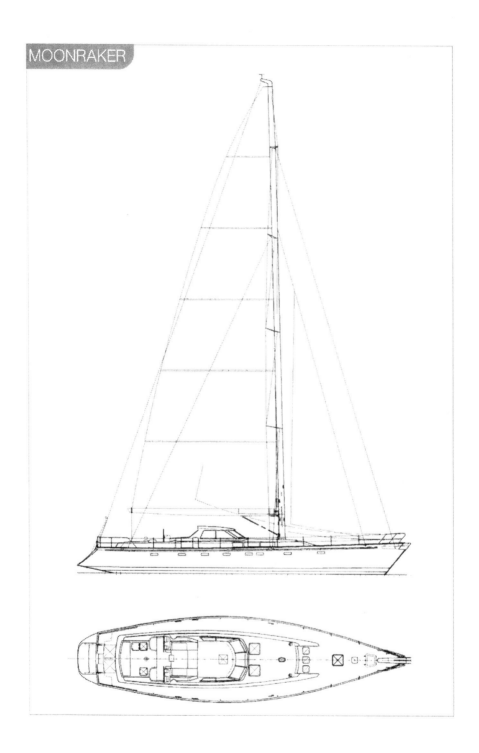

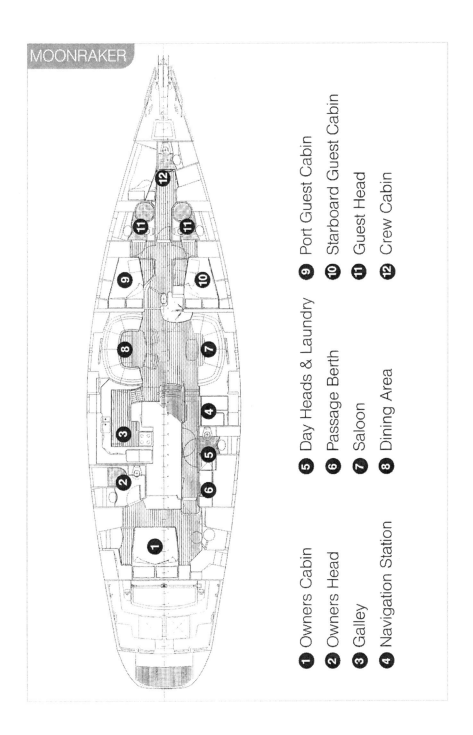

Appendix 1
Refit at Hinckley's Yard

The major work was in the cockpit. Most of the engine and sail controls were on a central pod at the end of the cockpit table. This was rather unusual, as they would usually be at the steering wheel so that the helmsman could reach them while steering. Obviously the first owner specified it this way for good reasons, and the second owner was happy with it, but it wasn't what we wanted. Essentially it seemed to me that the boat had been set up to be sailed on autopilot from the pilothouse, or maneuvered in harbour from a jog stick at the cockpit central control position. Luke and I decided to move all these controls to the two helm (steering) positions. The starboard side would have the engine controls, throttle, and autopilot, and the port side would have a new Furuno chart plotter/radar screen and repeat the throttle controls and autopilot.

The Brookes & Gatehouse wind and depth instruments were moved from the helm positions to the port and starboard sides of the pilothouse bulkhead, where they could be seen from inside the cockpit as well the wheel.

The jib and staysail furling buttons, which were also on the central pod, were moved next to their winches so that one person could operate the hydraulic furling button and sheet winch buttons at the same time to furl either headsail. The practical benefits of these changes were that the helmsman could manage most operations without leaving the wheel and we would be able to run single-person watches at night, although it would still need two people to reef the mainsail.

The cockpit table only seated four. We wanted to be able to seat six easily so that we could eat meals in the cockpit in comfort. A new table was designed and built in the same style but incorporated a refrigerator for soft drinks, beer, and wine. This meant we had more space for food in the main fridge.

The mast was taken out, inspected, and die tested, decks were sanded, the huge bank of batteries was replaced, a new washing machine was installed, and most of the electronics were upgraded. Finally the hull was cleaned, anti-fouled, and polished.

Appendix 2
Replacing a Through Hull Fitting in the Water

A major challenge was replacing the through hull fitting for the engine water exhaust. There was no crane big enough to haul our boat out in Grenada, and so the job would have to be done with the boat in the water but Luke was confident that he could do it.

Max had noticed that there were cracks in the through hull fitting pipe when we were in Antigua, and it was leaking below the seacock, which gave cause for concern. This pipe was bolted to the inside of the hull, allowing engine exhaust water to pass out. Max had made an emergency piece of board to fit and bolt over the hole in case the fitting broke open and let water flood in before it could be replaced. After doing some research Luke managed to locate the manufacturer of the part by e-mailing Graeme Henry, the project manager who built *Moonraker*. He was at sea in the Pacific on a yacht called *Stormvogel* at the time, but found the information we needed to order the new fitting from New Zealand.

Although Luke had thought the procedure through carefully, it still left me feeling rather nervous, because if he was wrong, we would have a spout of water three feet high and four inches wide coming into the boat. First a tapered wooden bung was made and covered in foam rubber for a tight fit. Max fitted it by diving under the boat and knocking it into the hole. He was using scuba gear and communicated with Luke using a predetermined code of knocks on the hull. Then Luke secured the bung by wiring it up from the inside to make sure it could not drop out and into the water. Although the operation had been well planned, something unexpected normally comes up—and it did! Some of the broken parts had been glued in to some of the parts we were reusing. They had to be very carefully cut out, making sure not to damage the bits we needed. At this point there was no turning back. If anything went wrong, water would have come in quicker than we could have pumped it out. If any of the parts didn't fit or broke then we would not have been able to move the boat for weeks until new parts were flown in. But finally, with everything secured, Luke was able to safely take off the seacock and remove and replace the cracked pipe. The cause of the cracking in the plastic pipe seemed to be corrosion between the hull and the fitting so this all had to be cleaned up. Holes were drilled into the new part to take the four bolts that secure it. Then it was fitted, the seacock replaced, and the bung removed. The whole operation took most of the day.

Appendix 3
Beaufort Wind Scale

Developed in 1805 by Sir Francis Beaufort of England

Force	Wind (Knots)	WMO Classification	Appearances of Wind Effects	
			On the Water	On Land
0	Less than 1	Calm	Sea surface smooth and mirror-like	Calm, smoke rises vertically
1	1-3	Light Air	Scaly ripples, no foam crests	Smoke drift indicates wind direction, still wind vanes
2	4-6	Light Breeze	Small wavelets, crests glassy, no breaking	Wind felt on face, leaves rustle, vanes begin to move
3	7-10	Gentle Breeze	Large wavelets, crests begin to break, scattered whitecaps	Leaves and small twigs constantly moving, light flags extended
4	11-16	Moderate Breeze	Small waves 1-4ft. becoming longer, numerous whitecaps	Dust, leaves, and small paper lifted, small tree branches move
5	17-21	Fresh Breeze	Moderate waves 4-8ft. taking longer form, many whitecaps, some spray	Small trees in leaf begin to sway
6	22-27	Strong Breeze	Larger waves 8-13ft, whitecaps common, more spray	Larger tree branches moving, whistling in wires
7	28-33	Near Gale	Sea heaps up, waves 13-20ft, white foam streaks off breakers	Whole trees moving, resistance felt when walking against the wind
8	34-40	Gale	Moderately high 13-20ft. waves of greater length, edges of crests begin to break into spindrift, foam blown in streaks	Whole trees moving, resistance felt when walking against the wind
9	41-47	Strong Gale	High waves 20ft, sea begins to roll, dense streaks of foam, spray may reduce visibility	Slight structural damage occurs slate blows off roofs
10	48-55	Storm	High waves 20-30ft. with overhanging crests, sea white with densely blown foam, heavy rolling, lowered visibility	Seldom experienced on land trees broken or uprooted, "considerable structural damage"
11	56-63	Violent Storm	Exceptionally high 30-45ft. waves, foam patches cover sea, visibility more reduced	
12	64+	Hurricane	Air filled with foam, waves over 45ft, sea completely white with driving spray, visibility greatly reduced	

Sources

Bonnette and Deschamps, *Guide to Navigation in French Polynesia*

Cornell, Jimmy, *World Cruising Routes,* Adlard Coles Nautical, 4th edition, 1998

Cornell, Jimmy, *World Cruising Handbook,* Adlard Coles Nautical, 2nd edition, 1996

Chester, Baumgartner, Frechoso and Oetzel, *The Marquesas Islands*, Mave Mai, Wandering Albatross, 1988

Clay, Warwick, *South Pacific Anchorages,* Imray Laurie Norie & Wilson Ltd, 2001

Gascoigne, John, *Captain Cook,* Hambledon Continuum, 2007

Hough, Richard, *Captain James Cook,* W.W. Norton & Company, 1997

Hogbin and Pocock, *The Pacific Crossing Guide*, Royal Cruising Club, 2nd edition, Adlard Coles Nautical

James Cook *The Journals*, Penguin Books, 2003

Neale, Tom, *An Island to Oneself,* Ox Bow Press, reprint, 1990

Nacy Schwalbe Zydler and Tom Zydler. *The Panama Guide,* Seaworthy Publications, Inc., 2006

Paul and Pham-Paul, *Guide to the Kingdom of Tonga,* Sailingbird Publications, Inc., 2004

Waterson and van der Reijden, *The ABC Islands,* Compass Consultants Ltd., 2006

El Canal de Panama, Bediciones Balboa, 2nd Edition, 2001

Fiji Leprosy Hospital Makogai Island 1911–1969, S/V Oblio and the Fiji Museum Archives

Lonely Planet, Panama, Tahiti & French Polynesia, Samoan Islands & Tonga, Lonely Planet Publications Pty Ltd., 2006

Landfalls of Paradise, Latitude 20, University of Hawai'i Press

Tonga Whale Watching Operators Association

The Daily Telegraph

Yachting Monthly

Yachting World